The Politics of Human Rights

Human rights is an important issue in contemporary politics, and the last few decades have also seen a remarkable increase in research and teaching on the subject. This book introduces students to the study of human rights and aims to build on their interest while simultaneously offering an alternative vision of the subject. Many texts focus on the theoretical and legal issues surrounding human rights. This book adopts a substantially different approach which uses empirical data derived from research on human rights by political scientists to illustrate the occurrence of different types of human rights violations across the world. The authors devote attention to rights as well as to responsibilities, neither of which stops at one country's political borders. They also explore how to deal with repression and the aftermath of human rights violations, making students aware of the prospects for and realities of progress.

Sabine C. Carey is Chair of Political Science at the University of Mannheim, Germany, and Senior Researcher at the Centre for the Study of Civil War at PRIO, Norway.

Mark Gibney is Belk Distinguished Professor in the Department of Political Science at the University of North Carolina-Asheville.

The late **Steven C. Poe** was Professor in the Department of Political Science at the University of North Texas.

The Politics
of Human Rights
The Quest for Dignity

Sabine C. Carey

Mark Gibney

Steven C. Poe

CAMBRIDGE
UNIVERSITY PRESS

CAMBRIDGE
UNIVERSITY PRESS

University Printing House, Cambridge CB2 8BS, United Kingdom

Cambridge University Press is part of the University of Cambridge.

It furthers the University's mission by disseminating knowledge in the pursuit of education, learning and research at the highest international levels of excellence.

www.cambridge.org
Information on this title: www.cambridge.org/9780521614054

© Sabine C. Carey, Mark Gibney and Steven C. Poe 2010
Part opening photograph: © Dragan Trifunovic/Shutterstock.

First published 2010
4th printing 2016

Printed in the United Kingdom by Clays, St Ives plc

A catalogue record for this publication is available from the British Library

Library of Congress Cataloguing in Publication data
Carey, Sabine C., 1974-
    The politics of human rights : the quest for dignity / Sabine C. Carey,
    Mark Gibney, Steven C. Poe.
        p.   cm.
    ISBN 978-0-521-84921-0 (hardback) - ISBN 978-0-521-61405-4 (pbk.)
    1. Human rights.   I. Gibney, Mark.   II. Poe, Steven C.   III. Title.
    JC571.C318 2010
    323-dc22   2010024608

ISBN 978-0-521-84921-0 Hardback
ISBN 978-0-521-61405-4 Paperback

To our students and teachers

Contents

Text boxes

Figures

Tables

Abbreviations

ANC	African National Congress		**IDP**	internally displaced person
ARV	antiretroviral		**IMT**	international military tribunals
CAT	Committee against Torture		**MDG**	Millennium Development Goals
CAVR	Commission for Reception, Truth and Reconciliation		**NGO**	non-governmental organisation
CPR	civil and political rights		**ODA**	Official Development Assistance
CRP	Community Reconciliation Processes		**OECD**	Organisation for Economic Co-operation and Development
DAC	Development Assistance Committee		**OGP**	Office of the General Prosecutor
ECHR	European Convention on Human Rights		**PTS**	Political Terror Scale
ECtHR	European Court of Human Rights		**R2P**	Responsibility to Protect
ESCR	economic, social and cultural rights		**SCFAIT**	Standing Committee on Foreign Affairs and International Trade (Canada)
FGM	female genital mutilation		**TRC**	Truth and Reconciliation Commission
GNI	gross national income			
ICC	International Criminal Court		**UDHR**	Universal Declaration of Human Rights
ICJ	International Court of Justice		**UNHCR**	UN High Commissioner for Refugees
ICTR	International Criminal Tribunal for Rwanda		**WTO**	World Trade Organization
ICTY	International Criminal Tribunal for the former Yugoslavia			

Introduction

This book is designed for a class on human rights or for the treatment of this subject in related courses. In our view, 'human rights' is one of the most important and most interesting subjects. After all, the study of human rights is essentially about how we treat all other people with whom we share this planet. In its essence, striving for the respect of human rights is a quest for human dignity. Human rights are about recognizing, honouring and protecting the human dignity of each one of the six billion people on this planet. When human rights are not protected, the victim's human dignity is thereby ignored. But what this also does is to deny the humanity in all of us.

In this book, we work under the assumption that students study human rights because they are deeply interested in making a positive contribution to the world. Our goal is to build on this interest and this passion. Along with this, our strong sense is that students want to 'get into' human rights immediately and we have structured this book with this goal in mind. In that way, this book is less theoretical and less historical than other books in this realm, and every effort has been made to focus on the humanity on which human rights is based.

The reader will also find a much different and more challenging conceptualization of human rights compared with the 'standard treatment' of human rights in other textbooks. The dominant approach is to recognize the universality of human rights, but then to go in the opposite direction by limiting the responsibility for protecting human rights solely to the territorial state. Under this approach, human rights will almost always be little more than a litany of 'horribles' carried out in distant lands by and against 'others'. Our approach to human rights is decidedly different. Much of what we present throughout this book is the notion that not only are human rights universal – but so is the obligation or the duty to protect and enforce these rights. Human rights are based on the notion of shared humanity but also of shared responsibility. In our view, any other approach to human rights is not deserving of the name.

Another distinguishing feature of this book is our use of quantitative methods. At a minimum, human rights brings together law, politics, history, economics, ethics, religion and morality, but we are also of the mind that the study of human rights is greatly enhanced through scientific method, including statistical analysis. Although this might sound off-putting at first – or worse, induce maths anxiety – you will soon discover how useful, informative (and even easy) this approach to human rights can be. Another novel aspect of our book is that not only do we provide suggestions of further books on the subjects covered in each chapter, but we also put together an extensive list of films that deal with the politics of human rights and emphasize, in a different way, the importance of human rights in order to respect and protect our human dignity.

In Part I we examine the nature of human rights as well as the different responsibilities to protect these rights. Chapter 1 provides a brief overview of the religious and philosophical roots of human rights and gives a short introduction to the main players in the human rights system. Chapter 2 focuses on the responsibilities of states to protect civil and political rights, as well as economic, social and cultural rights, while Chapter 3 discusses specific examples of state responsibilities, both domestic and international, in protecting human rights.

Part II introduces some quantitative measures of human rights to show how the respect for, and violation of, human rights can be traced across time and be compared across countries. In Chapter 4 we provide an overview of where different types of human rights are most at risk, using maps and tables when appropriate. In Chapter 5, we put forward several reasons why human rights are violated and empirically test these arguments, using quantitative analysis. Of course, no prior knowledge of these analytical tools is necessary in order to understand our arguments and presentation of results. We conclude this chapter with a brief case study of human rights in Nigeria, a country that has gone through the gamut of human rights practices (both good and bad) over the past few decades.

Part III focuses on how to restore human dignity when serious human rights violations have occurred. In Chapter 6 we discuss ways of halting ongoing human rights violations by presenting various humanitarian interventions, but also several 'non-interventions', since the 1970s, and we introduce the promising new project Responsibility to Protect. Chapter 7 focuses on the manner in which societies might re-establish trust and security in the aftermath of atrocities. We discuss and compare the retributive and restorative approach to justice, but we also highlight the difficult circumstances in which societies that try to establish transitional justice find themselves. Finally, in a brief conclusion, we highlight some of the progress that has been made in realizing the respect for human rights.

We end this introduction with a note about our co-author who is no longer with us. Steve Poe was a dear friend and trusted mentor to both of us. Steve not only recognized and honoured the dignity in all people, but his life was an embodiment of these values. In so many ways and for so many people, Steve was the personification of human rights.

part I

Human rights and state responsibilities

chapter **1**

The concept of human rights

We live in revolutionary times. For nearly all of human history, there was no such thing as 'human rights'. Rather, individuals had whatever 'rights' their own government decided to bestow upon them. But what if a state granted few rights – or worse, if it engaged in cruel and barbaric behaviour against its own citizens? Unfortunately, until a relatively short period of time ago, this was viewed as a purely 'domestic' or 'internal' matter between a government and its own people, and was thus treated as being outside the purview of the rest of the international community.

All this has changed, at least in theory. Certainly, the greatest impetus for the present-day human rights revolution was the Holocaust, when an estimated 6 million Jews were cruelly and systematically killed during the Second World War. Here was undeniable and incontrovertible proof that citizenship might offer absolutely no protection against a government that sought to make war on a particular group of people within a given society. Yet what the horrors of the Holocaust also showed was that this laissez-faire attitude regarding how a government treated its own citizens was simply no longer acceptable. Thus what emerged from what was arguably the darkest period in all human history was the present-day human rights revolution.

What are human rights?

The legal philosopher Michael Perry has summed up the essence of human rights by positing that there are certain things that ought never to be done to people and certain other things that should be done (Perry 1998). These 'things', then, are human rights and these rights are best spelled out in a number of international human rights instruments, most notably what has been termed the 'International Bill of Human Rights'. The first and most important component is the 1948 Universal Declaration of Human Rights (UDHR), which is often termed the 'Magna Carta' of human rights instruments. Not only did the Universal Declaration proclaim that all people have human rights – political and civil rights as well as economic, social and cultural rights – but it was the UDHR that set everything else in motion. In the words of Johannes Morsink, who has written the definitive account of the drafting history, the UDHR has 'profoundly changed the international landscape, scattering it with human rights protocols, conventions, treaties and derivative declarations of all kinds. At the end of the twentieth century there is not a single nation, culture, or people that is not in one way or another enmeshed in a human rights regime' (Morsink 1999: x).

The Universal Declaration is just that: a declaration. Thus it is not binding international law, although a strong argument could be made that it has now reached the status of customary international law, in the sense that its provisions are something that states feel they must abide by. However, the effort to then transform the UDHR resulted in two separate treaties, rather than a single entity: the International Covenant on Economic, Social and Cultural Rights (Economic Covenant), and the International Covenant on Civil and Political Rights (Political Covenant), which comprise the other two legs of the International Bill of Human Rights. Why was the UDHR broken down into two separate treaties? The 'standard' story is that this reflects Cold War tensions, with the Western democracies championing civil and political rights and the communist states supporting economic, social and cultural rights. However, Daniel Whelan's recent scholarship (2010) goes far in exposing this as myth. What Whelan has found instead is that there was near-universal support for both sets of rights, but also a general recognition that the two sets of rights were 'different' from one another – different in terms of the substance of the right involved, different in terms of the enforcement of those rights and, finally, different in terms of the levels of international assistance and co-operation that would be needed to protect these rights, especially with respect to economic, social and cultural rights. Thus, after extensive debate on the matter, the decision was made to have two separate treaties.

The larger point is that there is universal (or near-universal) agreement on the substance of what constitutes 'human rights'. Given below is a partial list of these rights taken from the UDHR:

a right to life, liberty and security of the person (Art. 3)

freedom from torture or cruel, inhuman or degrading treatment or punishment (Art. 5)

a right to equal protection against discrimination (Art. 7)

a right to an effective remedy for violations of fundamental rights (Art. 8)

freedom from arbitrary arrest, detention or exile (Art. 9)

a right to a fair and public hearing by an independent and impartial tribunal in criminal proceedings (Art. 10)

a right to freedom of movement (Art. 13)

a right to seek and enjoy asylum in other countries (Art. 14)

freedom of thought, conscience and religion (Art. 18)

a right to work, to free choice of employment, to just and favourable conditions of work and to protection against unemployment (Art. 23)

a right to education that is directed at the full development of the human personality and to the strengthening of respect for human rights and fundamental freedoms (Art. 26)

a right to social security, and the realization through national effort and international co-operation of the economic, social and cultural rights indispensable for a person's dignity and the free development of her personality (Art. 22)

the right to a social and international order in which rights and freedoms can be fully realized (Art. 28)

Box 1.1. **Children's rights**

Much is often made of the near-universal ratification of the Convention on the Rights of the Child (Children's Convention). Under the treaty, states parties obligate themselves to provide children with many of the same rights that adults have under other international treaties. Unfortunately, the perfunctory manner in which the treaty has been ratified – but then essentially ignored in practice – serves as a perfect example of much that is wrong with our present system of human rights protection. First, the treaty contains a provision that obligates states to take positive steps to make the Convention known. Article 42 provides: 'States Parties undertake to make the principles and provisions of the Convention widely known, by appropriate and active means, to adults and children alike.' This, however, has seldom happened, as evidenced by the fact that studies show that few children (and few adults, for that matter) know the first thing about the Children's Convention.

Yet there is at least some indication of important change, and this is the second point. In their book *Empowering Children: Children's Rights Education as a Pathway to Citizenship*, Howe and Covell (2005) report on the transformative effect that children's rights education can have. One of the biggest concerns with the notion of children having human rights is that they would not understand that with rights come certain responsibilities. However, studies from school districts in Belgium, Canada and the United Kingdom show that the reality is just the opposite:

> Rather than understanding that responsibilities are inevitably
> concomitants of rights, and rather than understanding rights as a
> foundation for democracy, children who have not received children's
> rights education tend to believe that having rights means being able
> to do what you want. Thus, a lack of, or avoidance of, rights education
> may be more likely to promote a culture of personal entitlement rather
> than a culture of democratic values. (Howe and Covell 2005: 15)

How does being a rights bearer manifest itself concretely? One of the nicest (and most stunning) examples involves the seemingly time-honoured practice of bullying. Remarkably enough, what studies show is that when children think of themselves as rights-bearers, bullying ceases almost altogether. The reason is that bullying is seen as a violation of human rights and children develop mechanisms to protect their own human rights – but also the rights of their classmates.

The universality of human rights

Despite its name, the Universal Declaration is not 'universal', in the sense that although no country voted against the Declaration, eight countries abstained. In addition, in 1948 large parts of the globe, particularly in Africa and Asia, were under colonial rule and thus were not truly represented, either in the drafting of the UDHR or when the document was voted on in the UN General Assembly.

Still, human rights are universal in the sense that all human beings possess human rights by the mere fact of their human existence. Like all other human rights instruments that have followed, the UDHR speaks in terms of protecting 'everyone' and denying human rights protection to 'no one'. What does not matter is where a person lives or the kind of government under which a person happens to live. What also does not matter is whether or not a particular state has agreed to be bound by any particular human rights treaty. In that way, then, although the United States is one of only two countries (Somalia is the other) that is not a state party to the Children's Convention (see Box 1.1), this does not mean that young people in the United States have no human rights. Rather, what this means is that these (human) rights will have to be protected solely through domestic (US) means.

There is a strong and unfortunate tendency to make the concept of human rights more difficult and more complicated than it should be. Furthermore, and perhaps because of this, human rights are often dismissed as being unrealistic and even utopian in nature. The reality, however, is much different from this. Human rights represent the bare minimum that is required for a person to live a human – as opposed to an inhuman – existence. Thus human rights are more properly thought of as establishing a floor below which no individual is to be allowed to fall. Yet human rights should not be viewed in terms of taking care of people. Rather, it is about creating conditions so that people can take care of themselves if they are able. More importantly, what human rights do is to create the (legal) guarantee that people will be able to provide for themselves. As the Nobel Prize recipient Amartya Sen (1981) has emphasized, hunger is not a simple by-product of the unavailability of food, but, rather, the unavailability of an entitlement to food.

One of the great misconceptions is to view human rights simply as moral rights or as rights based on certain religious or ethical principles – but nothing beyond that. Human rights are most certainly based on particular values of how people ought to live and how people ought to be treated, as we shall see in a moment. However, much of this book will be devoted to the idea that human rights are also legal rights. But we take this principle one step further by positing that states have certain well-defined legal obligations to protect those rights. Thus not only are human rights universal, but the responsibility to protect human rights is universal as well.

No doubt one of the problems in accepting the idea that human rights are legal rights comes from the enormous chasm between promise and reality – between the rights proclaimed by international human rights instruments and the cruel reality that a substantial portion of humanity is currently denied some form of human rights protection. How can there be a human right to food when upwards of 2 billion people in the world face food insecurity each day? How can there be a human right to be free from torture when literally scores of countries (many of which are states parties to the UN Convention against Torture and Other Cruel, Inhuman or Degrading Treatment or Punishment (Torture Convention)) continue to carry out this practice with impunity? How is it possible even to think about the human rights of women when one in three women has been beaten, coerced into sex or abused in some other way; when more than half the women in the world over the age of fifteen cannot read or write; and when a woman dies every minute of the day from preventable pregnancy-related causes? And, finally, how can anyone really take the provisions of the Children's Convention seriously despite the fact that there is near-universal ratification of the treaty, when over 100 million children of primary school age are out of school; when there are 250 million child labourers worldwide and every year 22,000 children die in work-related accidents; and when, in 2007 alone, 9.2 million children died before their fifth birthday, many of preventable causes?

We have several responses, although we admit that we are not adequately satisfied with any of them. The first is to point out that this disjunction between promise and reality is by no means confined to the realm of human rights. This same problem can exist under domestic law as well. For example, the Fourteenth Amendment of the US Constitution promises equal protection under the law. Yet, as Jonathan Kozol (1991) shows in his disturbing book *Savage Inequalities*, there is an enormous gap between the educational opportunities that rich children in the United States enjoy and those afforded to children from poor families. Does this disparate treatment prove that the Equal Protection clause of the Fourteenth Amendment is meaningless? Furthermore, does this mean that the language of rights should not be used in this particular context?

A second response is to admit what should be evident, namely that the greatest and gravest weakness in the entire realm of human rights concerns the lack of effective enforcement and protection of those rights. We repeatedly come back to this issue. While we acknowledge that some important gains have been made, it is crucial that the issue of human rights enforcement is addressed head-on. Our last response to the gap between human rights goals and practice is to caution against accepting this 'reality' as the way that the world has to be and always will be. Instead, we believe that the protection of human rights is not only something that should be achieved, but something that can be achieved.

In that vein, consider the substantial progress that has been made in addressing the issue of world poverty, but also be cognizant of how meagre our collective efforts really have been. In his book *The End of Poverty: Economic Possibilities for Our Time*, Jeffrey Sachs (2005) argues not only that economic development is real and widespread, but also that the extent of what he calls 'extreme poverty' is shrinking. Furthermore, Sachs maintains that it is quite realistic to think that extreme poverty could be eliminated completely by 2025. The good news, then, is that great progress has been made; and the better news is that we could quickly and rather easily achieve vastly more than we have done to date.

Yet we live in a world where an average of 30,000 Africans die needlessly and tragically every single day of diseases such as AIDS, tuberculosis and malaria, which Sachs compares to the 3,000 people who were killed in the horrific attacks on the United States on 11 September 2001. We know how various countries responded to the 9/11 attacks. But how do they respond to the deaths each day of ten times this number? Few could claim that we have done well. Sachs writes,

> Contrary to popular perception, the amount of aid per African per year is really very small, just under $30 per sub-Saharan in 2002 from the entire world. Of that modest amount, almost $5 was actually for consultants from donor countries, more than $3 was for food aid and other emergency aid, another $4 went to servicing Africa's debts, and $5 was for debt relief operations. The rest, $12, went to Africa. Is it really a surprise that we do not see many traces of that aid on the ground? If we want to see the impact of aid, we had better offer enough to produce results. (Sachs 2005: 310)

Sachs then focuses on the action – but in reality, the inactions – of one particular country, the United States:

> Since the 'money down the drain' argument is heard most frequently in the United States, it is worth looking at the same calculations for US aid alone. In 2002, the United States gave $3 per sub-Saharan African. Taking out the parts for US consultants, food and other emergency aid, administrative costs, and debt relief, the aid per African came to the grand total of six cents. It's hardly shocking that [US Treasury] Secretary O'Neill could find 'nothing to show for it'. (Sachs 2005: 310)

The philosopher Thomas Pogge (2002) presents a similar criticism of the lack of attention and effort by the West. As he writes in his book *World Poverty and Human Rights*,

> The disbursement of conventional development assistance is governed by political considerations: only 19 percent of the $56 billion in official development assistance (year 1999) goes to the 43 least developed countries. And only 8.3 percent is spent on meeting basic needs. (Pogge 2002: 207)

Pogge continues,

> All high-income countries together thus spend about $4.64 billion annually on meeting basic needs abroad – 0.02 percent of their combined GNPs, about $5.15 annually from each citizen of the developed world and $3.83 annually for each person in the poorest quintile. (Pogge 2002: 207)

As should be evident, scholars such as Sachs and Pogge believe that Western states and Western governments could be doing far more than we are at present to help eradicate extreme poverty. We certainly agree with this sentiment. However, we are also of the mind that the reason why we have not done much more is that, while we recognize this terrible state of affairs as a human rights problem, *it is only viewed as a human rights problem for some country other than our own*. As we shall explain later, we believe that this represents a fundamental misunderstanding of the meaning of human rights.

Box 1.2. **Millennium Development Goals**

The Millennium Development Goals (MDG) derive from the Millennium Declaration adopted by the UN General Assembly in 2000 at a special meeting attended by 147 heads of state. Human-rights scholar Philip Alston has described the MDGs as the 'single most important focus of international efforts to promote human development and dramatically reduce poverty' (Alston 2005: 755–6). The MDGs set forth eight fundamental goals (along with various accompanying targets), many of which had already been endorsed in a series of world conferences over the course of the preceding decade or more.

Goal 1. Eradicate extreme poverty and hunger.
Targets 1 and 2: halve, between 1990 and 2015, the proportion of people whose income is less than one (US) dollar a day, and the proportion of people who suffer from hunger.

Goal 2. Achieve universal primary education.
Target 3: ensure that, by 2015, children everywhere, boys and girls alike, will be able to complete a full course of primary schooling.

Goal 3. Promote gender equality and empower women
Target 4: eliminate gender disparity in primary and secondary education, preferably by 2005, and to all levels of education no later than 2015.

Goal 4. Reduce child mortality
Target 5: reduce by two-thirds, between 1990 and 2015, the under-five mortality rate.

Goal 5. Improve maternal health
Target 6: reduce by three-quarters, between 1990 and 2015, the maternal mortality rate.

Goal 6. Combat HIV/AIDS, malaria and other diseases

Targets 7–8: have halted by 2015 and begun to reverse the spread of HIV/AIDS, malaria and other major diseases.

Goal 7. Ensure environmental sustainability

Targets 9–11: adopt principles of sustainable development, halve by 2015 the proportion of people without access to safe drinking water, and by 2020 make a significant improvement in the lives of slum dwellers.

Goal 8. Develop a Global Partnership for Development

Targets 12–18: develop a predictable, non-discriminatory trading and financial system, address special needs of Least Developed Countries, deal comprehensively with debt problems, provide access to affordable, essential drugs in developing countries, make available the benefits of new technologies.

The biggest obstacle facing the fulfilment of the MDGs is that they have done little to change the dynamic of state responsibility. Thus, notwithstanding MDG # 8, which calls for a 'global partnership for development', Western states continue to operate under the premise that less developed countries have the primary (if not exclusive) responsibility of achieving these goals on their own. The (human) consequence of this is that the world is not that much closer to meeting these goals than when they were pronounced in 2000.

Where do human rights come from?

The human rights historian Paul Gordon Lauren (2003) has elegantly defined human rights as a concern with 'others'. When we say that the 'human rights revolution' began after the end of the Second World War, we are of course not suggesting that there was never a concern for 'others' before this time – or that there has been any kind of full-blown concern with 'others' since then. What Lauren does in his book *The Evolution of Human Rights: Visions Seen* is to provide a wonderful account of the 'visions' of human rights that have arisen at various times in history and in so many different cultures, religions and philosophical approaches. Unfortunately, the brave and relentless visionaries who sought to carry out these precepts – those who fought against the international slave trade, those who promoted equal rights for men and women, those who opposed colonial rule, those who sought to eradicate genocide, hunger, torture and so on – were repeatedly met with derision, opposition or worse. Yet it is only through the tireless and, at times, seemingly futile efforts of these visionaries that the concept of human rights exists today.

Religion

Hinduism is the world's oldest religion, having been founded approximately 4,500 years ago. It teaches that all human life is sacred and should therefore be treated with an immutable respect and love. Indeed, the first principle of Hinduism is ahimsa, or doing no harm to others. In Judaism (founded approximately 3,300 years ago), the first book of the Old Testament, the Book of Genesis, speaks of the value and sacredness of all God's children, but also of the clearly defined responsibility that human beings have towards each other. This responsibility to others is most forcefully illustrated in Cain's cry to the Lord, 'Am I my brother's keeper?' In Christ's teaching, approximately 2,000 years ago, he repeatedly spoke of the need to take care of the poor, the sick and the hungry, and the necessity of welcoming strangers, perhaps best illustrated in the parable of the Good Samaritan.

Buddhism (founded approximately 2,500 years ago) is based on the universal issues of human relationships, a profound respect for the life of each person and compassion in the face of pain suffered by fellow human beings. Siddhartha Gautama, the founder of this religion, rejected the harsh caste system in place in India and instead asserted the worth of all human beings, regardless of their social position. At about the same time as the emergence of Buddhism in India, Confucianism was founded in China, emphasizing personal and government morality and social justice. The basis of all these teachings can be found by following Jen ('benevolence' or 'humanity'), which names the universal relationship between human beings. It is the manifestation of the best in humans, extending beyond the personal in its capacity to care for others, and is perhaps best summed up by this well-known Confucian expression: 'If there be righteousness in the heart, there will be beauty in the character. If there is beauty in the character, there will be harmony in the home. If there be harmony in the home, there will be order in the nation. If there be order in the nation, there will be peace in the world.'

Finally, there is Islam, founded approximately 1,500 years ago. The prophet Muhammad, to whom the tenets of this religion were revealed, preached in favour of an absolute equality among races and that religious toleration should be guaranteed. The Koran, the sacred book of Islam, addresses the sanctity of life, compassion and obligation to one's fellow human beings. One of the pillars of Islam is the notion of charity as a way of lifting the burdens of those that are less fortunate. Being not just a prophet and teacher but a government administrator as well, Mohammed recognized the inextricable link between religion and politics. He preached of freedom from the injustices perpetuated by social privilege, arguing that all men are equal in the eyes of Allah.

Philosophy

It is the very nature of philosophy to attempt to address the most difficult questions regarding human relationships. For centuries, moral and political philosophers from various traditions, cultures and historical periods have dealt with questions of justice and a person's responsibility to their fellow human beings. As we shall see, philosophers from a wide array of cultures espoused principles that we would now associate with human rights.

The duty towards others: the ancient world

We begin in ancient China, where, nearly twenty-four centuries ago, Mo Zi, the founder of the Mohist school of moral philosophy, taught the importance of duty, self-sacrifice and an all-embracing respect towards all others, not merely friends and family, but 'universally throughout the world'. Less than one hundred years later, Mencius, a Confucian-inspired sage, wrote extensively on human nature, arguing that humans are fundamentally good, but that this goodness had to be nourished and protected. A government ruled for the well-being of its citizens, and when it failed to do so it forfeited the right to rule.

Similar philosophies regarding social justice and morality developed in other regions of the world including Africa, the Americas and the Middle East. In ancient Babylon, King Hammurabi developed his still well-known legal code based on broad principles of justice among people. One of the first written sets of laws in recorded history, Hammurabi's Code, sought to give 'the oppressed man' equal protection under the law. In the sixth century BC, Cyrus the Great, founder of the Achaemenid Persian Empire, promulgated the 'Charter of Cyrus'. The Charter recognized certain rights such as liberty, freedom of religion and certain economic and social rights.

In Greece, around the same time as Mencius, an early Western tradition was developing predicated centrally on the notion of a universal law (what is now often referred to as natural law) of nature or god that pervaded all creation. This law governed the universe in all facets and gave a basis for egalitarian society founded on respect for citizens and for equality. These philosophers were concerned with the cultivation of virtue on both an individual scale and the scale of the city-state. In *The Republic*, Plato argued in favour of a universal justice that transcends one's immediate circumstances. Aristotle, one of the most pivotal Greek philosophers, contributed significantly to theories of natural right and politics. The virtues Aristotle advocated include charity and concern for others.

The Roman stoics broadened the scope of rights in practical application to include more beneficiaries than in the Greek tradition. They expanded views of nature to create theories of classical natural law. Cicero argued that this supreme natural law provided the source of real justice. He developed a theory of universal justice that guided human nature to act justly and be of service to others, claiming that the natural law binds all human society together. The body of law known as *jus gentium* (law of nations), developed by Roman jurists, expanded on this theory, asserting that the duties and rights imposed by this natural law far exceeded those acquired by citizenship alone.

From duties to rights: the Middle Ages, the Reformation and the Enlightenment

These early philosophies, which put forth a number of formative theories of human rights, ultimately hinged on universal responsibilities and duties, rather than on what we now refer to as rights. The modifications of theories and the transformation of theories into practice have long been tied to political, economic and social conflict. It took centuries of turmoil to pave the way for concepts of natural rights to emerge. The decline of feudalism gave rise to a middle class with political and economic power. The Renaissance and the Reformation liberated the individual from prior spiritual constraints and religious intolerance, and the citizenry became increasingly critical of tyrannical leaders.

Thomas Aquinas, the influential thirteenth-century philosopher and theologian, made lasting contributions to ethics and theories of natural law and politics. Aquinas translated and interpreted many of Aristotle's works, dealing especially with Aristotle's notion of natural right. Aquinas stated that natural law was divinely willed and posited a duality in which people were subject to the authority of both humankind and God. According to Aquinas, to live out of a sense of justice towards others was to live divinely. This helped natural law theory support the important human rights principle that every person is an individual apart from membership in a particular state.

Christian humanists and reformists in the late fifteenth to early sixteenth centuries further expanded rights theory by drawing on both the duty and compassion that religion impelled, as well as principles of moral philosophy in championing reform in political and economic arenas. The scientific revolution encouraged the belief that reason could discover natural law in human affairs. There was also a growing rejection of the notion of the 'divine right' of kings, and the increased recognition that all human beings are endowed with natural rights.

The Enlightenment facilitated a palpable shift in view from natural law as duties to natural law as rights. Enlightenment thinkers focused not so much on 'pure' scientific discovery and abstract system-building, but instead on applied science and reforms related to human nature and long-standing issues of human exploitation. John Locke, an English philosopher and one of the most pivotal thinkers of the seventeenth century, attempted to weave universal natural law and natural rights together. In his *Second Treatise on Government*, Locke emphasizes not interfering with another's rights, arguing that every human being in the 'state of nature' possesses certain 'natural rights'. People are born in a 'perfect state of equality, where naturally there is no superiority or jurisdiction of one over another'. All people are therefore entitled to enjoyment of all rights and privileges of the law of nature. It then follows that individuals form a government in order to preserve the natural rights of man (life, liberty and estate). His insight that all people are possessed of like faculties and that reason reveals a law higher than government provides tools with which to criticize governments and other power structures that might oppress people.

Several others of Locke's contemporaries expressed similar philosophical values regarding rights. In France, Jean-Jacques Rousseau, one of the major figures of the Enlightenment, argued that 'man is born free'. He and his intellectual peers, including Voltaire, the Baron de Montesquieu and David Hume, espoused the use of human reason and knowledge to free individuals from dogma and absolute authority. The German philosopher Immanuel Kant developed the notion of a 'categorical imperative', based on the principle of treating others as ends and not as means.

In the United States many thinkers, including John Adams and Thomas Jefferson, drew heavily on the principles of the Enlightenment for their political philosophy. The Declaration of Independence (1776) begins in decidedly Lockean language: 'We hold these truths to be self-evident, that all men are created equal, that they are endowed by their Creator with certain unalienable rights, that among these are life, liberty and the pursuit of happiness.' The Declaration was radical in its assertion of independence from Britain, but also in terms of its declaration of rights for all. In England, Thomas Paine's *Rights of Man* drew on theory of natural law and rights. Paine introduced the specific expression 'human rights', claiming that man entered society to have his natural human rights better secured.

The Second World War period

We now move to the period of the Second World War and focus on three documents. The first, but least well known, of these is President Franklin Roosevelt's address to Congress in January 1944, which has been described by the legal philosopher Cass Sunstein (2004) as the 'greatest speech of the 20th century'. What Roosevelt called for in his speech was for the creation of an Economic Bill of Rights as a natural complement to the original Bill of Rights in the US Constitution. Under this proposed Economic Bill of Rights, which remains unfulfilled to this day, all Americans would be entitled to

> the right to a useful and remunerative job in the industries or shops or farms or mines of the nation;
>
> the right to earn enough to provide adequate food and clothing and recreation;
>
> the right of every farmer to raise and sell his products at a return which will give him and his family a decent living;
>
> the right of every businessman, large and small, to trade in an atmosphere of freedom from unfair competition and domination by monopolies at home or abroad;
>
> the right of every family to a decent home;
>
> the right to adequate medical care and the opportunity to achieve and enjoy good health;
>
> the right to adequate protection from the economic fears of old age, sickness, accident, and unemployment;
>
> the right to a good education.

Sunstein notes that what motivated Roosevelt was not some idea of economic equality – but freedom. Roosevelt believed that people who live in 'want' are simply not free people. In addition, and just as important, Roosevelt was also of the view that 'want' is anything but inevitable. For Roosevelt, the US Constitution was an incomplete document. What was needed to complete the American Revolution was his proposed Economic Bill of Rights. Although his proposal has never been seriously pursued in the United States, the idea behind it played an enormously important role in the drafting of the Universal Declaration.

The second document is the United Nations Charter. In some ways the UN Charter is nothing more than a political document establishing a political institution: the United Nations. Yet the Charter can also be seen as a philosophical, historical, moral and legal document, created from the hell of the Second World War but also setting forth a vision of a future world. The Preamble of the UN Charter is certainly deserving of being quoted in full:

We the Peoples of the United Nations determined:

to save succeeding generations from the scourge of war, which twice in our lifetime has brought untold sorrow to mankind, and

to reaffirm faith in fundamental human rights, in the dignity and worth of the human person, in the equal rights of men and women and of nations large and small, and

to establish conditions under which justice and respect for the obligations arising from treaties and other sources of international law can be maintained, and

to promote social progress and better standards of life in larger freedom, And for these ends:

to practice tolerance and live together in peace with one another as good neighbours, and

to unite our strength to maintain international peace and security, and

to ensure, by the acceptance of principles and the institution of methods, that armed force shall not be used, save in the common interest, and

to employ international machinery for the promotion of the economic and social advancement of all peoples,

Have Resolved to Combine Our Efforts to Accomplish These Aims

Accordingly, our respective Governments, through representatives assembled in the city of San Francisco, who have exhibited their full powers found to be in good and due form, have agreed to the present Charter of the United Nations and do hereby establish an international organization to be known as the United Nations.

The final document is the Universal Declaration of Human Rights itself. At the present time, the UDHR has taken on an almost mythical importance. On one level, perhaps, this is a positive development, in the sense that governments and people the world over look to the document for guidance and inspiration. But in another way this view of the UDHR is detrimental to the protection of human rights, because the document is treated as more inspirational and aspirational than real. This is certainly not what the drafters intended. What they sought to establish was what Morsink describes as an 'aggressive' approach to human rights, and what they wanted to create, above all else, was a much better world than what they had lived through. Has the UDHR and all of the other international human rights instruments achieved this? Given the levels of starvation, extrajudicial killings, illiteracy, maternal deaths, torture and so on, that continue to afflict hundreds of millions of people, we believe that it is fair to say that the drafters of the UDHR would be appalled and outraged that their painstaking efforts have apparently amounted to so little.

Human rights and the West

Our discussion thus far should not be interpreted to mean that human rights are not a contested concept. One of the most compelling and intelligent critiques of 'human rights' has been given by Makau Mutua (2001), who has developed what he terms the savages–victims–saviours (SVS) metaphor in his criticism of the dominant approach to human rights. The *savage* in this model consists of non-Western states – but really, non-Western cultures – that refuse to follow the dictates of the European/US model. The *victims* are the nameless masses of sympathetic but helpless innocents who are thought to suffer under the misrule and misdeeds of these savage states. The third and final component is the *saviour*, which is made up of various Western institutions including the United Nations, Western countries (most notably the United States) and non-governmental organizations such as Amnesty International and Human Rights Watch that are based in the West. According to Mutua, 'human rights' is based on the un-stated precept that the saviour must protect the victim from the cruelties of the savage.

Mutua argues that what is so often missing from any discussion of human rights is a much broader historical and political context. In his view, what those who promote human rights systematically ignore is the long and ugly history of Western intervention – whether through colonial rule or the so-called 'civilizing' goal of Christian missionary work, and so on – that has brought great harm to non-Western people, but which has always been carried out under the banner of providing help and assistance to these 'unfortunate people'. Mutua describes what he sees as a seemingly incurable virus: 'the impulse to universalize Eurocentric norms and values by repudiating, demonizing, and "othering" that which is different and non-European' (Mutua

2001: 210). According to his analysis, what we now know as 'human rights' is little more than just another attempt by the West to exert its control over and influence on people and governments in all other parts of the world – but done under the guise of so-called 'universal' values. Mutua maintains that while Western people are quite enamoured of the human rights edifice that they have constructed, non-Western people are able to see right through this, which is why (in his view at least) the concept of human rights has virtually no legitimacy outside the West itself.

Another perceived element of Western hypocrisy involves the lack of Western self-examination or self-criticism. Thus while Western institutions are desperately intent on exposing the horrors carried out in 'savage' societies, these same institutions are either unable or unwilling to recognize the wrongs that they themselves commit. Thus, while discrimination against and abuse of females in non-Western countries is fodder for investigation and recrimination by the various 'saviour' institutions, what is systemically ignored are all the forms of discrimination and abuse suffered by females in Western states.

Finally, Mutua addresses the 'typical' white American high school or college student who earnestly joins the local chapter of Amnesty International, and in the course of doing so protests against such things as female genital mutilation in faraway lands or writes letters of protest to political or military leaders with names that do not easily roll off the English-speaking tongue, as Mutua describes it. Mutua honours the work of such students, but he provides this criticism and caution:

> The zeal to see all humanity as related and the impulse to help those defined as in need is noble and is not the problem addressed here. A certain degree of human universality is inevitable and desirable. But what that universality is, what historical and cultural stew it is made of, and how it is accomplished make all the difference. What the high school or college student ought to realize is that her zeal to save others – even from themselves – is steeped in Western and European history. If one culture is allowed the prerogative of imperialism, the right to define and impose on others what it deems good for humanity, the very meaning of freedom itself will have been abrogated. That is why a human rights movement that pivots on the SVS metaphor violates the

very idea of the sanctity of humanity that purportedly inspires it. (Mutua 2001: 219)

Without question, Makau Mutua presents an extraordinarily powerful and disturbing challenge to the entire notion of human rights, one that all those who believe in human rights (or say they do) need to confront and address. In contrast to this is the work of Michael Ignatieff (2001), a human rights scholar, activist and now a leading Canadian politician, and one of the great defenders of human rights and its values.

Ignatieff does not deny the primacy of Western states (and Western lawyers) in the drafting of the Universal Declaration of Human Rights. Yet, rather than proclaiming Western superiority, Ignatieff sees this document, written in the wake of the massive horrors of the Second World War, in just the opposite light: as a frank and painful acknowledgment of the enormous failures of the West. He writes,

> The Declaration may still be a child of the Enlightenment, but it was written when faith in the Enlightenment faced its deepest crisis of confidence. In this sense, human rights is not so much the declaration of the superiority of European civilization as a warning by Europeans that the rest of the world should not seek to reproduce its mistakes. (Ignatieff 2001: 65)

To be clear, this recognition of the shortcomings of the West does not mean that human rights are not based on certain Western values. Ignatieff takes the position that the most important value of all – protecting the individual from powerful oppressive forces within a given society – is a decidedly Western concept and there is no need to apologize for this. However, Ignatieff argues that these (Western) values have now become universal values, and this has been achieved by empowering the powerless and by giving voice to the voiceless in places the world over. Furthermore, Ignatieff adamantly opposes the notion that human rights are in any way an attempt to fundamentally change these societies – or the people who live there. What human rights do, instead, is provide the choice of opting out, but only when the individual himself or herself finds it necessary to do so. He writes,

> It is simply not the case, as Islamic and Asian critics contend, that human rights forces the Western way of life upon their societies. For all its individualism, human rights does not require adherents to jettison their other cultural attachments ... What the Declaration does mandate is the right to choose, and specifically the right to *leave* when choice is denied. (Ignatieff 2001: 70)

Thus while Makau Mutua sees human rights as a cover for the continued domination of Western interests and Western values, Michael Ignatieff sees human rights as transcending these things, and providing a common language for an equally shared, but contentious, conversation of how people are to be treated:

> But once this universal right to speak and be heard is granted, there is bound to be tumult. There is bound to be discord. Why? Because the European voices that once took it upon themselves to silence the babble with a peremptory ruling no longer take it as their privilege to do so, and those who sit with them at the table no longer grant them the right to do so. (Ignatieff 2001: 94)

We leave it up to the reader to determine who has the better reasoned argument. Like Ignatieff, we believe that there is certainly no need to apologize for defending and promoting human rights – if anything, there should be an apology for not doing vastly more than we do. However, one thing that concerns us about Ignatieff's approach is that it all sounds so easy: what human rights does is to provide an 'out' for those who face oppression. What we fail to see is this exit. For sure, Western states provide refugee protection to some small number of individuals seeking safety in another land, but, other than that, the sort of protection that Ignatieff is talking about seems much more theoretical than real.

In terms of Mutua's approach, we agree that the concept of human rights is riddled with hypocrisy and inconsistencies. In addition, we believe that it is essential that human rights be viewed with a cynical eye and that it is vitally important to place it within a broader historical context. However, one of our concerns about Mutua's approach is that it can easily lead to an excuse for doing nothing, the rationale being that any Western involvement in attempting to eliminate human rights violations in a non-Western country would only be another form of 'Western imperialism'. The point is that the policies of

Western states already have a profound effect on human rights practices in developing countries. To ignore those realities and to remove ourselves from any participation in preventing these wrongs is, in a word, a cop-out.

Box 1.3. Human rights and the 'War on Terror'

In an influential book *The Lesser Evil: Political Ethics in an Age of Terror*, Michael Ignatieff (2004) argues that Western states might have to resort to 'evil' measures in order to protect themselves from international terrorism. He writes,

> It is tempting to suppose that moral life can avoid this slope simply by avoiding evil means altogether. But no such angelic option may exist. Either we fight evil with evil or we succumb. So if we resort to the lesser evil, we should do so, first, in full awareness that evil is involved. Second, we should act under a demonstrable state of necessity. Third, we should choose evil means only as a last resort, having tried everything else. Finally, we must satisfy a fourth obligation: we must justify our actions publicly to our fellow citizens and submit to their judgment as to their correctness. (Ignatieff 2004: 19)

What is to prevent Western states from going 'too far'? Ignatieff answers that it is democracy itself that will do so. What do you make of Ignatieff's position? Can we – and should we – sacrifice some element of 'human rights' in order for greater societal security? Note, however, whose human rights would be forfeited. Note also that the democratic check that Ignatieff proposes would only include the voices and the interests of our own Western states.

International human rights law

International human rights law serves as the cornerstone of human rights. Without this law, human rights would be confined to the moral realm. With this law, there is both the hope and the possibility – but more importantly, the obligation – to make these ideals into reality.

Box 1.4. **Human rights timeline**

1945	UN Charter
1945–6	Nuremberg Trials
1948	Universal Declaration of Human Rights
1948	Convention on the Prevention and Punishment of the Crime of Genocide
1949	Geneva Conventions
1950	European Convention on Human Rights (entered into force 1953)
1951	UN Convention Relating to the Status of Refugees (entered into force 1954)
1965	International Convention on the Elimination of All Forms of Racial Discrimination (entered into force 1969)
1966	International Covenant on Economic, Social and Cultural Rights (entered into force 1976)
1966	International Covenant on Civil and Political Rights (entered into force 1976)
1969	American Convention on Human Rights (entered into force 1978)
1976	African Charter on Human and Peoples' Rights (entered into force 1986)
1979	Convention on the Elimination of All Forms of Discrimination Against Women (entered into force 1981)
1984	UN Convention against Torture and other Cruel, Inhuman or Degrading Treatment or Punishment (entered into force 1987)
1990	UN Convention on the Rights of the Child (entered into force 1990)
1990	UN Convention on the Protection of the Rights of All Migrant Workers and Members of Their Families (entered into force 2003)
2006	UN Convention on the Rights of Persons with Disabilities (entered into force 2008)

Yet, notwithstanding what is now a wealth of international human rights treaties, there are several misunderstandings about them. The first is the idea that there is a sharp demarcation between domestic and international law. Furthermore, the former is invariably treated as being 'real' law, while the latter is almost never viewed in the same way. This represents a misreading of both domestic and international law. Rather, when a country becomes a state party to an international human rights treaty – that is, when the government of a country signs and then ratifies a particular human rights instrument – what this state is thereby doing is incorporating this particular component of international law into its own domestic law. In that way, there is no distinction or separation between the two. Instead, the two become one and the same.

Consider the US accession to the Torture Convention. The UN General Assembly adopted the treaty without a vote on 10 December 1984 and it was then opened for signature on 4 February 1985. Article 27 specifies that the treaty will enter into force thirty days after the twentieth state has signed and ratified the treaty, and this was achieved on 26 June 1987. The United States signed the treaty on 18 April 1988. Under the US Constitution, Article II, Section 2, in order for a treaty to become part of United States law, the US Senate must give its 'advice and consent'. The US Senate did so 21 October 1994. At this point this international human rights treaty became a part of US domestic law.

Perhaps a more serious misconception about international human rights law concerns its scope and meaning. As a general, if not universal, rule, states operate under the belief that their obligations under international human rights law only apply to their actions within their own domestic realm, but that these same human rights obligations do not bind them when they act outside their own territorial borders. Certainly, the starkest example of this approach to human rights was the policy of the Bush administration to house 'enemy combatants' at Guantánamo Bay, Cuba, rather than in federal prisons within the United States. The rationale behind this policy was that the US government would not have the same human rights obligations towards these individuals if they were housed at Guantánamo Bay that they would if they were placed in detention somewhere within US territorial boundaries. It is noteworthy that governments the world over sharply criticized the United States for these practices. However, what also has to be said is that all states operate under this very same assumption.[1]

---

1 Within hours of taking office, US President Barack Obama ordered a suspension of the military tribunals in Guantánamo Bay. However, his plans of closing the prison by January 2010 have been complicated by resistance from US, British and French politicians to move the detainees to prisons on their own soil, despite widespread domestic and European support for the plans.

We strongly oppose a vision of human rights that provides two different sets of standards, one at home and another when a country operates outside its own territorial borders. As we will explain throughout this book, international human rights law – *all* international human rights law – gives rise to both domestic and international obligations (or what we shall call extraterritorial obligations).

To clarify our point, we use the Torture Convention as an example. We begin our analysis by asking this simple question: why would a country become a state party to the Torture Convention? The answer seems obvious. A country becomes a state party in order to prevent or eliminate torture. Yet if a state were interested only in preventing torture within its own domestic borders – but were completely indifferent to whether this odious practice was carried out in any other place – why would it go to all the trouble of signing and ratifying an international human rights instrument? Why not simply ban torture through domestic legislation and leave matters at that?

Our answer is that international human rights treaties mean something more than this. In becoming a state party to an international human rights treaty, each state party is committing itself not only to protecting human rights within its own territorial borders, but also to helping to work towards the elimination of violations of human rights, no matter where these might take place. It is this aspect, more than anything else, that truly makes human rights so revolutionary.

Introducing the major players

· ·

There are a multitude of institutions and actors involved in human rights. We close this chapter by introducing briefly some of the major players.

The United Nations human rights system

The protection of human rights is one of the primary objectives of the United Nations and there are a number of bodies within it that address human rights issues, either directly or indirectly.

The Human Rights Commission/Council

Arguably, the principal UN organ dealing with human rights is the Human Rights Commission, which was replaced by the Human Rights Council in 2006. The Commission's contribution to human rights cannot be overstated. It was, after all, the Human Rights Commission that did the vital and painstaking work of initiating the drafting of nearly every one of the international human rights treaties, including the International Bill of Rights.

However, the Commission did not become (and was not allowed to become) the Great Defender of human rights that people around the world wanted it to become, as evidenced by the tens of thousands of petitions it received each year from victims of human rights abuse. This changed, at least to a certain degree, starting in 1967, when the Commission was given some authority to discuss human rights violations with particular countries, and in 1970 it was authorized to investigate complaints (but not individual complaints) where there was evidence of 'a consistent pattern of gross and reliably attested violations of human rights and fundamental freedoms'. However, this process has been both time-consuming and anything but transparent.

Still, the Commission/Council has produced some important and innovative work – most notably in establishing human rights standards, but also in subjecting human rights abusing states to some level of scrutiny and, at times, condemnation. The Commission/Council's various Working Groups and Special Rapporteurs also carried out groundbreaking work, some of which we shall see in Chapter 3.

The UN Human Rights Council came into existence in 2006 as a replacement for the Commission. It is made up of forty-seven member states (and not independent experts as are the treaty bodies described below) that are elected annually by majority vote. The rationale behind the change is that the Commission had become too 'politicized', and, more particularly, that countries that were some of the worst violators of human rights were being elected to serve on the Commission – and the United States was not (Alston 2006). Perhaps the most novel aspect of the new Council is that it has been designated with subjecting each country to a 'universal periodic review', based on objective and reliable information, of the fulfilment of each state of its human rights obligations. However, this procedure has just started and it is not clear how well the Council will be able to perform this task.

The High Commissioner for Human Rights

This position was created following the 1993 World Conference on Human Rights in Vienna, with the idea of having a single office serving as a focal point for human rights activity in the UN system. To a certain extent this has been the case, although the power of the position has seemingly waxed and waned depending on the political skills but also the visibility of the High Commissioner.

The human rights treaty bodies

The UN has established treaty bodies to monitor and administer the major international human rights treaties. With the exception of the Political Covenant (which is monitored and implemented by the Human Rights Committee, not to be confused with the Human Rights Commission/Council), the name of each treaty body is virtually the same as the treaty itself. Thus the Committee Against Torture (CAT) is responsible for administering the Torture Convention, the Committee on Economic, Social and Cultural Rights is responsible for the Economic Covenant, and so on. Unlike the Human Rights Commission/Council whose membership is made up of state representatives, each of the treaty bodies comprises 'independent experts'.

The states parties to each treaty are obligated to file periodical reports with the appropriate treaty bodies. In turn, the treaty body offers commentary on these reports in the form of 'Concluding Observations'. Beyond this, some of the most important work of the treaty bodies has come in the form of 'General Comments', some of which we shall examine in Chapter 3. Finally, several of the treaties also provide for a system of individual complaints (but only when a state has agreed to be subject to this procedure), and the treaty bodies deal with these complaints as well.

The Security Council

The UN Security Council has primary responsibility for maintaining international peace and security. It is the only UN body that can authorize the use of force, and in that way it can be instrumental in the protection of human rights, although, as we see in

Chapter 6, the Council has often been accused of shirking this duty, its non-response to the Rwandan genocide in 1994 and its present non-response to gross and systematic human rights violations in the Darfur region of the Sudan serving as two of the more glaring examples.

The Secretary-General

The Secretary-General of the United Nations is the head of the Secretariat (one of the principal organs of the organization) and acts as the leader and spokesperson of the United Nations. Article 97 of the UN Charter defines the Secretary-General as the 'chief administrative officer', but the role of the Secretary-General goes far beyond this, particularly the Secretary-General's ability to direct the spotlight on to the world's troubled areas.

The General Assembly

The General Assembly's competence is unlimited, and under Article 13 it can 'initiate studies and make recommendations' for the purpose of 'Assisting in the realization of human rights and fundamental freedoms for all without distinction as to race, sex, language, or religion'. The most direct role that the General Assembly has played in the protection of human rights is by means of a number of declarations passed by the General Assembly that have eventually become binding international human rights treaties.

The International Court of Justice

The International Court of Justice (ICJ) is the principal judicial body of the United Nations and it is housed in The Hague, Netherlands. Not to be confused with the International Criminal Court (ICC), the ICJ attempts to settle legal disputes submitted to it by UN member states, and it also gives advisory opinions on legal questions submitted by authorized international organs and the General Assembly.

We shall be referencing several ICJ opinions in various places in this book. In Chapter 2 we analyse the Court's 2007 decision in *Bosnia v. Serbia*, which deals with the responsibilities of states under the Genocide Convention, and in Chapter 3 we discuss the ICJ's holding in the *Arrest Warrants Case (Democratic Republic of the Congo v. Belgium)*, which deals with immunity of state officials. Unlike in domestic courts, there is no hierarchy of international tribunals.

However, the International Court of Justice, which is the successor of the Permanent Court of International Justice under the League of Nations, is certainly the most visible and prestigious international judicial body.

The International Criminal Court

The International Criminal Court (ICC) is a permanent tribunal established in 2002 by the Rome Statute of the International Criminal Court, and it also is based in The Hague. The ICC prosecutes individuals while the ICJ deals with state–state disputes. The ICC's authority is derived from Article 5 of the Rome Statute and it grants jurisdiction over four types of crime: genocide, crimes against humanity, war crimes and crimes of aggression (although it should be noted that the Statute does not explicitly define the crime of aggression, and therefore the ICC cannot prosecute it until states parties to the Statute agree on a definition). Although the ICC has got off to a slow start, in spring 2009 it issued its first indictment against a sitting head of state, President Bashir of Sudan.

Regional and country-specific international tribunals

Prior to the establishment of the ICC, the United Nations created two regional bodies to prosecute war criminals in two particular conflicts: the International Criminal Tribunal for the former Yugoslavia (ICTY), which also is housed in The Hague, and the International Criminal Tribunal for Rwanda (ICTR), which is based in Arusha, Tanzania. In addition to this, the United Nations helped establish the so-called 'hybrid' tribunal in Sierra Leone, the Special Court for Sierra Leone – hybrid because it had both international and domestic (Sierra Leone) judges. Finally, in early 2009 a UN-backed court – the Extraordinary Chambers in the Courts of Cambodia – brought its first criminal proceedings against Khmer Rouge leaders who had carried out genocide in that country more than three decades previously.

Regional actors

Some of the most important human rights work has been done under regional human rights instruments and by various regional actors.

The African Charter on Human and Peoples' Rights

Also known as the Banjul Charter, the African Charter was created by the Organization of African Unity (since replaced by the African Union). In a 1979 Assembly of Heads of State and Government a resolution was adopted for a committee to draft a continent-wide human rights instrument like those existing in Europe and the Americas. In 1986 the African Commission on Human and Peoples' Rights was created as a judicial body to enforce the provisions of the Banjul Charter. However, unlike its American and European counterparts, the African human rights court has not accomplished much.

The American Convention on Human Rights

The American Convention was adopted in San José, Costa Rica, in 1969 and came into force in 1978. The purpose of the Convention is 'to consolidate in this hemisphere, within the framework of democratic institutions, a system of personal liberty and social justice based on respect for the essential rights of man'. The American Convention is implemented at the first level by the Inter-American Commission on Human Rights, which then determines what cases are to be brought before the Inter-American Court of Human Rights.

The European Convention on Human Rights

The European Convention on Human Rights (ECHR) was adopted under the aegis of the Council of Europe in 1950 to protect human rights and fundamental freedoms. Notably, the Convention established the European Court of Human Rights, which many consider to be the single most important human rights adjudicatory body in the world. We analyse several of the ECHR rulings.

Non-governmental organizations

Finally, some of the most important players regarding all of human rights are the non-governmental organizations (NGOs) that push and prod states, the United Nations, international financial institutions, the media and so on, in the cause of human rights. There are literally thousands of NGOs, and thus it is only possible to list a very few of the better known ones: Amnesty International, Human Rights Watch, Doctors without Borders, Oxfam and so forth.

Conclusion

In this chapter we have shown that the principles and ideas of human rights can be found throughout human history, across time and space, and in different cultures and religions. The entitlement to human rights was institutionalized on an international level with the Universal Declaration of Human Rights, at a point in time when humankind had witnessed and experienced one of the worst atrocities in history. Since then, a new framework of international, regional and national structures has developed, as well as a network of varied institutions and organizations, which are aimed towards realizing the right to a life of dignity for every human being. Acknowledging the existence of universal human rights is an important step towards this goal, but it is only the first one. What must follow is the realization of the responsibilities that such rights bring with them. In the next chapter, we discuss the responsibilities of states to protect these universal human rights and evaluate various aspects of their track record to date.

FURTHER READING

The evolution of human rights

- Lauren, Paul Gordon. 1998. *The Evolution of International Human Rights: Visions Seen*. Philadelphia: University of Pennsylvania Press.
  This beautifully written book remains *the* definitive text on the historical development of human rights principles.

- Morsink, Johannes. 1999. *The Universal Declaration of Human Rights: Origins, Drafting, and Intent*. Philadelphia: University of Pennsylvania Press.
  Morsink's book offers a highly readable and insightful analysis detailing every step of the drafting process of the UDHR.

Poverty eradication

- Pogge, Thomas. 2002. *World Poverty and Human Rights: Cosmopolitan Responsibilities and Reforms*. Cambridge: Polity Press.
  The question Pogge addresses is, why isn't world poverty the single most pressing ethical issue of our time?

- Sachs, Jeffrey. 2005. *The End of Poverty: Economic Possibilities for Our Time*. New York: Penguin Press.
  Sachs uses some of his own experiences as a government consultant to explain how extreme poverty could be reduced substantially with relatively slight increases in Western foreign aid.

- Collier, Paul. 2007. *The Bottom Billion: Why the Poorest Countries Are Failing and What Can Be Done about It*. Oxford University Press.
  Collier's analysis is based on the idea that poor countries fall into various 'traps' – the conflict trap, the dependence on one natural resource trap, the landlocked trap, and the bad governance trap – that makes economic development maddeningly difficult to achieve.

- Sunstein, Cass. 2004. *The Second Bill of Rights: Why We Need It More than Ever*. New York: Basic Books.
  Sunstein argues that the only reason why economic rights were not included in the US Constitution is its timing as the earliest constitution in the world. The book focuses on Roosevelt's idea that those who are wanting are not 'free' people, and his proposal for a second Bill of Rights that would be focused on economic protection. Although this has never happened, at least not in the United States, many of Roosevelt's ideas (and those of his wife Eleanor) were reflected in the Universal Declaration of Human Rights.

Philosophical approaches to human rights

- Donnelly, Jack. 2007. *International Human Rights*, 3rd edn.
  Donnelly and his early collaborator, Rhoda Howard-Hassmann, remain two of the giants in the field of human rights. One of the arguments Donnelly is best known for is his passionate defence of the principle of the universality of human rights.

- Ignatieff, Michael. 2001. *Human Rights as Politics and Idolatry*.
  Ignatieff defends human rights against the charge that they promote Western values. His argument, instead, is that they are a reaction to the enormous failures of these values.

- Mutua, Makau. 2002. *Human Rights: A Political and Cultural Discourse.* Mutua's book presents one of the great challenges to human rights. According to his argument, 'human rights' is simply another attempt by Western powers to extend their domination over non-Western people. This truly is one of the most thought-provoking and challenging books on human rights.
- Shue, Henry. 1980. *Basic Rights: Subsistence, Affluence, and US Foreign Policy.* Although nearly three decades old, *Basic Rights* continues to be one of the most widely cited and most influential books in the entirety of human rights literature. Shue develops not only the idea of human rights but, just as importantly, the responsibility to protect those rights.

RELATED WEBSITES

- Human Rights Council, http://www2.ohchr.org/english/bodies/hrcouncil/.
- International Court of Justice, http://www.icj-cij.org/.
- International Criminal Court, http://www.icc-cpi.int/.
- Amnesty International, http://www.amnesty.org/.
- UN High Commissioner for Human Rights and Human Rights Bodies http://www.ohchr.org/EN/Pages/WelcomePage.aspx.

RELATED FILMS

The Holocaust

- **Schindler's List** (Steven Spielberg, 1993). This Academy Award-winning film remains unmatched in terms of its ability to convey the horror of the Holocaust. The film focuses on Oskar Schindler, who at the beginning of the film is a man with extensive business dealings with the Nazi regime. Schindler slowly becomes transformed and he ends up risking his life and his fortune to save the lives of his Jewish workers.
- **Night and Fog** (Alain Resnais, 1955). This stark and unsparing documentary released in the mid-1950s provided the broader public indelible images of the horrors of the 'Final Solution'.
- **The Pianist** (Roman Polanski, 2002). This is the story of Wladyslaw Szpilman, a brilliant Jewish musician who goes from a world of concert halls and acclaim to the confines of the Warsaw Ghetto and then the destitution and ruins of war-ravaged Europe. Szpilman is played brilliantly by Adrien Brody, who was awarded the Oscar for best actor, and *The Pianist* is able to show the horrors of the Holocaust by focusing on the suffering of one person.
- **Shoah** (Claude Lanzmann, 1985). This nine-hour documentary is a series of interviews with people who were involved in the Holocaust or affected by it – as well as those who still deny knowing that it was happening right in front of them.
- **Sophie's Choice** (Alan J. Pakula, 1982). This film is not about the Holocaust as such, but about a Holocaust survivor (Meryl Streep) who is faced with making two impossible decisions in her life. What makes the film so terribly effective is that the enormous crimes of the Nazis can be seen in both of these.

chapter **2**

State responsibilities

Our focus in the previous chapter was on the meaning of human rights. In the present chapter we examine the question of state responsibility. What obligations do states have to protect human rights, and when are states responsible for violating human rights? According to Article 1 of the International Law Commission's (Draft) Articles on State Responsibility, which were presented to the UN General Assembly in 2001, 'Every internationally wrongful act of a State entails the international responsibility of that state' (Crawford 2002). But when does a state commit an 'internationally wrongful act'? And what does it mean to be 'responsible' for this?

In most cases, establishing state responsibility for human rights violations will not be difficult, although states will do everything in their power to hide their actions from worldwide scrutiny. Imagine a situation where security officers of state A torture political dissidents in that country. This behaviour becomes public and the actions of the individuals involved are tracked back to the political leaders. State A is responsible for committing an internationally wrongful act and is thereby acting in violation of international law.

However, there will be other instances where establishing and assigning responsibility will be much more difficult. This is especially the case when a state acts outside its own territorial borders, or when a state's domestic policies have severe negative human rights consequences for those living in other countries. In terms of the former, for example, suppose that state A's agents had engaged in torture outside the territorial boundaries of state A. Has state A committed an internationally wrongful act in the same manner as when torture was carried out inside state A's borders? And would it matter if the torture victims were not citizens of state A?

This example can be extended. Suppose that agents of a neighbouring country (state B) provide training in torture techniques to agents of State A. Or imagine that state C provides equipment to State A (cattle prods were a common example in the 1980s), with full and complete knowledge that agents of state A were using this equipment to carry out torture. Or suppose that agents from state A frequently travel to state D – but authorities in state D make no effort to initiate any legal proceedings against these torturers. Or suppose that one of the torture victims travels to state E and files a legal claim against state A in the domestic courts of state E – but this suit is dismissed on the basis of the doctrine of sovereign immunity. Are any of these other states responsible, in some manner, for torture?

Freedom from torture is a civil and political right (CPR), but of course responsibility arises in the context of economic, social and cultural rights (ESCR) as well. Suppose that, in an attempt to reduce government expenditures, a state institutes a policy of charging school fees that has the effect of substantially reducing the number of young people receiving an education. This state is responsible for committing an internationally wrongful act and this state is acting in violation of international law. In particular, the state is failing to meet its obligations to protect the human right to an education. But to complicate matters slightly, what if the school fees were instituted at the behest of the International Monetary Fund (IMF) as part of a structural adjustment programme (SAP)? Can it be said that the IMF – and its constituent states – is also responsible for violating the education rights of these children?

Positive and negative obligations

One of the more useful ways of approaching this issue of responsibility is to think in terms of positive and negative obligations. A negative obligation is an obligation not to do something, while a positive obligation is an obligation to do something. Despite this simple classification, there will be instances where there will be elements of both involved.

Negative obligations

The most important negative obligation is the duty not to harm others. Negative obligations are universal and it is easy to see why. A person has an obligation not to harm other individuals, and location simply does not matter. Thus, all of us have a negative obligation not to harm other people, whether these individuals are family members, neighbours or people who live half the world away. Or as the philosopher Henry Shue has pithily stated, 'I can easily leave alone at least five billion people, and as many more as you like' (Shue 1988: 690). The obligation for states is the same. In that way, the prohibition against torture means that the United Kingdom is not only prohibited from torturing British subjects, but it is prohibited from torturing all individuals who are within its territorial borders.

Lopez Burgos v. *Uruguay* (1981)

But does this same obligation exist outside a country's territory? This issue was directly addressed by the UN Human Rights Committee in *Lopez Burgos* v. *Uruguay* (1981). The *Lopez Burgos* case arose out of the 'dirty wars' in the various Southern Cone countries in the late 1970s and early 1980s. The applicant, a Uruguayan national, claimed that Uruguayan agents had kidnapped her husband and had secretly detained him in Argentina. The Uruguay government denied these allegations, but it also held that the claim should be dismissed as inadmissible, because the International Covenant on Civil and Political Rights (Political Covenant) does not apply to actions taken by a state outside its own territorial jurisdiction. Article 2 of the Political

Covenant provides, 'Each State Party ... undertakes to respect and to ensure to all individuals within its territory and subject to its jurisdiction the rights recognized in the present Covenant'. The argument of the Uruguayan government was that while in Argentina, Mr Lopez Burgos was thereby not within Uruguay's 'territory and jurisdiction', and thus not within the purview of the Political Covenant (at least with respect to Uruguay).

The Human Rights Committee roundly rejected this position. It held that this language simply imposes a mandate on the state parties to uphold the provisions of the Covenant within its own territory, but that it says nothing that would permit states to perpetrate violations in the territory of another state. The Human Rights Committee went on to hold that 'it would be unconscionable to so interpret the responsibility under Article 2 of the Covenant to permit a State party to perpetrate violations of the Covenant on the territory of another State, which violations it could not perpetrate on its own territory' (para. 12.3).

The position of the Uruguayan government might not seem tenable, but also note that this idea that a state's human rights obligations are substantially different (and perhaps even non-existent) outside its own territorial borders is still very much with us. In fact, the policy decision of the US government to house 'enemy combatants' at Guantánamo Bay, Cuba, rather than in some location in the United States, was in large part premised on the idea that the country's human rights obligations toward these detainees would be considerably different in a prison 90 miles from the United States.

What makes *Lopez Burgos* (and the Guantánamo situation) easier to conceptualize is that it involves a single state acting directly – albeit outside its own territorial borders. However, there are other situations either where a state acts through other entities (either another state or through non-state actors), or where two (or more) states are acting at the same time, or where a state is responsible for violating human rights without being 'responsible' for those actions under a particular human rights treaty. In all of these situations, responsibility will be much less direct and much less certain. We illustrate this with three judicial rulings. The first (*Soering*) provides a very expansive reading of state responsibility, while the second (*Bosnia*) offers a decidedly narrower vision of state responsibility. The last case (*Bankovic*) is an example where a group of European states is 'responsible' for violating human rights, at least in a theoretical sense, but where there is no judicial body available to hold these states legally accountable for these actions.

Soering v. *United Kingdom* (1989)

Soering v. *United Kingdom* is generally regarded as one of the landmark holdings of the European Court of Human Rights (ECtHR). Jens Soering is a German national who was accused of committing a double murder in the US state of Virginia, but who then fled to the United Kingdom, where he was taken into custody. Authorities in Virginia sought Soering's return, and the question for the ECtHR was whether extraditing Soering, with the likely prospect that he would eventually be placed on death row under conditions the Court ruled amounted to torture and degrading treatment, would constitute a violation of Article 3 of the European Convention, which prohibits such treatment.

In terms of our discussion of state responsibility, the position of the British government is particularly interesting. The United Kingdom argued that after an extradition was carried out, it would not bear any responsibility for the manner in which Jens Soering might subsequently be treated, because at that point any harm done to him would be carried out on foreign (US) soil and at the hands of non-British actors. The ECtHR flatly rejected this position. It held that extradition under circumstances where torture and/or degrading treatment might ensue would violate the 'spirit and the intention' of Article 3 specifically and the European Convention more broadly.

Bosnia v. *Serbia* (2007)

The second decision is the International Court of Justice (ICJ) ruling in *Bosnia* v. *Serbia* from 2007. The principal issue in this case is whether Serbia, which had provided massive amounts of political, economic and military assistance to various Bosnian Serb paramilitary forces that had committed genocide, had thereby violated the Genocide Convention. Article 1 of the Convention provides, 'The Contracting Parties confirm that genocide, whether committed in time of peace or in time of war, is a crime under international law which they under-take to prevent and to punish.' Article 3 makes the following acts punishable as well: conspiracy, incitement, attempts to commit geno-cide and complicity in genocide.

To the disbelief of much of the international community, the ICJ ruled that Serbia was not responsible for committing genocide itself or for 'aiding and assisting' or 'complicity' in genocide. However, in a separate (and largely ignored) section of its ruling, the Court held that by not attempting to use its considerable influence over its Bosnian Serb allies, Serbia had not met its obligation to 'prevent' genocide; and through its failure to arrest war criminals for proceedings before the International Criminal Tribunal for the former Yugoslavia, it had not met is obligation to 'punish' those who had engaged in genocide.

Bosnia v. *Serbia* is perhaps the strongest and clearest affirmation by any adjudicatory body to date that human rights treaties give rise to both domestic and extraterritorial obligations. In this case, not only are the states parties under an obligation not to commit genocide themselves, but they are also under a legal obligation to do every-thing in their power to 'prevent' genocide in other countries. On the other hand, in terms of being responsible for 'complicity' in genocide (and perhaps for all other kinds of human rights violations as well), the ICJ set forth a nearly insurmountable standard, demanding not only that the sending state must control virtually all the activities of the recipient entity, but also that it must have been aware of the recipient's specific intent and, presumably, that it shared this intent. Under the ICJ's approach there are only two distinct and separate cat-egories: those states that (somehow) have met this 'effective control' standard, and then a separate category consisting of all those states that have not. The problem with this either-or approach is that under the Court's ruling, Serbia was no more 'responsible' for genocide in Bosnia and Herzegovina than Argentina or Canada, or a multitude of other states that had no connection at all to the gruesome events in that country.

Banković et al. v. Belgium et al. (2001)

The third and final case is another landmark decision of the European Court of Human Rights, only *Bankovic* v. *Belgium* takes a decidedly different approach to the issue of state responsibility than does *Soering*. *Bankovic* arose out of a NATO bombing mission over Serbia in 1999 that resulted in the death or injury of thirty-two civilians. Article 1 of the European Convention provides, 'The High Contracting Parties shall secure to everyone within their jurisdiction the rights and freedoms defined in ... this Convention.' The issue addressed by the Court was whether these civilians, who lived in a country that was not a state party to the European Convention, had thereby been brought within the 'jurisdiction' of these European states for purposes of Convention protection.

The ECtHR ruled that they were not and it dismissed the claim as inadmissible. The Court based its decision on the principle that the European Convention was only intended to apply to the 'legal space' of Europe. On the other hand, the Court acknowledged that the Convention had been given an extraterritorial reading in the past, most notably in a series of cases involving Turkey's occupation of part of Cyprus. In those cases, the Turkish government claimed that the European Convention did not apply to its actions in Cyprus because they were outside Turkey's territorial borders. However, in large part based on the need to avoid a 'legal vacuum', both the former European Commission of Human Rights and the European Court of Human Rights consistently held that the Convention did apply to Turkey's activities in Cyprus. Seemingly to accommodate these previous holdings, in *Banković* the Court ruled that the European Convention was 'essentially' or 'primarily' territorial, but that it could be applied to events outside Europe when one of the European states had exercised 'effective control' over individuals in these other countries. The ECtHR never spelled out what this entailed. However, in its dismissal of the case, what we do know is that dropping bombs and killing individuals is *not* exercising 'effective control' over the affected individuals.

Yet the ECtHR is not saying that the European states are not responsible for violating human rights, but rather that the European Convention does not apply to actions such as this that occur outside the 'legal space' of Europe. However, the ECtHR maintained that other human rights treaties are also without extraterritorial effect. This, of course, is the same position espoused by Uruguay in the *Lopez Burgos* case, but rejected by the Human Rights Committee.

To sum up, a negative obligation is an obligation not to do something and the most important negative obligation is not to harm others. We have argued that this obligation is universal in the sense that it applies to everyone. To a certain extent, international human rights law seems to follow this principle. Thus in *Lopez Burgos* the Human Rights Committee held that Uruguayan authorities could not do things in another country that it was prohibited from doing back home. In its *Soering* decision, the ECtHR even seemed to take this position a step further by ruling that the United Kingdom would be responsible for violating the European Convention simply by placing an individual in a situation – in another country and under the custody of foreign officials – where this person might subsequently face torture or degrading treatment.

The approach taken by the International Court of Justice offers two completely different views. In that part of its ruling in *Bosnia* v. *Serbia* dealing with the issue of 'complicity', the Court set forth an extraordinarily demanding standard, thereby failing to assign responsibility even in a situation where one state (Serbia) had provided enormous levels of military, economic and political support to an obviously dangerous and genocidal group of paramilitary forces in another country (Bosnia). On the other hand, the ICJ's ruling with respect to the obligation to 'prevent' genocide sets forth a quite revolutionary standard. According to the Court, each state has to do everything in its power to prevent genocide – no matter where this genocide takes place, no matter if these efforts would ultimately prove to be successful, and no matter whether other states were meeting their own obligations under the treaty. In its decision the ICJ held that Serbia had failed to meet this responsibility and because of this it had violated the Genocide Convention. However, what also needs to be said is that there are other states, the European countries and the United States in particular, that seemingly did not do all that they could to prevent genocide in Bosnia in 1995, or in Sudan since 2003 either.

Finally, the *Banković* decision shows us another side of state responsibility. The ECtHR did not seem to question or challenge the notion that European states had carried out human rights violations in a country outside Europe. However, the Court ruled that these acts by themselves did not bring the affected individuals within the jurisdiction of the European countries. Thus the European states have violated their negative obligation not to harm others – but they are not 'responsible', at least under the European Convention, for these actions. Of course, what remains unclear is where these violating states would be or could be held responsible – and under what law.

Positive obligations

Positive obligations are different from negative obligations in two ways. First, as noted before, while a negative obligation is an obligation not to do something, a positive obligation is an obligation to do something. In terms of the division of human rights, negative obligations are generally associated with civil and political rights, while positive obligations are generally associated with economic, social and cultural rights. Or, to state this even more simply, a state has a (negative) obligation not to torture a person and a (positive) obligation to feed those who are without food.

A second difference relates to the extent of the obligation. While negative obligations are universal, positive obligations are not. The essential reason for this is resource limitations. No individual has the duty to provide for all – and no state does either. Yet, because human rights are universal, what is demanded is a system that protects everybody. Shue describes this as establishing a system of 'full coverage':

> Universal rights … entail not universal duties but full coverage. Full coverage can be provided by a division of labor among duty bearers. All negative duties fall upon everyone, but the positive duties need to be divided and assigned among bearers in some reasonable way. Further, a reasonable assignment of duties will have to take into account that the duties of any one individual must be limited, ultimately because her total resources are limited and, before the limit is reached, because she has her own rights, which involve perfectly proper expenditures on some resources on herself rather than fulfilling duties toward others … One cannot have substantial positive duties toward everyone, even if everyone has basic rights. The positive duties of any one individual must be limited. (Shue 1988: 690)

Shue's comments relate specifically to the obligations of individuals, but the obligations of states run pretty much along the same lines. The world is divided into individual nation-states, and human rights protection is premised on each state being (primarily) responsible for protecting the human rights of all those within its territorial borders.

As mentioned above, positive obligations are more obviously related to ESCR, and the main international human rights treaty in this realm is the International Covenant on Economic, Social and Cultural Rights (Economic Covenant). Article 2(1) of the Economic Covenant provides,

> Each state party ... undertakes to take steps, individually and through *international assistance and cooperation*, especially economic and technical, to the maximum of its available resources, with a view to achieving progressively the full realization of the rights recognized in the present Covenant by all appropriate means ... (emphasis added)

One of the major distinctions between the Political Covenant and the Economic Covenant is that while the former demands immediate results, the latter does not. In other words, the Economic Covenant acknowledges the reality that a poor state cannot suddenly be expected to provide such things as the 'highest attainable standard of health care' to its entire population. However, what is expected is a 'progressive realization' towards that goal, meaning that next year is expected to be better than this year, but also that richer states have a responsibility for achieving these goals sooner than poorer states.

Thus the Economic Covenant provides states with a certain degree of leeway. However, large numbers of states have still not come anywhere close to meeting their obligations. One of the most tragic examples of this is Zimbabwe. In 2000–1, the Mugabe government instituted a disastrous land reform programme that resulted in the immediate decline of maize production of about 28 per cent. In addition to this, the country experienced a severe drought in 2002. The combination of these two events resulted in half the country's population becoming 'food insecure'. However, what made matters considerably worse is that rather than seeking international assistance and co-operation as mandated by Article 2(1), the Zimbabwean government placed restrictions on food aid to the country. Finally, the government used food as a political weapon by denying foodstuffs to its political opponents. Smita Narula has provided this analysis of the extent of Zimbabwe's failure to meet its human rights obligations:

> As a party to the ICESCR [International Covenant on Economic, Social and Cultural Rights], among other relevant international treaties, the Zimbabwean government's actions were in clear violation of international law. The government violated its duty to respect, protect and fulfill the right to food in significant ways. When it took measures to prevent access to adequate food it failed in its duty to respect the right to food. When it allowed other actors to deprive individuals of their access to adequate food it failed in its duty to protect the right to food. And when it refused to provide food for those who were unable to feed themselves, or to facilitate access to food by proactively engaging in activities aimed at strengthening people's utilization of resources and means to ensure their livelihood, it violated the duty to fulfill the right to food.
> (Narula 2006: 709–10)

Narula continues,

> Even where resource constraints existed, the government of Zimbabwe was obligated to meet its core obligation to ensure freedom from hunger. In addition, the government was under an obligation to guarantee, with immediate effect, that the right of food was exercised without discrimination of any kind, including discrimination on the basis of political or other opinion. The ESCR Committee has also emphasized that 'food should never be used as an instrument of political and economic pressure.' The government was clearly in violation of this norm.
> (Narula 2006: 710)

A domestic example such as this is relatively straightforward. And the fact that the Zimbabwean government actively pursued a number of inhumane policies makes assigning responsibility that much easier. However, even if the government had not done any of these things, it would still have a (positive) obligation to protect the economic rights of all those within its territorial borders by doing everything in its power to provide food to those in need.

Our discussion thus far has been limited to a state's domestic obligations. But is this the extent of a state's obligations, or does it have human rights obligations that extend outside its own borders? The apparent position of states, or at least Western states, is that they do not have any human rights obligations (or at least any positive human rights obligations) beyond their own borders. This position was most clearly expressed during the course of a country study of Sweden conducted by Paul Hunt, the former Special Rapporteur on the Right to Health. Sweden has long been among the most 'generous' countries in the world, and in 2007 it ranked second (behind Norway) in terms of the amount of foreign aid it provides in relation to its gross national income (GNI). However, when Hunt pressed Swedish officials whether they were under a *legal* obligation to provide such aid, the answer he received was negative. In his report Hunt takes strong exception to this position. He writes,

> [I]f there is no legal obligation underpinning the human rights responsibility of international assistance and cooperation, inescapably all international assistance and cooperation is based fundamentally upon charity. While such a position might have been tenable 100 years ago, it is unacceptable in the twenty-first century. (Hunt 2008: 28)

Which view is correct? The first thing to note about the Economic Covenant is that there is simply no mention (as there is in many other international human rights treaties) of either 'territory' or 'jurisdiction'. The second point is that the language in the Covenant is relatively straightforward: states clearly obligate themselves to provide 'international assistance and co-operation' in order to help achieve the full realization of the rights listed in the Economic Covenant.

Sigrun Skogly has undertaken the most thorough and searching analysis of the drafting of the Economic Covenant. Her conclusion is that there was a 'general consensus' among the drafters of the Covenant that the economic, social and cultural rights set forth in the treaty could only be protected through international means. Skogly writes,

> [T]he drafting history of Article 2 (1) shows that there are some inconsistencies in the approaches held as to the concrete meaning of *through international co-operation and assistance*. However, it seems that the delegations were quite agreed that international co-operation and assistance is needed for the full implementation of the rights, and that the resources available based upon this co-operation and assistance should be part of the resources used for the full realization of these rights. (Skogly 2006: 86, emphasis in original)

The idea that states have human rights obligations outside their own borders has started to gain more common acceptance. The current Special Rapporteur on the Right to Food, Olivier de Schutter, and his immediate predecessor, Jean Ziegler, have been among the strongest proponents of the idea that under the Economic Covenant states have both territorial and extraterritorial obligations. For example, Ziegler (2005) describes the fact that 'in a world richer than ever before, millions of children still starve to death' as 'scandalous'. He points out that every day more than 17,000 children under the age of five die from hunger-related diseases and that more than 5 million 'tiny children' will be killed by the end of the year.

> And every day, hundreds of millions of children do not get enough to eat to sustain a normal life, leaving them mentally and physically disabled. This is not only immoral. It is illegal according to international human rights law. It violates the right to food, the right to health, and eventually the right to life. (Ziegler 2005: 4)

In terms of specific obligations, Ziegler points out that states without sufficient resources have an obligation to seek international support, and 'States which are in a position to assist others have an obligation to do so' (Ziegler 2005: 15).

Box 2.1. **How generous?**

The University of Maryland Center for International and Security Studies and the Center for the Study of Public Attitudes has conducted studies concerning public attitudes and knowledge of US foreign aid programmes. In a 1995 study, when asked what percentage of the US federal budget went to foreign aid, the median response was 15 per cent. Nearly three-quarters of the respondents thought that US foreign aid was 'too high'. When asked what the 'right' amount would be, the median response was 5 per cent of the federal budget, and that 3 per cent would be 'too low'. This study was replicated in February 2001. This time the median response was that 20 per cent of the federal budget was spent on foreign aid.

How much does the U.S. government actually spend on foreign aid? Less than 1 per cent of the federal budget.

Ziegler's successor, Olivier de Schutter, has made it one of his top priorities to instruct governments on the two sets of obligations, one domestic and one extraterritorial, that states possess under the Economic Covenant. He writes,

> [T]he right to food imposes on all States obligations not only towards the persons living on their national territory, but also towards the populations of other States.
>
> These two sets of obligations complement one another. The right to food can be fully realized only when both national and international obligations are complied with. (De Schutter 2008: 6)

Box 2.2. **Official Development Assistance**

Most aid flows from the developed world are distributed as Official Development Assistance (ODA), which is monitored and recorded by the Development Assistance Committee (DAC) of the OECD. The graph shows how much aid countries distributed during 2007, calculated as a percentage of their current gross national income. Only Norway, Sweden, Luxembourg, Netherlands and Denmark are above the target of 0.7 per cent agreed to by the United Nations, while 50 per cent of countries contributed less than 3.8 per cent of their GNI.

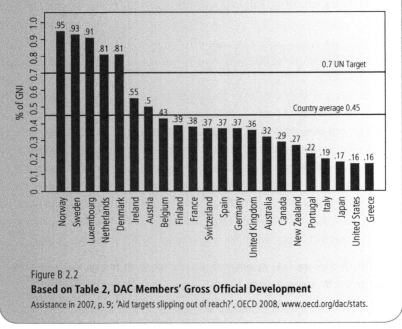

Figure B 2.2
Based on Table 2, DAC Members' Gross Official Development
Assistance in 2007, p. 9; 'Aid targets slipping out of reach?', OECD 2008, www.oecd.org/dac/stats.

The Committee on Economic, Social and Cultural Rights, the UN body that is responsible for implementing the Economic Covenant, has also started to push the notion that the Economic Covenant gives rise to both domestic and what it calls 'international obligations', or what we have termed 'extraterritorial obligations'. In one of its earliest General Comments (No. 3, 1990), the Committee explained that the term 'maximum available resources' in Article 2(1) referred to resources 'existing within a State and those available from the international community through international co-operation and assistance' (para. 1). The Committee then proceeded to explain,

> It is particularly incumbent upon those states that are in a position to assist others in this regard ... It [the Economic Covenant] emphasizes that, in the absence of an active programme of international assistance and co-operation on the part of all those States that are in a position to undertake one, the full realization of economic, social and cultural rights will remain an unfulfilled aspiration in many countries. (para. 14)

The Committee has repeatedly returned to this theme. In its General Comment on the Right to Food (No. 12, 1999), the ESCR Committee stressed that states parties have an obligation to 'take steps to respect the enjoyment of the right to food in other countries, to protect that right, to facilitate access to food and to provide the necessary aid when required' (para. 12). In its General Comment on the Right to Health (No. 14, 2000), the Committee noted that 'depending on the availability of resources, States should facilitate access to essential health facilities, goods and services in other countries, wherever possible and provide the necessary aid when required' (para. 39). Finally, in its General Comment on the Right to Water (No. 15, 2002), the Committee held that 'international assistance should be provided in a manner that is consistent with the Covenant and other human rights standards and sustainable and culturally appropriate. The economically developed States parties have a special responsibility and interest to assist the poorer developing States in this regard' (para. 34).

The Committee has started to use its Concluding Observations for the same purposes. For example, in its Concluding Observations to Ireland's 2002 treaty report, the Committee 'encouraged' the Irish government, as a member of both the World Bank and the International

Monetary Fund, to 'do all it can do to ensure that the policies and decisions of those organizations are in conformity with the obligations of the States parties under the Covenant, in particular the obligations … concerning international assistance and co-operation'. The Committee also 'urged' the Irish government to ensure that its contribution to international development co-operation reached 0.45 per cent of its gross national product (GNP) by the end of that year (2002), 'and that this annual figure increases as quickly as possible, to the United Nations target of 0.7 per cent of GNP'. In 2007, Ireland's aid contribution was 0.55 per cent.

In sum, states have not only negative obligations but also positive obligations. To use Michael Perry's conception of human rights, not only are there certain things that ought not to be done to people – but there are certain other things that should be done. Providing food, shelter, social security, schooling and so on are some of the 'things' that states are obligated to provide to those without. Moreover, a state's failure to use its maximum available resources to meet these obligations constitutes a violation of international human rights law.

We also questioned whether a state's human rights obligations ended at its own territorial borders. In terms of negative obligations, there seems to be almost universal agreement that negative obligations are both territorial and extraterritorial in nature. Thus, a state cannot torture an individual within its own domestic realm – or anywhere else. In terms of positive obligations, on the other hand, Western states seem to take the position that their human rights obligations are exclusively territorial. Under this approach, no state is (legally) obligated to provide any kind of foreign aid. However, this position has recently come under challenge.

Contested responsibilities

We close this chapter by turning to several examples where the issue of state responsibility has been contested. Each of the following examples involves some aspect of extraterritoriality. These certainly can be difficult issues to deal with, but, as globalization proceeds apace, such examples will multiply greatly. So the question is, what countries are responsible – and responsible for what?

Civil and political rights

We begin with examples of CPR. We do so not because we intend to give primacy to this set of rights, but on the basis that assigning state responsibility seems more intuitive in this realm. It is seemingly easier to assign responsibility when a country drops bombs on and kills civilians in another country than it would be where a country institutes economic sanctions and in the course of doing so helps bring about similar results. Human rights consequences will often be just as cruel and devastating when economic, social and cultural rights are violated. For example, compare the number of Iraqi deaths (between 350,000 and 500,000) that resulted from economic sanctions that were applied against that country from 1991 to 2003 with the number of civilian deaths (between 100,000 and 600,000) that have resulted from the current ongoing conflict.

Arms sales

The first of the two examples we use involves arms sales. In theory, there is nothing inherently wrong with selling arms to another country, especially if the recipient has a strong human rights record and the seller can reasonably assume that these weapons will be used only for defensive purposes. However, there are multiple examples where arms have been sold to countries with less than stellar human rights records. Lerna Yanik (2006) has provided a number of such examples. We highlight two. The first example involves the competition between a number of Western states (France, the United Kingdom, the Soviet Union, the United States and West Germany in particular) to arm and equip Saddam Hussein throughout the course of the 1980s – during a period when Iraq was fighting a deadly war with Iran, but also during a time when Hussein was conducting a genocidal campaign against Kurds in the northern part of the country. A second example used by Yanik is Rwanda, where a host of states (South Africa, Israel, France and Bulgaria) 'showered' weapons on this country just before the 1994 genocide, when ethnic tensions were on the brink of explosion. These are just two examples, but, as she readily admits, 'the examples of arms transfers to countries with problematic human rights records are countless' (Yanik 2006: 358).

Perhaps the most startling thing is that, with the exception of China, the other permanent members of the UN Security Council were the biggest arms dealers in the world for the period of her study (1999–2003). According to Yanik's data, the following countries were the largest arms dealers in the world during this period of time, with the percentage of the world market in parentheses:

United States (34.0%)

Russia (30.0%)

France (7.2%)

Germany (5.9%)

United Kingdom (4.8%)

Ukraine (2.5%)

Italy (1.9%)

China (1.7%)

Netherlands (1.4%)

Canada (1.4%)

Most countries (Russia, China and the Ukraine being the exceptions) have some human rights conditionality in their arms export laws. That is, arms are not (supposed) to be sold to countries that violate human rights. Yet this is exactly what has taken place. In her analysis Yanik applied the Freedom House Report categorization of whether states were *free, partly free* or *not free*. These three categories capture the extent to which political rights and civil liberties are respected in a particular country.[1] Yanik also accounted in her analysis for whether the country receiving arms was experiencing a war or conflict. She then examined arms sales on the basis of this. For the period 1999–2003 she found that nine (of thirty-five) countries to which the United States sold arms either were experiencing a military conflict or were classified as either *not free* or *partly free*. The number for Russia was nine; for France twelve; for Germany five; for the

---

1 More information about Freedom House and its reports can be found at http://www.freedomhouse.org/.

United Kingdom nine; for the Ukraine ten; for Italy nine; for China five; for the Netherlands six; and for Canada three.

Our question is whether the selling states are, or should be, responsible, in some manner, for the violations in these recipient states, especially those with egregious human rights records. This is not to suggest that the sending state would be as responsible as the receiving state. However, the present approach that seemingly assigns no responsibility to the selling state defies not only common sense but the demands and objectives of international human rights law itself.

Extraordinary rendition

The second example where countries might be responsible for the violation of civil and political rights occurring outside their own borders is 'extraordinary rendition', which already has gained a certain amount of notoriety in the 'war on terror' (Association of the Bar of New York City 2004). In the usual practice, extraordinary rendition occurs when an individual is kidnapped in one state, flown to one or more other countries, and subsequently 'interrogated' (meaning tortured) in a country like Egypt, Syria, Thailand or Pakistan (Mayer 2008). One of the more (in)famous examples involved Maher Arar, a Canadian national who was taken off an aircraft at John F. Kennedy airport, New York, during what was intended as a brief stopover. Arar was subjected to nearly two weeks of questioning by US agents, subsequently flown to Italy and then to Jordan, and eventually driven to Syria, where he was detained for more than a year and subjected to repeated torture. After his release, the Canadian government conducted an investigation of this matter and exonerated him of any wrongdoing. In addition, it issued an apology and paid him $10.5 million in compensatory damages. However, Arar's suit in a Canadian court against Jordan and Syria for the torture inflicted on him was dismissed by the Ontario Superior Court in February 2005 on the basis of sovereign immunity. We return to the issue of sovereign immunity in the context of torture in the next chapter.

The reaction of the US government has been considerably different. To this day, the United States has not offered any apology or any form of compensation to Arar and he remains on the country's terror watch list. Arar has filed a suit in a US federal court against various federal officials, alleging gross violations of his civil and human rights. This case was dismissed by the court on the basis that any litigation would entail having to divulge 'state secrets'. This decision was upheld by the US Court of Appeals. In June 2010 the US Supreme Court denied Arar's writ of certiorari, thus the dismissal of his suit stands.

What states are responsible for violating Arar's human rights? The most obvious case would be Syria. This is the country where the torture was carried out and it was also Syrian agents who apparently carried out the torture. Beyond this, a strong case could be made for US responsibility, although the ICJ's decision in *Bosnia* v. *Serbia*, discussed earlier in this chapter, might rule out US responsibility on the basis that the United States had not exercised the requisite degree of 'effective control' over Syrian officials who were physically carrying out the torture. But what about Italy and Jordan? Political and military leaders in both countries most assuredly knew where Arar was ultimately being sent and the fate that awaited him in Syria. On the other hand, it also seems both illogical and counterproductive to hold these countries anywhere near as 'responsible' for torture as Syria and the United States would be.

Economic, social and cultural rights

In this last section we examine violations of ESCR. We have already noted that one of the problems in assigning responsibility in this realm is that the actions (or inaction) of one state will often be much less direct and take place over a much longer period than in situations involving CPR. Another problem in assigning responsibility in the context of ESCR is that many of the actions that could give rise to human rights violations might be the result of policies that, at least on the surface, appear to be quite benign – and perhaps even good public policy. An excellent example of the latter is the rush by a number of Western states to develop a biofuel industry in order to reduce greenhouse gas emissions (as well as dependence on foreign oil). As countries began to rely heavily on certain foodstuffs as a biofuel source (maize in particular), food prices rose precipitously, resulting in widespread violations of the human right to food in a number of developing countries.

The Global Gag Rule

The first situation we look at comes from a study conducted by the Crowley Program in International Human Rights at Fordham University Law School, which is reported in the article 'Exporting Despair: The Human Rights Implications of US Restrictions on Foreign Health Care Funding in Kenya' (Hoodbhoy et al. 2005). The goal of the study was to measure the impact in one country (Kenya) of the 'Global Gag Rule', or Mexico City Policy, which was an executive order issued by George W. Bush on 22 January 2001. The Global Gag Rule formally reinstated a set of restrictions, first promulgated in 1984 by the Reagan administration, which prohibits foreign non-government recipients of USAID money from promoting or advocating abortion either as a means of family planning or, in all but potentially fatal cases, as a procedure to safeguard a woman's health.[2]

To put this example into context, in 2001–2 Kenya spent 17.6 per cent of its GDP on health, although this amounted only to $6.20 per person due to the country's extreme poverty. In addition, multilateral donors contributed 16 per cent of all health care funding in Kenya, USAID being the largest and most significant provider. After the issuance of the Global Gag Rule, two of the leading Kenyan health organizations, Marie Stopes International and Family Planning Association of Kenya, refused to sign the pledge required under the Mexico City Policy. As a consequence, both organizations suffered a significant loss of funding, which resulted in a severe reduction of staff and services. These two NGOs provide vital services to women throughout Kenya and often serve as the sole source of health care for poor and rural women. Thus the closure of the clinics had a severe impact upon the women in the communities they serve.

Kenya is a state party to the Economic Covenant. Article 12(1) proclaims the 'right of everyone to the enjoyment of the highest attainable standard of physical and mental health'. Article 12(2) specifies that among the steps necessary to achieve the full realization of this right is 'the creation of conditions which would assure to all medical service and medical attention in the event of sickness'.

---

2 One of the first things President Obama did when he entered office was to revoke the Global Gag Rule, as President Clinton had done before him.

Kenya's responsibility under the Economic Covenant to protect the right of everyone in Kenya to the 'enjoyment of the highest attainable standard of physical and mental health' is not being questioned. What is also not being questioned is Kenya's failure to meet this obligation. However, the question that the authors of this report raise is whether the United States was also 'responsible' for the increased ESCR violations that occurred in Kenya following the cut-off of USAID funding:

> Holding Kenya responsible for the effects of a policy instituted by the United States may appear beside the point in any setting other than international law. As this Report notes, Kenya has assumed binding obligations to realize the right to health, the elimination of discrimination based upon gender, and freedom of expression. As this Report further documents, the impact of the Mexico City restrictions within the country suggest that, in the first instance, the Kenyan government has failed to make good on these legal obligations. (Hoodbhoy et al. 2005: 91)

The report continues,

> This legal conclusion, however, begs the practical reality. But for the Mexico City Policy, the reductions in health and reproductive care, disproportionate impact on women, and attempted censorship of reproductive medical information described here would not have occurred. This is not to say the Kenyan government was powerless to anticipate and mitigate these effects. Yet at the end of the day, the effective causes for the challenges under review comprise the funding restrictions, USAID, and the United States. (Hoodbhoy et al. 2005: 91–2)

Despite this seemingly cause-and-effect relationship, the authors conclude that the United States was not responsible for the increased ESCR violations in Kenya, relying in large part on the fact that the United States is not a state party to either the Economic Covenant or the Convention on the Elimination of Discrimination against Women (CEDAW).

European Union sugar policy

The second example involves European Union (EU) sugar subsidies that have played a central role in making the EU the second-largest exporter of sugar into the world, with an annual surplus of 5 million tons of sugar that is sent out in the world market at artificially low prices. At first glance this scenario might simply look like business as usual, and perhaps it is business as usual. However, as Wouter Vandenhole has pointed out in his study of this policy, 'Because the viability of sugar industries is strongly influenced by world market conditions (one quarter of sugar output is traded internationally), the distorting effects of the EU subsidies on world prices had a considerable negative impact in the South' (Vandenhole 2007: 76–7). Not only are sugar farmers in the South not able to compete with subsidized EU sugar in the international market, but they are experiencing great difficulty competing with EU sugar within their own domestic markets as well. This, in turn, has led to widespread economic devastation in a number of sugar-producing states: 'Subsidies for surplus production and export dumping interfere with the right to an adequate standard of living of these individuals in the South who would otherwise be able to make a living from sugar production' (Vandenhole 2007: 90).

All twenty-five member states of the EU are states parties to the Economic Covenant. Article 11(1) of the Economic Covenant provides,

> The States Parties to the present Covenant recognize the right of everyone to an adequate standard of living for himself and his family, including adequate food, clothing and housing, and to the continuous improvement of living conditions. The States Parties will take appropriate steps to ensure the realization of this right, recognizing to this effect the essential importance of international co-operation based on free consent.

Vandenhole asks whether the overproduction of sugar, which is a direct result of EU policy, violates the Economic Covenant. He argues that it is:

> In conclusion, given the harmful effects of subsidies for surplus dumping on the right of farmers in the South to an adequate living and the lack of acceptable justification for these subsidies, it can be concluded that the EU sugar production and export subsidies that lead to surplus dumping in the South are in violation of the ICESCR. The EU itself seems to acknowledge that its agricultural subsidies have a detrimental impact on development in the South for, in the current WTO Doha Development Round of negotiations, it has offered to abolish its export subsidies, albeit on the condition of reciprocity. (Vandenhole 2007: 91–2)

Vandenhole continues,

> In light of this acknowledgement, the third state obligations to respect the right of individuals in the South, such as small sugar producers or labourers in the sugar industry, to an adequate standard of living can hardly be considered excessively demanding or unrealistic for it does not lead to a blanket rejection of all subsidies but only of those that relate to surplus dumping in the South. The consequences of this obligation are, moreover, in full accordance with sound economic analysis as the current regime leads to unfair competition with more efficient producers in the South and higher prices for consumers in the North. (Vandenhole 2007: 92)

Canadian mining operations

The last example is of a Canadian mining project on the island of Mindanao in the Philippines, which was reported by Sara Seck (2008). In 2004 a delegation of community members from Mindanao came to Canada, where they expressed concerns about environmental and health violations at the Canatuan mining project, which is owned by the Canadian mining company TVI Pacific, and also related concerns about Canadian government support for the mine. In March 2005, two community members travelled to Canada and testified before the Parliamentary Subcommittee on Human Rights and International Development and the Standing Committee on Foreign Affairs and International Trade (SCFAIT). In June 2005, SCFAIT adopted a report of the Subcommittee and presented it to the Canadian Parliament. The SCFAIT Report states as fact that

> [M]ining activities in some developing countries have had adverse effects on local communities, especially where regulations governing the mining sector and its impact on the economic and social wellbeing of employees and local residents, as well as on the government, are weak or non-existent, or where they are not enforced. (SCFAIT Report 2005, Introduction)

The Subcommittee expressed concern that Canada has no laws to ensure that the activities of Canadian mining companies in developing countries conform to human rights practices and standards, and it called for 'clear legal norms' in order to hold Canadian corporations and residents accountable. However, in October 2005, the government tabled such a measure and rejected many of the recommendations in this report. The Government Response noted that the international community is still in the 'early stages of defining and measuring' corporate social responsibility, particularly in the area of human rights. The call for establishing clear legal norms of accountability was rejected. Instead, the government committed itself only to examining the 'best practices of other states'.

At the time of writing, Canada does not regulate the environmental and health standards of Canadian mining corporations operating in developing countries. However, no other country applies its environmental and health laws in this fashion either. Thus, with respect to extraterritorial operations, the 'best practices' of Western states are really 'no practices', in the sense that no country has made an effort to regulate the operations of its own multinational corporations in this realm.

We return to the question raised earlier: which countries are responsible for committing human rights violations – and responsible for what? The easiest cases involve the practices of home states. In each instance, the home state is not meeting its obligation to protect ESCR within its own borders. In the examples given above, Kenya is not meeting its obligations under the Economic Covenant and neither is the Philippines. The same would no doubt be true in countries where sugar farmers have lost their livelihood.

But what about the other countries involved? We can begin with the Global Gag Rule. Is the United States 'responsible' for the increased violations of ESCR that resulted from the closure of clinics due to withdrawn funding from the United States, even if it was known ahead of time that there was a strong likelihood that the cut-off of USAID funding would lead to this result? But what about the responsibilities of other donor countries? Could it be said that after the US government had substantially reduced its aid, that these states now had a greater responsibility to help protect human rights in Kenya and presumably in other countries similarly affected by the Gag Rule?

In terms of EU sugar policy, Vandenhole concludes that overproduction of sugar is deliberate and that the EU proceeded with this policy even when the member states were fully aware of the severe negative human rights consequences for sugar farmers in developing countries. Vandenhole concludes that the EU (and its member states) is responsible for failing to protect the human rights of sugar farmers in developing countries. Is this conclusion correct?

Finally, despite the entreaties of affected populations, Canada has pointedly refused to regulate the behaviour of Canadian mining companies operating in other lands. One of the concerns of the Canadian government is that this would place Canadian concerns at a competitive disadvantage. Is Canada (and seemingly a host of other countries as well) 'responsible' for not taking measures that might lead to better environmental practices and better human rights practices in other countries?

Conclusion

This chapter has explored the issue of state responsibility for violating international human rights standards. Within a domestic setting, state responsibility is relatively easy to determine. Thus if a state (through its agents) carries out torture, it is thereby committing an internationally wrongful act. Or, to use an example from the realm of economic, social and cultural rights, if a state institutes school fees that has the effect of substantially reducing the number of children who are to receive an education, this country is likewise committing an internationally wrongful act.

What is much more difficult to discern is when a state pursues policies that have human rights consequences in another country. How does the practice of extraordinary rendition square with the obligation of countries to protect the human rights of individuals? In doing so, countries seem to do everything in their power to avoid responsibility altogether. Still, assigning responsibility in these situations would not seem to be a difficult task, although not all states involved in this should be responsible in the same manner and to the same degree. Thus a state whose agents carry out the torture would be more responsible than a state that served as a refuelling site for a 'torture flight'. What remains unclear is the level of responsibility that exists for the country that set all of these operations in motion, which was the United States in our particular example.

The question of responsibility is more difficult to establish for violations of ESCR, particularly when the actions (or inactions) of one country have severe implications for the enjoyment of these rights outside its borders. Yet difficulty alone in establishing responsibility for human rights violations does not automatically relieve a country from this responsibility.

FURTHER READING

Economic rights

- Hertel, Shareen and Lanse Minkler (eds.). 2007. *Economic Rights: Conceptual, Measurement, and Policy Issues.*
  This volume is divided into three parts: conceptual issues, measurement issues and, finally, policy issues relating to economic rights. The book represents an important effort to bring economic rights into the mainstream of the human rights literature.

Children's rights

- Howe, R. Brian and Katherine Covell. 2005. *Empowering Children: Children's Rights Education as a Pathway to Citizenship.*
  Howe and Covell breathe life into the Convention on the Rights of the Child. Perhaps the most compelling feature of the book is the multitude of studies the authors are able to reference showing how a true human rights education can be enormously beneficial to young children.

Extraterritorial obligations

- Skogly, Sigrun. 2006. *Beyond National Borders: States' Human Rights Obligations in International Cooperation.*
  Skogly's scholarship is vital to our understanding of the nature and scope of human rights. Her focus is on the drafting of the International Covenant on Economic, Social and Cultural Rights. She found that there was a general consensus that economic human rights could only be protected by means of international assistance and co-operation. Skogly's research provides some of the strongest support for the proposition that human rights are not territorially based.

- Coomans, Fons and Menno Kamminga (eds.). 2004. *Extraterritorial Application of Human Rights Treaties.*
  The essays in this volume present some of the clearest thinking in terms of the scope of a state's human rights obligations.

- Gibney, Mark. 2008. *International Human Rights Law: Returning to Universal Principles.*
  Gibney argues that there has been a fundamental misreading of international human rights law, and he suggests ways of going back to the original intent and meaning behind human rights.

- Kuper, Andrew (ed.). 2005. *Global Responsibilities: Who Must Deliver on Human Rights?* This collection is one of the few books that take up the argument of where responsibility lies to protect human rights.

RELATED FILMS

Economic, social and cultural rights

- **Darwin's Nightmare** (Hubert Sauper, 2004). A. O. Scott of the *New York Times* has described this Academy Award nominee as a 'masterpiece', and this might well be an understatement. There are no 'talking heads' in this film. Rather, the viewer watches this morality tale unfold as European concerns remove several tons of Nile Perch fish from Lake Victoria each day – at the same time that Tanzania is experiencing a famine. No one in the film can seem to make any kind of connection between these two things.

- **Black Gold** (Nick Francis and Marc Francis, 2006). Although coffee has become a worldwide commodity, what this movie explores is how desperately poor most coffee growers are. The film also looks at the manner in which the World Trade Organization maintains this status quo.

- **Mardi Gras: Made in China** (David Redmon, 2004). This story is told in two parts, and in seemingly two different worlds. The first is the revelry and drunkenness of Mardi Gras, marked by the colourful beads that are tossed around, particularly for those willing to remove their clothing. The other world is the Chinese factory where these beads are made, under conditions that most viewers could not comprehend.

- **Crude** (Joe Berlinger, 2009). This gripping film is focused on the legal battle over what has been termed the Amazon Chernobyl. The plaintiffs are a group of Ecuadoran citizens who claim that Exxon/Mobil has created an environmental disaster the size of the state of Rhode Island. What the viewer witnesses is the actual court proceedings held in the rainforest, as well as the political and judicial machinations that take place behind the scenes.

- **Born Into Brothels** (Zana Briski and Ross Kaufman, 2003). This film follows the otherwise bleak fortunes of a group of children from Calcutta's red light district. The moving force here is Briski, a professional photographer, who teaches the children her craft and then has their work displayed before a world audience. Of course, implicit in the movie is the idea of the countless millions of children born into similar circumstances who will never be afforded such opportunities.

- **In This World** (Michael Winterbottom, 2002). Filmed in quasi-documentary style, this story begins in a refugee camp in Pakistan and it provides the harrowing journey of young Afghans attempting to gain entry into the United Kingdom in order to seek asylum. Even the most hardened nativist will come to understand the forces that propel poor and dispossessed people the world over to seek life in the West.

chapter 3

Rights with responsibilities

One of the definitions of human rights that we presented in Chapter 1 was Michael Perry's notion that there are certain things that ought not to be done to people and certain other things that should be done. As we said then, these 'things' are generally what we mean by human rights. Perry approaches human rights on religious grounds. His conception of human rights is based on the idea that human beings are 'sacred', and because they are sacred they must be afforded certain protections. The secular approach puts forward that each and every human being possesses an inherent dignity. Human rights are the tools to respect and maintain this dignity.

In this chapter we examine the content and meaning of several specific rights, although it is important to understand that every human right is related to all others. We cannot cover the entire range of human rights, but we sample both categories of civil and political rights (CPR) and economic, social and cultural rights (ESCR), and outline the responsibilities and obligations that states have to protect those rights.

The first right we discuss is one that we have touched on previously, freedom from torture. One of the most publicized examples of torture in recent years has been the images of prison abuse – torture – at Abu Ghraib, where Iraqi citizens were subjected to severe physical and psychological pain and treated as disposable playthings for the amusement of US service personnel. After that we look at refugee protection. Refugees could be considered as the most desperate people of all because the basis of refugee protection is that a person has lost all human rights protection from his or her own government and is in search of such protection in some other country. Yet, as Andrew Shacknove (1985) has explained, refugees might also be seen as occupying a preferred position, as they at least have recourse to international assistance and protection, something that most victims of human rights abuse do not have.

We then turn to two related ESCRs: the right to health and the right to food. The numbers here are simply staggering. An average of 50,000 people die each day of preventable causes, and a substantial portion of this toll is due to disease and hunger. Children, especially those under the age of five, are the most likely victims, and it is not possible to imagine a more horrible existence than that of a small child who is allowed to die from either malnutrition or disease.

The last right we examine is the right to have an effective remedy. Another way of expressing this is the right to enforce your human rights. The tragic and repeated problem is that there is a double victimization at work here. The first involves the original human rights violation, while the second is the denial of redress or remedy that is promised in the human rights instrument itself.

Freedom from torture

The right to be free from torture is arguably the most widely recognized and universally accepted human right. Like most other human rights, the prohibition against torture exists in several international and regional human rights instruments, including the Universal Declaration and the Political Covenant. However, for purposes of simplicity, most of our discussion will be based on the Convention Against Torture and Other Cruel, Inhuman or Degrading Treatment or Punishment (Torture Convention).

What is torture?

Under Article 1, torture is defined as

> any act by which severe pain or suffering, whether physical or mental, is intentionally inflicted on a person for such purposes as obtaining from him or a third person information or a confession, punishing him for an act he or a third person has committed or is suspected of having committed, or intimidating or coercing him or a third person, or for any reason based on discrimination of any kind, when such pain or suffering is inflicted by or at the instigation of or with the consent or acquiescence of a public official or other person acting in an official capacity. It does not include pain or suffering arising only from, inherent in or incidental to lawful sanctions.

There are several aspects of this definition that we want to highlight. First, in order for some action to be classified as 'torture', the pain or suffering involved must be 'severe'. Anything less than this does not give rise to torture, although it might constitute cruel or degrading treatment. For some period of time, torture and cruel and degrading treatment were viewed as being one and the same. However, what has changed at least some of the thinking in this area is the 1978 decision by the European Court of Human Rights in *Ireland* v. *United Kingdom*, where the Court ruled that 'five techniques' – wall-standing, hooding, subjection to noise, deprivation of sleep, and deprivation of food and drink – did not constitute torture, but rather, cruel and degrading treatment.

When is pain or suffering 'severe'? It is, of course, impossible to say in the abstract when the threshold for torture is reached in a particular case. In that regard, one of the issues raised repeatedly during the course of the Bush administration's conduct of the 'war on terror' was whether 'waterboarding' (repeatedly pouring water into the mouth of a person held under restraint) constituted torture or not, Vice President Dick Cheney repeatedly (and rather infamously) claiming that it was not.

The Bush administration tried to redefine torture so that only treatment whose consequences could be death, organ failure or permanent impairment of a significant bodily function would constitute torture. However, one might argue that actions that fall under this very restricted category constitute only a small sub-group of actions that cause 'severe pain or suffering' as identified in the Torture Convention. Beyond this, the Bush administration also sought to establish the idea that when the president is acting as commander in chief, he is not bound by domestic or international prohibitions against torture. However, if this were the case, and if all heads of state maintained this position (and many still do), most torture in the world would not be illegal.

Second, torture can be either physical or mental. However, as the sadomasochistic images from the Abu Ghraib prison in Iraq show, torture will often have elements of both. Finally, there is a 'state action' requirement. This is generally interpreted as meaning that torture occurs only if state officials are involved, but it is important to note that private acts can also be considered 'torture' if the state has an apparent policy of allowing these practices to occur.

Domestic obligations

What are the duties and obligations of the states parties? Among others, countries obligate themselves to take effective measures to prevent acts of torture in any territory under their jurisdiction (Art. 2); to make acts of torture punishable under domestic law (Art. 4); to investigate allegations of torture (Art. 12); to establish a mechanism by which victims of torture are able to obtain redress and have an enforceable right to fair and adequate compensation (Art. 14); and to train police and security personnel properly so that they do not engage in torture (Art. 10).

While this list of duties and obligations is impressive, empirical evidence suggests that being a state party to the Torture Convention does not ensure that a particular government will not use torture as a political tool. In fact, 81 per cent of states that have adopted the Convention Against Torture violate it in the same year they ratify the treaty (Powell and Staton 2009). In a provocatively entitled article, 'Do Human Rights Treaties Make a Difference?', Oona Hathaway (2002) concludes that international human rights treaties such as the Torture Convention do make some difference – but not nearly as much as one might think. Emilia Powell and Jeffrey Staton (2009) conclude that only those states that have an effective and strong *domestic* legal enforcement system will honour their *international* obligations that follow from being states parties to the Torture Convention.

Extraterritorial obligations

In Chapter 1 we asked why countries become states parties to international human rights treaties, and argued that in becoming a state party to the Torture Convention a country is obligating itself to work towards the elimination of this egregious practice no matter where this takes place. The Preamble of the Torture Convention spells out this goal quite succinctly: 'Desiring to make more effective the struggle against torture and other cruel, inhuman or degrading treatment or punishment throughout the world.' Beyond this, the Torture Convention contains several provisions that explicitly set forth international or extraterritorial obligations for all states parties. We take up three of these: non-refoulement, the 'prosecute or extradite' provision and the inter-state complaint system. A fourth provision, the right to an effective remedy and redress for those who have been tortured, will be treated later in this chapter.

The first extraterritorial obligation we take up is the principle of non-refoulement. Article 3 of the Torture Convention provides that 'No State Party shall expel, return ('refouler') or extradite a person to another State where there are substantial grounds for believing that he would be in danger of being subjected to torture.'

The prohibition against non-refoulement is absolute, in the sense that it protects everyone, even those who have committed human rights violations themselves (including torture). However, the universality of this principle has now come under challenge. In *Suresh* v. *Canada*, the Canadian Supreme Court ruled that 'We do not exclude the possibility that in exceptional circumstances, deportation to face torture might be justified' (para. 78). The Human Rights Committee and the Committee Against Torture have both sharply criticized the Canadian government for this position, with the former making these pointed remarks in its Concluding Observations to Canada's state report:

> The Committee is concerned by the State party's policy that, in exceptional circumstances, persons can be deported to a country where they would face the risk of torture or cruel, inhuman or degrading treatment ... The State party should recognize the absolute nature of the prohibition of torture, cruel, inhuman or degrading treatment, which in no circumstances can be derogated from. Such treatments can never be justified on the basis of a balance to be found between society's interest and the individual's rights ... No person, without any exception, even those suspected of presenting a danger to national security or the safety of any person, and even during a state of emergency, may be deported to a country where he/she runs the risk of being subjected to torture or cruel, inhuman or degrading treatment. The State party should clearly enact this principle into its law. (UNHRC 2006: para. 15)

Beyond *Suresh*, as we saw in Chapter 2, the practice of extraordinary rendition has severely tested the meaning of Article 3, as several Western states, the United States in particular, have engaged in far-ranging as well as far-flung programmes that have resulted in those suspected of supporting international terrorism being sent to countries that have a long and ugly history of carrying out torture.

Another kind of extraterritorial obligation under the Torture Convention is the obligation of each state party either to prosecute all alleged torturers who are within the country's territorial jurisdiction, or to extradite these individuals to a country that will prosecute. This duty arises even if the state party has no connection whatsoever with the torture that has taken place in the sense that neither the victim nor the torturer is a national of that country. Instead, it is the torturer's mere presence in this country that gives rise to this legal obligation. In that way, based on the principle of 'universal jurisdiction', what the Torture Convention effectively does, at least in theory, is to establish an international constabulary force to eliminate torture.

In the United States an historical prosecution occurred in January 2009, when Charles 'Chucky' Taylor, a US citizen and the son of the former president of Liberia, Charles Taylor, was convicted in a Miami courtroom of leading a vicious paramilitary unit that routinely tortured and killed civilians in Liberia. Taylor was sentenced to ninety-seven years in prison. This has been the only time that US officials have brought criminal charges under the 1994 criminal law that prohibits torture, despite estimates that there are literally scores of torturers presently living in the United States. However, there is no indication that the Taylor prosecution will prompt the US government to begin initiating proceedings against these other individuals, or that it will seek extradition for these same purposes. Chucky Taylor's American citizenship should not matter. Rather, like all other states parties, the United States is obligated to prosecute or extradite all alleged torturers within its jurisdiction.

A similar case arose several years ago in the United Kingdom, involving the prosecution of Faryadi Sarwar Zardad, a former Afghan warlord who was responsible for carrying out torture in his own country. After applying for asylum in the United Kingdom in 1986, Zardad was arrested in London. British authorities invested more than £3,000,000 in collecting evidence against him in Afghanistan in preparation for this trial. In July 2005, Zardad was convicted in the London Central Criminal Court (Old Bailey) of conspiring to torture and other crimes against Afghan nationals, and he was sentenced to twenty years' imprisonment.

The final extraterritorial provision is the inter-state complaint system. Under Article 21, the Torture Convention allows a state to file a complaint against another state on the grounds that the latter is not fulfilling its obligation under the Convention. But to date there has never been a single complaint filed under Article 21 – but this is certainly not because torture has disappeared from the face of the earth. The inter-state complaint procedure is based on the idea that each state party has a vested interest in ensuring that other countries carry out their own obligations under the treaty. The fact that states have not (yet) employed this mechanism should not detract from this broader principle.

The *Filartiga* principle

Despite the widespread inaction over punishing perpetrators of torture, there have also been some positive examples where individuals who were responsible for inflicting 'severe pain or suffering' on people were either prosecuted criminally or else held civilly liable.

Perhaps the most famous case involving the latter is the *Filartiga* case. Dolly Filartiga, a Paraguayan national who had been living in the United States, brought a private civil complaint against a police official (Pena-Irala) who had directed her brother's torture and killing in Paraguay, but who was visiting the United States at the time that the suit was filed. In an historic ruling the Second Circuit Court of Appeals held that the prohibition against torture is universal, and that foreign nationals who are victims of this practice can use US federal courts and sue under a federal law (Alien Tort Statute), when those who directed and/or carried out torture are present in the United States and properly served. In this case, the Filartiga family was awarded a $10 million default judgment, although they have yet to collect any of this money from the defendant.

One of the outcomes of this ruling has been that a multitude of cases against individuals who directed or carried out gross and systematic human rights abuse have since been brought to US courts from human rights victims around the globe. This is no small victory for human rights and the pursuit of dignity, even if the judgments are almost all symbolic in the sense that compensation has rarely reached the victims.

The Pinochet principle

The second principle comes from the international effort to criminally prosecute the former Chilean dictator Augusto Pinochet. During a visit to the United Kingdom, British authorities placed Pinochet under arrest on 16 October 1998, at the request of the Spanish magistrate Baltasar Garzón, who was seeking Pinochet's extradition.

Over the course of the next eighteen months, the UK House of Lords issued three historic decisions, ultimately holding that as a state party to the Torture Convention, Pinochet could be extradited to Spain in order to be tried in that country for crimes committed in Chile. However, basing his decision on 'humanitarian' considerations relating to Pinochet's physical and mental state, the UK Home Secretary Jack

Straw ultimately declined to send Pinochet to Spain and allowed him to return to Chile. After his return, Pinochet spent much of the rest of his life fending off legal proceedings brought by Chilean officials.

The Pinochet case is one of the important victories in human rights. However, two issues should be highlighted. First, the Pinochet case certainly did not lead to a surge in prosecutions against those who directed or carried out torture. In fact, an interesting comparison can be made with the case of Hissène Habré, the former dictator of Chad, whose regime systematically practised torture in the 1980s (Brody 2006). Habré was overthrown in 1990 and he then fled to Senegal, where he has resided ever since. In 2000, Chadian victims and various NGOs filed a criminal complaint in Dakar, which even led to Habré's arrest and indictment, although he was soon released. In 2005, the Belgium government sought his extradition, but this request was rejected. However, after being criticized by the Committee Against Torture (CAT), in 2007 the Senegalese government finally began the process of instituting criminal proceedings against Habré under the universal jurisdiction principle. At the time of writing Habré's trial had still not commenced, although one of the more noteworthy developments is that in early 2009 Belgium filed a claim against Senegal before the International Court of Justice on the basis of the latter's unwillingness to proceed against Habré.

Second, the Pinochet ruling does not apply to current heads of state or ministers. In the *Arrest Warrant* case (*Democratic Republic of the Congo* v. *Belgium*), the International Court of Justice ruled that sitting government officials are immune from prosecution in domestic courts in foreign countries. Instead, the ICJ ruled that such proceedings can only take place before the International Criminal Court (ICC) or some other international tribunal (such as the International Criminal Court for Rwanda or for the former Yugoslavia), or in the courts of the home country itself. Charles Taylor, the former president of Liberia (and Chucky Taylor's father), is presently being tried before the ICC following an indictment handed down by the Special Court in Sierra Leone for his involvement in the civil war in that country. And in early 2009, the ICC handed down its first indictment against a sitting head of state, President Omar Hassan al-Bashir of Sudan, for war crimes stemming from the conflict in the Darfur region of that country.

Torture justified?

One might argue that torture could and should be justified if it would protect public safety. This is exactly what the Israeli Supreme Court held in *Public Committee Against Torture* v. *Israel*. Although the Supreme Court affirmed the principle that torture is prohibited under international law, it also ruled that there might be instances where state authorities could engage in such practices – the so-called 'ticking time bomb'.

The appeal of this position is obvious: large numbers of innocent people can be saved from dying by torturing one person – presumably one bad person. However, there are strong arguments that can be made against this position. The first is that the assumption in this scenario is always that security officials have the 'right' person. In other words, state officials know (somehow) that the person they are about to torture does in fact possess vital information. What is seldom considered is the possibility – the very real possibility as we know from some of the extraordinary rendition cases – that state officials have the 'wrong' person in their custody. Of course, one reason why they might have the wrong person is that after being subjected to torture, people will confess to just about anything and implicate just about anyone. Again, we know this to be true from a number of extraordinary rendition cases.

The second point relates to actual state practice. Under the 'ticking time bomb' scenario it is always a single individual who is tortured in an effort to save the lives of countless numbers of people. However, consider the widespread and systematic torture at Abu Ghraib. Did US officials truly believe that each one of these individuals had knowledge of a 'ticking time bomb'? Or were US officials simply on some kind of perverse fishing expedition – but at the expense of the well-being of innocent Iraqi civilians, and in violation of both domestic and international law?

The last point is to posit a counter-example to the 'ticking time bomb'. In this alternative scenario, government officials arrest a young man and subject him to repeated torture in the belief that he is a terrorist and that this treatment will elicit the information they deem vitally necessary. Instead, this person has been a law-abiding citizen – until he is subjected to torture. After his eventual release, he decides to strike out against those who wrongfully tortured him and he becomes a feared 'terrorist' who is singlehandedly responsible for a string of bombings that cause enormous human carnage. So does torture still seem justifiable?

Refugee protection

The second right we examine is refugee protection. As we noted before, a refugee is a person who has lost human rights protection in his or her own country and is in need of another home in order to enjoy such protection. Article 14 of the Universal Declaration provides that 'Everyone has the right to seek and enjoy in other countries asylum from persecution.' 'Asylum' is simply another word for refugee protection. Although an individual has the right to seek asylum, it is generally agreed that no state has a legal obligation to provide refugee protection. However, as we shall explain in a moment, states are obligated not to send an individual back to a country where this person's life or well-being would be threatened.

Who is a refugee?

In order to qualify as a refugee a claimant must be (i) outside her country of nationality, and (ii) have a well-founded fear of persecution that is (iii) based on one of the five following factors: race, religion, nationality, membership of a particular social group or political opinion.

The first requirement is that a person be outside her country of origin. There are many instances where individuals who face persecution are either not allowed or are not able to flee their home state. Those individuals who are in a refugee-like situation but who have not left their own country are generally termed 'internally displaced persons' (IDPs). There are now more IDPs in the world than there are refugees, and some states, such as Iraq, produce large numbers of both.

The second requirement is that the individual must have a 'well-founded fear' of persecution. Although there is disagreement in this area, the dominant view is that this standard has both an objective and subjective element, and the refugee claimant must prove both of these. The key is that the refugee claimant must show the prospect of future harm if returned to her country. This does not mean that past harm is not important. For one thing, evidence of past persecution may constitute strong evidence that the fear of future persecution is real. On the other hand, the absence of past persecution does not mean that a person will not face such treatment in the future.

How much 'risk' is necessary in order to have the required 'well-founded fear' of persecution? While the mere chance or remote possibility of being persecuted is insufficient to establish a well-founded fear, the applicant need not show that there is a 'clear probability' that he or she will be persecuted. Rather, the general rule is that the applicant must show a 'real chance' or 'reasonable possibility' of being persecuted.

What is 'persecution'? Oddly enough, there is no universally accepted definition of this term. However, it can be inferred that a threat to life or freedom constitutes 'persecution'. Although it is common to think of 'persecution' as human rights violations involving imprisonment or violations of the physical integrity of the individual such as torture, there is nothing in the definition that would restrict persecution in this manner. Rather, the dominant view is that the notion of persecution also includes other forms of ill-treatment, although there is widespread disagreement as to what the minimum level of severity this should be to qualify as persecution. Do all instances of human rights violation constitute persecution? If not, which instances of human rights violation should?

State practice shows a decided bias towards violations of CPR. Individuals fleeing from economic deprivation are invariably termed 'mere' economic refugees – which is to say that they are not refugees at all. The thinking behind this is that individuals fleeing from economic deprivation are better protected in their country of origin. There is no question that this is true and that a vastly more efficient and humane system would be to protect economic rights *in situ*, as it is referred to under international law. However, what if this is not done? Is it still justifiable to deny refugee protection on this basis?

The last component is the so-called 'nexus' requirement. In order to be a refugee under international law, the claimant must establish that the persecution she faces is based on one of five enumerated factors: political opinion, religion, race, nationality or membership of a particular social group. These terms are all self-explanatory except 'membership of a particular social group'. This category was introduced late at the drafting of the Refugee Convention and there is little indication of what it was intended to cover. Although adjudicators and scholars alike have struggled with this notion, the most common view is that the term does not encompass every definable group in a population but, rather, only groups defined by certain kinds of characteristic. One understanding defines such a common characteristic as one that the members of the group either cannot change (because it is an innate unalterable attribute or because the attribute that defines the group refers to some past actions or experience shared by the members) or should not be required to change because it is so fundamental to their identities.

Gender persecution has presented some of the most vexing issues in this area. In the *Kasinga* case, US immigration authorities granted asylum to a woman from Togo who had fled that country because of her fear of facing female genital mutilation (FGM) if she were returned to that country. The 'social group' in this case consisted of young women who feared FGM. On the other hand, US authorities rejected the asylum claim of an Iranian woman who had strong objections to wearing a burka, and who expressed a fear of the harsh consequences she would suffer if she were returned to Iran and refused to dress in that manner. Because of the difficulty of establishing a social group, one suggestion has been to change the refugee definition specifically to include a gender component. Yet another goes in the opposite direction. It would remove the nexus requirement altogether and grant refugee status simply on the basis of a well-founded fear of persecution.

Refugee numbers

According to data from the Office of the UN High Commissioner for Refugees (UNHCR), at the end of 2007 there were 11.4 million refugees and 13.7 million internally displaced persons. Where do refugees come from? According to UNHCR data, the largest number (3 million) were from Afghanistan and the next highest figure is the

2.3 million refugees from Iraq (this does not take into account Palestinian refugees, who are not under the UNHCR's mandate, but who would otherwise constitute the largest population of refugees). Thus, nearly half the world's refugees are presently from two countries experiencing war. These two countries are then followed by Sudan (523,000), Somalia (457,000), Burundi (376,000) and the Democratic Republic of the Congo (370,000).

Where do refugees go to? Although there is a great deal of discussion about the 'compassion fatigue' of Western states, it is important to point out that the vast majority of refugees in the world are being housed in non-Western states. The UNHCR estimates that approximately 9.3 million refugees (82 per cent) are being hosted in developing states, and that the fifty least developed countries host 18 per cent of the world's refugees. In short, while many Western countries have made a significant contribution in protecting the world's refugee population, much of this burden has been left to other states.

State responsibilities

The most critical of all refugee rights is protection against refoulement, which we have seen before in our discussion of the Torture Convention. The only important difference is that there is no nexus requirement under the Torture Convention, while there is one under the Refugee Convention. Article 33(1) provides,

> No Contracting State shall expel or return ('refouler') a refugee in
> any manner whatsoever to the frontiers of territories where his life or
> freedom would be threatened on account of his race, religion, nationality,
> membership of a particular social group or political opinion.

Article 33 prohibits refoulement 'in any manner whatsoever'. This means that not only are direct forms of refoulement prohibited, but also more indirect actions taken by a state or omissions that would have the effect of sending an individual back to her country of origin.

The principle of non-refoulement only prohibits return to territories where the applicant faces a serious prospect of harm. The principle does not prevent a state from sending a person to a country where this person would not face such a risk. Most Western states have denied access to asylum procedures in situations where responsibility for assessing an application for asylum could have been assumed by another state. This is generally known as 'first country of asylum' and it is based on the idea that the applicant could have (and should have) requested asylum if s/he passed through a safe country before arriving at the state where asylum is being sought.

In addition to the 'safety' of states that asylum seekers have passed through, many countries have also developed the notion of 'safe countries of origin'. Towards that end, receiving states have drafted an extensive list of countries thought to be 'safe'. If a country of origin is on this list, this will either serve to bar an asylum claim altogether or else result in accelerated procedures and/or different evidentiary standards being applied. In theory there is much to commend the idea that receiving states should not be wasting valuable administrative resources on asylum claims from individuals from 'safe countries'. The thinking behind this policy is that countries such as New Zealand do not produce refugees and receiving states should not be forced to spend time and resources on claims from individuals from such states. On the other hand, what is troubling is that some of the states that have appeared as 'safe countries' were anything but safe. A prime example was Algeria's inclusion on safe country lists throughout the 1990s.

Stemming refugee flows: the other side of extraterritoriality

We have made repeated reference to a state's extraterritorial obligations, positing that a state has human rights obligations not only to those within its own territorial borders, but also to those who reside in other countries. Refugee protection is perhaps the ultimate recognition of this principle, in the sense that it entails a transfer of the primary obligation to protect an individual's human rights from one country to another.

There is, however, another aspect of extraterritoriality that relates to the manner in which would-be receiving states have started to apply their immigration laws well outside their own national borders. In *Sale* v. *Haitian Ctrs. Council* (1993), the US Supreme Court held that the US Coast Guard's interdiction programme that stopped Haitian rafts in the Atlantic Ocean and then returned these passengers to that country was not in violation of the principle of non-refoulement. In an 8–1 opinion, the Court held that this provision in US law applied only to individuals who were within or right at the territorial boundaries of the United States – but that the prohibition against returning a person to a country where his life or well-being might be threatened did not apply to those who never made it to US territory.

The United States is not the only country that has extended the reach of its immigration laws (Gammeltoft-Hansen forthcoming). Australia has instituted the so-called 'Pacific Solution', which consists of intercepting unauthorized migrant vessels in international waters and sending refugee claimants to third countries for asylum processing. In southern Europe, migration control on the high seas has been carried out by Italy in the Adriatic Sea, by France and Greece in the Mediterranean, and by Spain both in the Mediterranean and in the Atlantic Ocean outside the Canary Islands. Beyond this, several states have claimed that 'international zones' or 'transit areas' in ports and airports do not form part of the national territory of the state in which they are situated. For example, the United Kingdom has taken the position that an asylum seeker arriving at one of its airports has not reached UK territory until he or she encounters immigration authorities. Finally, several European states have instituted carrier sanctions against airlines that bring 'unauthorized' migrants, thus providing a strong incentive for airline companies to restrict those who are allowed to travel to those states. All of these policies constitute a way in which destination states are extending the scope of their immigration control laws well beyond their own territorial borders – arguably all the way to the ports and air terminals of sending countries.

The right to health and the right to food

We now turn to two related ESCR rights: the human right to health and the right to adequate food. Article 25(1) of the Universal Declaration treats the two (and other) rights together: 'Everyone has the right to a standard of living adequate for the health of himself and his family, including food, clothing, housing and medical care and necessary social services.'

Health

These two rights are treated separately under the Economic Covenant. In terms of the right to health, Article 12.1 provides, 'The States Parties ... recognize the right of everyone to the enjoyment of the highest attainable standard of physical and mental health.' Beyond this, the right to health is also recognized in other international human rights treaties, including the Convention on the Elimination of All Forms of Racial Discrimination, the Convention on the Elimination of All Forms of Discrimination against Women, and the Convention on the Rights of the Child. In addition, an increasing number of countries (such as South Africa) now have this right enshrined in the national constitution itself (Kinney and Clark 2004).

The right to health is important not only in its own right, but also in terms of the ability of individuals to enjoy other human rights. The Committee on Economic, Social and Cultural Rights has described this interconnectedness in this manner: 'Health is a fundamental human right indispensable for the exercise of other human rights. Every human being is entitled to the enjoyment of the highest attainable standard of health conducive to living a life in dignity' (CESCR 2000: para. 1). The Committee goes on to say:

> The right to health is closely related to and dependent upon the realization of other human rights, as contained in the International Bill of Rights, including the right to food, housing, work, education, human dignity, life, non-discrimination, equality, the prohibition against torture, privacy, access to information, and the freedoms of association, assembly and movement. These and other rights and freedoms address integral components of the right to health. (UNCESCR 2000: para. 3)

Like all ESCRs, the right to health is subject to 'progressive realization', based on a country's 'available resources'. The Economic Covenant recognizes that ESCRs cannot be met immediately in many poorer states, but governments are under an obligation to make continual progress toward this end.

Notwithstanding this, some of the data are nothing short of horrific. Consider maternal mortality as just one example. Each year there are over 500,000 maternal deaths in the world, or the equivalent of one maternal death every minute. Some 95 per cent of these deaths are in Africa and Asia, and while women in some rich countries have a 1 in 8,700 chance of dying in childbirth, women in some low-income countries have a 1 in 10 chance.

Surely this represents a human tragedy of the highest order? Yet there has been a strong tendency to see this kind of situation as 'only' a health issue – not as a human rights issue. Paul Hunt, the first UN Special Rapporteur on the Right to Health, responds in this manner:

> [M]aternal health is not just a health issue, it is a human rights issue. Avoidable maternal mortality violates women's rights to life, health, equality and non-discrimination. Moreover, the scale of maternal mortality is just as large as – if not larger than – many of the extremely serious human rights issues that, for many years, have attracted much of the attention of established human rights NGOs. For example, several of these organizations campaign against the death penalty. In 2005, about 2,500 people under sentence of death were executed. This is almost certainly an underestimate, so assume this figure might be multiplied tenfold to 25,000. How many maternal deaths were there in the same period? About 500,000. (Hunt 2007: para. 34)

State obligations

As for all human rights, the primary responsibility for protecting the human right to health resides with the territorial state. Some states provide excellent protection, while others provide almost none. One of the most important considerations is the allocation of resources a government is willing, or able, to devote to these purposes. In the 1990s, for example, sub-Saharan African countries typically spent less than 3 per cent of their budgets on health. However, by 2003, many of the countries in this region spent between 11–13 per cent of their national budget on health-related goods and services (Garrett 2007). Although this is an important start, the overall poverty of these countries will continue to place severe constraints on the ability of those states to protect ESCRs.

What about other countries? In Chapter 2 we made reference to Paul Hunt's country report on Sweden. Undoubtedly the most unusal aspect of this study is that not only did he visit Sweden, he also travelled to Uganda and then to the World Bank in Washington, DC, in order to determine whether Sweden was also meeting its extraterritorial obligations. Hunt generally gave high marks to Sweden's work, although in his report he made several suggestions on how Swedish authorities could better incorporate human rights principles into their overseas initiatives. However, where Hunt strongly disagreed with Swedish policies was in respect to whether as a state party to the International Covenant on Economic, Social and Cultural Rights (Economic Covenant) Sweden was under a legal obligation to provide such assistance.

HIV/AIDS

One of the world's great health and human rights challenges involves HIV/AIDS, which has already killed 25 million people and presently afflicts another 33 million individuals, nearly all of whom (96 per cent) live in low- and middle-income countries, especially in sub-Saharan Africa.

Until the mid-1990s there was no effective treatment for AIDS and those who contracted the disease were consigned to a horrible death. In 1996, at an international AIDS meeting in Vancouver, scientists presented evidence of a new combination of drugs, known as antiretrovirals (ARVs), that were proven to extend the lives of those infected with this disease. However, the price of the drugs at that time was $14,000 per person per year, which made this drug financially out of the reach of all but a relatively small number of people in developing states.

Since then there has been greatly increased attention to this issue as well as increased funding. For example, the UN Global Fund to Fight AIDS, Tuberculosis and Malaria was created in 2002, and by 2007 it had approved more than $6.6 billion in proposals and dispersed $2.9 billion. In the United States, in his 2003 State of the Union address, President Bush called for the creation of a $15 billion, five-year programme for AIDS, tuberculosis and malaria, resulting in the creation of the President's Emergency Plan for AIDS Relief (PEPFAR), which primarily provides money for ARVs to infected individuals in sixteen countries. Yet, despite these and other efforts, in 2006 fewer than 25 per cent of Africans in need of ARVs were receiving them, and in rural areas that number was under 5 per cent (Farmer 2007). The target for Millennium Goal Number 6 is to 'have halted by 2015 and begun to reverse the spread of HIV/AIDS'. The great unanswered question, of course, is how (and who) has the responsibility for achieving this.

Box 3.1. **The 2004 tsunami and the recognition of extraterritorial obligations**

On 26 December 2004 a 9.0-magnitude earthquake on the floor of the Indian Ocean set off a series of tidal waves through the Bay of Bengal and as far as east Africa. Walls of water up to 65 feet high swept across the coastlines of Indonesia, Sri Lanka, Thailand and India, leaving more than 225,000 people dead and an additional 1.8 million homeless. What eventually ensued from this great tragedy was one of the largest humanitarian aid efforts in world history. Immediately following the tsunami, President George W. Bush declared that the United States would provide $15 million. This, however, created enormous criticism of the 'stinginess' of Western states generally and the United States in particular. The US commitment was increased to $350 million on 31 December 2004 and then to $950 million in February 2005.

The international response to the 2004 tsunami is one of the clearest examples of an extraterritorial obligation to fulfil. States that did not provide (enough) aid were roundly condemned – and most (if not all) quickly changed policy. This principle was subsequently strengthened by the international responses to the cyclone in Myanmar and the earthquake in China, both of which occurred in 2008. An obligation to provide assistance to those affected by natural disasters seems rather firmly in place. What would it take to recognize this same principle more generally – and outside the context of natural disasters?

Food

The second ESCR we examine is the right to food. The basis of this right should be obvious. People cannot live if they do not have adequate food, but the right to food goes much further than that. Even if individuals have enough to eat somehow to survive, the lack of proper nutrition has a serious debilitating effect on a person's overall health and well-being. Finally, individuals who do not know when (or even if) their next meal is coming are, in that way, reduced to a subhuman existence. There simply is no human dignity in suffering from starvation or malnutrition.

Box 3.2. **A story**

Uwem Akpan is one of the great chroniclers of life on the African continent. Akpan's stories are known for removing all vestiges of sentimentality – and perhaps even hope. The following excerpt comes from the short story 'An Ex-mas Feast' that is part of his anthology *Say You're One of Them*. The story concerns a squatter family in Nairobi, Kenya, living in almost unimagined destitution. It is Christmas time, but it is not clear whether Maisha, the family's twelve-year-old prostitute daughter, will be able to turn enough tricks that the family will have the means to enjoy a 'proper' holiday meal. To help ward off the family's hunger, the mother takes out sniffing glue (*kabire*). The story is told by Maisha's younger brother:

> Mama smiled at the glue and winked at me, pushing her tongue through the holes left by her missing teeth. She snapped the tin's top expertly, and the shack swelled with the smell of shoemaker's stall. I watched her decant the *kabire* into my plastic 'feeding bottle.' It glowed warm and yellow in the dull light. Though she still appeared drunk from last night's party, her hands were so steady that her large tinsel Ex-mas bangles, a gift from the church Ex-mas party, did not even sway. When she poured enough, she cut the flow of the glue by tilting the tin up. The last stream of the gum entering the bottle weakened and braided itself before tapering in midair like an icicle. She covered the plastic with her palm, to retain the glue's power. Sniffing it would kill my hunger in case Maisha did not return with an Ex-mas feast for us. (Akpan 2008: 7)

The human right to food is provided for in a number of international human rights instruments, most notably in Article 11(1) of the Economic Covenant, which reads,

> The States Parties to the present Covenant recognize the right of everyone to an adequate standard of living for himself and his family, including adequate food, clothing and housing, and to the continuous

improvement of living conditions. The States Parties will take appropriate steps to ensure the realization of this right, recognizing to this effect the essential importance of international co-operation based on free consent.

Despite this guarantee, it is estimated that nearly 900 million people in the world are chronically hungry, and the majority of these live in rural areas and half of them live in smallholder farming households. It is almost always assumed that this is because there is not enough food to feed everyone. This, however, is not the case. The human right to food is not merely about everyone being fed. Instead, it is about the entitlement to have access to food, or sufficient purchasing power to buy the food that a person and his or her family needs.

State responsibilities

Food is a commodity that is bought and sold in a global market, where the actions and activities in one part of the world can have a tremendous effect on the availability of food in countries all over the world. The present world food crisis is the epitome of this vast interconnectedness. Henry Shue pointed out more than two decades ago that 'A vote in Washington to change the wheat price support in Nebraska can change the price of bread in Calcutta and the price of meat in Kiev' (Shue 1988: 694).

Notwithstanding this, each state has the primary responsibility to ensure that the right to adequate food is protected for all those within its own territorial borders. This entails three types or levels of obligation: to respect, to protect and to fulfil. The obligation to *respect* means that states will not take measures that would reduce access to food – at home or in some other state. This is analogous to part of the Hippocratic Oath: do no harm. The obligation to *protect* requires that states ensure that enterprises or individuals do not deprive people of their right to adequate food. Thus, under the duty to protect, a state has a responsibility to ensure that its multinational corporations do not engage in practices in other countries that reduce access to food for nationals of this other state. Finally, there is the duty to *fulfil*, which means that a state has a positive obligation to help provide access to adequate food, if and when the situation warrants it.

Under a territorial approach to human rights, each state is responsible for meeting the right to food of those who are within its territorial boundaries. However, as we posit throughout this book, this provides an incomplete and even misleading view of human rights. Rather, as explained by Olivier de Schutter, the UN Special Rapporteur on the Right to Food, states have two related sets of rights:

> [T]he right to food imposes on all States obligations not only towards the person living on their national territory, but also towards the populations of other States. These two sets of obligations complement one another. The right to food can be fully realized only when both national and international obligations are complied with. (de Schutter 2008: para. 10)

The right to an effective remedy

Like all rights, violations of human rights demand some form of redress. A right without a remedy is no right at all, and this is true of human rights as well. Under the Political Covenant (Art. 3) the states parties agree to ensure an 'effective remedy' to those whose CPRs have been violated, while the states parties to the Torture Convention (Art. 14) obligate themselves to 'ensure that the victim of an act of torture obtains redress and has an enforceable right to fair and adequate compensation, including the means for as full rehabilitation as possible'.

The problem with this is that the state that has carried out the first human rights violation is invariably placed in the position of investigating itself. To be sure, certain mechanisms have been created that would remove at least some of the self-interest and bias that would otherwise be at work here. For example, the Political Covenant and the Torture Convention both have an individual complaint mechanism allowing victims to file a claim before the appropriate treaty body, assuming that the state has signed the Optional Protocol. Still, it is fair to say that the vast majority of human rights victims in the world have no realistic place to press their human rights claim.

An interesting scenario developed a few years ago involving Houshang Bouzari, an Iranian businessman who alleged that he had been tortured. Bouzari was eventually able to flee from Iran and move to Canada. After living there for a few years he brought a suit against the Iranian government in the Canadian courts. The basis of Bouzari's suit was that as a state party to the Torture Convention, Canada had an obligation to ensure for him some form of redress and compensation. While Article 13 of the Torture Convention provides for a remedial system for 'any individual who alleges he has been subjected to torture in any territory under its jurisdiction', Article 14 (see above) makes no mention of either 'territory' or 'jurisdiction'. What it refers to instead is 'the victim'.

The drafting of the Convention is also instructive. The drafters considered briefly, adopted without discussion and then abandoned one year later a proposal by the Netherlands to restrict the unconditional obligation in Article 14 to torture committed in territory under the jurisdiction of the state party (Hall 2007). Furthermore, there was no indication by the Working Group responsible for drafting the Convention that this lack of any geographic scope posed any special problem. Rather, the only country that has consistently given Article 14 an exclusively territorial reading has been the United States, which ratified the Torture Convention with this 'understanding' of its scope.

Notwithstanding this, Canadian courts dismissed Bouzari's claim on the grounds of sovereign immunity protection. However, following this, the UN Committee against Torture expressed concern at Canada's failure to provide a civil remedy for all victims of torture. In its 2005 Concluding Observations to Canada's report, CAT recommended that Canada 'review its position under Article 14 of the Convention to ensure the provision of compensation through its civil jurisdiction to all victims of torture' (UNCAT 2005: para. 5). At this point there is a disjuncture between the views of the CAT, the UN body that has been assigned to implement and monitor the Torture Convention, and various judicial bodies that have granted sovereign immunity protection for states accused of carrying out torture (Orakhelashvili 2007).

One of the great fears in all this is that the judicial systems in various countries will quickly become overwhelmed with cases from all four corners of the globe. We certainly can be sympathetic to this claim, although we hasten to add that we are also convinced that human rights violations in the world would drop dramatically if and when states were actually held accountable for their egregious actions. Nonetheless, there has come to be some discussion of other ways to help provide a forum to provide an effective remedy for victims. One such proposal (Gibney 2002) calls for the creation of an International Civil Court – not to be confused with the International Criminal Court, which already exists. Such a court is premised on the reality that nearly every victim of human rights abuse has no place to pursue her claim. In nearly every instance, pursuing a claim in the judiciary of the home state would be bordering on the suicidal. How can a victim of torture expect to be provided with an effective remedy by the state that is responsible for carrying out the torture in the first place? Furthermore, as we have seen here, other states have readily provided sovereign immunity protection to even the most abusive state. What the International Civil Court is intended to do is to provide a forum where victims of human rights violations would be able to pursue their claims.

A similar proposal has recently been made by the UN Special Rapporteur on Torture, Manfred Nowak, who has called for the establishment of a World Court of Human Rights within the United Nations itself (Nowak 2007). Under this proposal, the World Court would be based on a new international treaty – the Statute of the World Court of Human Rights – that would enter into force after a sufficient number of states had ratified the treaty. What is different about Nowak's plan is that each state would be able to determine which of the human rights treaties the Court would be able to exercise jurisdiction over. Thus a country might make itself subject to cases arising under the Torture Convention but not the Convention on the Rights of the Child.

Despite some differences, both proposals are based on two important principles. The first is the recognition that victims of human rights have no place to take their claim. The second principle is that a right without a remedy is really no right at all.

Conclusion

Human rights exist to preserve and to protect the inherent dignity in each one of us. Achieving this end without human rights would not be possible. Human rights are not merely about being fed, having shelter, not being tortured and so on. Rather, human rights are also about having the right or the entitlement to these things. Only in this way is a person's true humanity honoured and respected.

In this chapter we focused on five distinct human rights: freedom from torture, refugee protection, the right to health, the right to food and finally the right to redress or an effective remedy. We did this not because these rights are in any way different from or more important than any other, but rather in an attempt to make human rights more concrete. However, we approached this with the full understanding that each of these rights is related to one another – as well as to all other human rights.

We also examined state responsibilities for protecting and enforcing human rights. Each state has the primary responsibility for ensuring that human rights – all human rights – are protected for those within its territorial boundaries. However, state responsibilities to protect human rights do not arbitrarily end at their own territorial border. This is perhaps easier to see with respect to CPRs. The obligation not to torture applies not only within a state's domestic realm but outside it as well. Otherwise it would be permissible for a state to simply carry out torture in another country or somewhere out on the high seas. This result would be entirely inconsistent with the object and purpose of international human rights law.

Beyond this, we discussed the specific extraterritorial provisions in the Torture Convention, the 'prosecute or extradite' provision, the non-refoulement principle and the inter-state complaint system. We noted the dispute concerning whether states have an obligation to provide redress to all torture victims, and the manner in which this squares (or does not square) with the principle of sovereign immunity.

Furthermore, we outlined the right to seek asylum. Although a person cannot demand refugee protection in a particular country, all people enjoy the right not to be sent back to a country where her life or well-being would be threatened. Finally, we examined two ESCRs, the right to food and the right to health. No one could claim that those without food or those left to die or suffer from preventable diseases are living lives of human dignity. We have seen that there is an increased effort by some of the poorest countries to devote considerably more resources to meet the right to health. However, given the abject poverty of so many countries, these efforts do not go very far in terms of protecting these, and other, human rights.

The Economic Covenant demands that a state devote the 'maximum available resources' to meeting the rights in the treaty. In addition to its own resources, a state that is unable to protect the rights of all those within its territorial borders is obligated to seek international assistance for those purposes. There are two ways of determining a state's 'maximum available resources'. One is to compute only the resources that a particular state has at its disposal. The second, and more appropriate, way is not only to compute this amount, but also the resources that come from outside states that have an obligation under the Economic Covenant to provide 'international assistance and co-operation'. We would argue that the amount that is 'available' in these two scenarios will differ enormously.

FURTHER READING

State responsibility

- Crawford, James. 2002. *The International Law Commission's Articles on State Responsibility.*
  Crawford, who served as Special Rapporteur for the International Law Commission, has compiled the Articles on State Responsibility and their accompanying Commentary.

'The War on Terror'

- Mayer, Jane. 2008. *The Dark Side: The Inside Story of How the War on Terror Turned into a War on American Ideals.*
  Mayer presents an exhaustive study of the manner in which US laws, ideals and values were swept away by the 'war on terror'.

Refugees and internally displaced persons

- Zolberg, Aristide, Astri Suhrke and Sergio Aguayo. 1999. *Escape from Violence: Conflict and the Refugee Crisis in the Developing World.*
  Escape From Violence provides both a theoretical approach and a case study analysis of the causes and consequences of refugee flight.

RELATED FILMS

'The War on Terror'

- **The Road to Guantánamo** (Michael Winterbottom, 2005). This film presents the story of the 'Tipton Three', three British Muslim men who travelled to Afghanistan for fun and wound up being detained at Guantánamo Bay, Cuba. The film blurs the line between what is 'real' and what is not, as it combines actual documentary footage of interviews with the three former detainees with re-created scenes.

- **Taxi to the Dark Side** (Alex Gibney, 2007). The movie explores the American practice of torture by focusing on the killing of an innocent Afghan taxi driver at Bagram Air Base. Winner of the 2007 Academy Award for best documentary feature.

- **USA v. Al-Arian** (Line Halvorsen, 2007). This is a spellbinding film that covers the case of a University of South Florida professor who is accused of providing 'material support' to Palestinian terrorists. Just when it seems that the situation for the defendant and his family could not get worse, he is essentially forced to plead guilty – to charges of which he has already been acquitted by a jury in Tampa. This is a deeply disturbing and moving film that makes the term Kafkaesque seem inadequate.

- **State of Fear** (Pamela Yates, Paco de Onis and Peter Kinoy, 2005). Although this film focuses on the Peruvian government's brutal response to the terror threat posed by the Shining Path, it serves as a cautionary tale for all countries facing what is too easily termed 'international terrorism'.

- **Why We Fight** (Eugene Jarecki, 2006). The title comes from Frank Capra's propaganda films for the US government during the Second World War. It places the latest US foreign intervention in Iraq in a much broader historical context.

Refugee Protection

- **Mrs Goundo's Daughter** (Barbara Attie and Janet Goldwater, 2009). This documentary focuses on a mother's effort to keep her daughter in the United States as a refugee in order to avoid facing FGM if sent back home.

- **Well-founded Fear** (Shari Robertson and Michael Camerini, 2000). In order to meet the refugee standard, an individual must be able to show that she/he has a 'well-founded fear' of persecution. This insightful but discomfiting film follows the fortunes of people from various countries as they make their claim for refugee protection in the United States.

part **II**

Empirical representations and explanations of human rights violations

chapter

4

Where are human rights violated?

In the preceding three chapters we argued that all indviduals have unalienable rights simply because they are human. Respecting these rights is essential for individuals to have the chance of living a life in human dignity. States have a responsibility and obligation to protect these rights, primarily within, but also outside, their own borders. Yet, as we have already shown with various examples throughout this text, for many people the protection of their human rights is a very distant ideal. Most people have at least some of their rights violated most of the time. In this chapter, we show which countries provide better, or worse, protection for specific human rights in the twenty-first century compared with other countries. Related to this, we touch on issues of measuring human rights and human rights violations. We discuss why one might want to measure and quantify the concept of human rights and then show examples of how this has been done in the study of human rights. The first section focuses on civil and political rights, before we turn to economic, social and cultural rights in the second half of this chapter.

Measuring exactly which rights of which individuals are violated when and by whom is an impossible undertaking. However, many attempts have been made to capture the extent to which certain groups of rights are violated in specific countries. We see this as an important and crucial step towards protecting human rights in the future, and to have a starting point for doing justice to those whose rights are currently violated. If we want to find out how we can prevent the suffering people endure, for example when they are tortured, imprisoned without a fair trial, or denied basic commodities such as food, water and housing, we need to investigate the causes of such ill-treatment and the failure to provide and protect these rights.

So where are human rights violated at the beginning of the twenty-first century? What countries top the list of 'worst human rights performers'? And what, if any, characteristics do these countries have in common, where people are unable to live a life in dignity and security? What can we learn from these cases, especially when we compare them with those countries in which people live secure and safe lives? In order to answer these questions, we need to be able to compare the human rights conditions across countries using some standard measures. Being able to compare human rights records of countries across time and space enables us to find commonalities that might explain why some countries perform better and others perform worse – which is the necessary first step towards preventing human rights violations in the first place.

In the following discussion we focus on measurements that use country-years as the unit of analysis. This means that the human rights situation is evaluated for each country as a whole in a given year. Then one value on a predefined scale is chosen to represent the overall human rights situation in this particular country during that particular year. This approach has several weaknesses. First, representing a country with just one figure does not tell us anything about potentially drastic variations within that country. The human rights violations might be concentrated in a geographically small area and occur only very rarely in the rest of the country. For example, the human rights condition of individuals in India varies drastically between different regions within the country. Similarly, in the United Kingdom between the late 1960s and the 1980s, the risk of suffering violence at the hands of the police was far higher in Northern Ireland than in the rest of the country. Another example is the treatment of the right against arbitrary imprisonment in the United States overall and in Guantánamo Bay in particular. More common, however, is the fact that the violation of human rights is not concentrated within a specific geographical area, but is focused on a particular group within that country, for example, by limiting access to food and shelter and restricting civil liberties for certain ethnic or religious groups. In these cases, where there are vast differences in the human rights condition within one country, it is very difficult to present an adequate and 'correct' picture for the whole country. However, to date these country-level data are generally the best measures that are available if we want to compare human rights conditions across the globe.

Civil and political rights

As discussed in Chapter 1, the UN Covenant on Civil and Political Rights details a wide range of basic civil and political rights of nations and individuals. It includes the right to life, freedom from torture, slavery or arbitrary arrest, and freedom of opinion and expression, among many others. There have been various attempts to create a measure of the respect, or violation, of civil and political rights across the globe. In this section we show the extent to which political rights and civil liberties are protected around the globe. To illustrate the respect for these rights, we use the Freedom House measure of civil liberties and political rights.

Box 4.1. **Freedom House reports**

Since the 1970s Freedom House has published yearly reports on *Freedom in the World*, which measure the respect for political rights and civil liberties. These reports contain survey ratings and narrative reports by regional experts on almost 200 countries. The reports capture political rights and civil liberties; the political rights focus on the electoral process, political pluralism and participation and the functioning of government. Civil liberties are clustered into four groups: freedom of expression and belief; associational and organizational rights; the rule of law; and personal autonomy and individual rights. Each sub-category is made up of several questions, which are answered by regional experts. You can find more information about the organization and about their reports at the Freedom House website at http://www.freedomhouse.org/.

Freedom House reports capture a specific subset of the rights that are included in the Covenant on Civil and Political Rights. More specifically, as stated by Freedom House on their website,

> Political rights enable people to participate freely in the political process, including the right to vote freely for distinct alternatives in legitimate elections, compete for public office, join political parties and organizations, and elect representatives who have a decisive impact on public policies and are accountable to the electorate. Civil liberties allow for the freedoms of

expression and belief, associational and organizational rights, rule of law,
and personal autonomy without interference from the state.[1]

Countries that ensure that their citizens can enjoy civil liberties and
political rights are classified as 'free'; countries where these rights are
virtually absent are classified as 'not free'; and those in the middle
are labelled as 'partly free'. Figure 4.1 shows how many countries
Freedom House has put into the three categories over time. Since the
beginning of their reports in 1972, the number of not free countries
has declined, making up 46 per cent of all countries in 1972 (69 countries) but only 22 per cent in 2008 (42 countries). At the same time,
the number and proportion of free countries has risen from 29 per
cent in 1972 (44 countries) to 46 per cent in 2008 (89 countries). Over
the same time period, the number of countries in the middle, those
classified as 'partly free', has increased from 38 (25 per cent) to 62 (32
per cent). Clearly, respect for civil liberties and political rights, for
example as granted under democratic political systems, has increased
over the past thirty years, but for many countries there is still a long
way to go. Figure 4.1 also shows that after the collapse of the Soviet

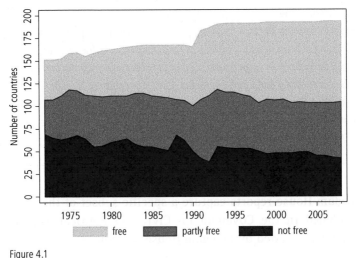

Figure 4.1
Freedom House classification of countries over time
Source: Freedom House. 2008. *Freedom in the World.*

---

1 See http://www.freedomhouse.org/template.cfm?page=351&ana_page=354&year=2009.

Union and the end of the Cold War, the number of free and partly free countries increased quite suddenly, while the number of not free countries declined.

Physical integrity rights

The second group of human rights we present are physical integrity rights. This set of rights is also based on the Covenant on Civil and Political Rights, but it focuses on a different subset from the Freedom House reports. Physical integrity rights refers to the right to be free from political violence and terror, such as torture, arbitrary imprisonment and extrajudicial killings. To show where and to what extent these physical integrity rights have been violated, we use the Political Terror Scale (PTS).[2]

This scale codes reports that are compiled by Amnesty International and the US Department of State. Both Amnesty International and the US State Department issue yearly reports on virtually every country in the world, and in these reports they describe the human rights situation in these countries, including the extent to which these rights to physical integrity have been violated. The reports are evaluated by coders and then each country for each year is assigned a number on a scale from 1 to 5 as follows:

Level 1   Countries under a secure rule of law; people are not imprisoned for their views, and torture is rare or exceptional. Political murders are extremely rare.

Level 2   There is a limited amount of imprisonment for non-violent political activity. However, few persons are affected, and torture and beatings are exceptional. Political murders are rare.

---

2 This scale captures repression and political violence, for example in the form of torture or political imprisonment. Therefore 'Political Terror' refers to the violation of physical integrity rights, which is separate from the meaning of 'terror' as it is commonly understood post-11 September 2001.

Level 3   There is extensive political imprisonment, or a recent history of such imprisonment. Execution or other political murders and brutality may be common. Unlimited detention for political views, with or without a trial, is accepted.

Level 4   Civil and political rights violations have expanded to large numbers of the population. Murders, disappearances and torture are a common part of life. In spite of its generality, on this level terror affects those who interest themselves in politics or ideas.

Level 5   Terror has expanded to the whole population. The leaders of these societies place no limits on the means or thoroughness with which they pursue personal or ideological goals.[3]

As with the Freedom House measure, this scale tries to evaluate the human rights situation across whole countries using one scale, so that countries can more easily be compared across time and space.

Before comparing the violations of physical integrity rights along these dimensions, we briefly outline how these human rights reports are compiled, since they form the basis of this Political Terror Scale. When the US State Department began writing country reports in 1976, Congress wanted to make sure that the United States was not giving foreign aid to countries that grossly and consistently violated human rights. Over time, the reports became more comprehensive both in the number of countries they covered and in the types of human rights on which they focused. In the overview for the 2008 country reports, the US Department of State describes the way in which these reports are compiled:

> Our overseas US missions, which prepared the initial drafts of the reports, gathered information throughout the year from a variety of sources across the political spectrum. These sources included government officials, jurists, the armed forces, journalists, human rights monitors,

---

3 Source: www.politicalterrorscale.org. This website also provides further information about the Political Terror Scale. For an alternative measure of human rights, which also uses the US State Department and Amnesty International country reports as sources, see the CIRI Human Rights Project, http://ciri.binghamton.edu/.

academics, and labor activists. This information gathering can be hazardous, and US Foreign Service personnel regularly go to great lengths, under trying and sometimes dangerous conditions, to investigate reports of human rights abuse, monitor elections, and come to the aid of individuals at risk, such as political dissidents and human rights defenders whose rights are threatened by their governments.

After completing their drafts, State Department missions abroad sent them to Washington for review by the Bureau of Democracy, Human Rights and Labor, in cooperation with other Department of State offices. As they worked to corroborate, analyze, and edit the reports, Department officers drew on their own sources of information. These included reports provided by US and other human rights groups, foreign government officials, representatives from the United Nations and other international and regional organizations and institutions, experts from academia, and the media. Officers also consulted with experts on worker rights, refugee issues, military and police topics, women's issues, and legal matters. The guiding principle was to ensure that all information was assessed objectively, thoroughly, and fairly.[4]

Like the US State Department, Amnesty International issues an annual report which catalogues human rights abuses around the world. The Amnesty International reports concentrate more narrowly on physical integrity rights. For these reports, the Amnesty International research teams focus on particular countries and investigate and check a variety of sources and information, including statements from prisoners and survivors of abuse, lawyers, journalists, refugees, community works and other human rights organizations. For countries that deny access to Amnesty International, the organization relies on information from outside the country, such as media reports or information from refugees.

Clearly, it is very difficult to compose a report that accurately reflects the human rights situation on the ground, particularly since the human rights abuses that these reports focus on are generally carried out in secret, and perpetrators are keen to avoid these abuses coming to light. Yet especially under these circumstances it is important to try to find out how individuals and their right to physical integrity are treated. When human rights are most under threat

---

4 For full details, see www.state.gov/g/drl/rls/hrrpt/2008/frontmatter/118983.htm

or actually violated, when individuals are denied their rights, it is most important to re-emphasize that they possess these rights. Jack Donnelly (2003) calls this the 'possession paradox'. This means that the importance of a right becomes more pressing when the enjoyment of the right is denied.

The Political Terror Scale uses both the US State Department country reports and the Amnesty International annual reports to code the violation of physical integrity rights around the globe. Elsewhere, we have compared these two reports and found that while the State Department reports have at times treated US friends and trading partners favourably compared with Amnesty International reports, their evaluations of the respect for physical integrity rights largely overlap.[5]

To show how the Amnesty International and the State Department reports have been used to place countries on the Political Terror Scale, we indicate how selected countries have been described in the reports for 2007, and what coding on the PTS scale these reports have triggered.

The State Department Human Rights Report for Uruguay in 2007 describes the human rights situation in the country as follows:

> There were no reports that the government or its agents committed arbitrary or unlawful killings. ...
>
> There were no reports of politically motivated or other disappearances. ...
>
> The law prohibits [torture and other cruel, inhuman, or degrading treatment or punishment], and there were no reports that government officials employed them. ...
>
> Ministry officials stated that there were no complaints of police abuse in prisons during the year. However, on October 10, a detainee died from strangulation at a police station within hours of his arrest. At year's end authorities were prosecuting five police officers for their alleged involvement. ...
>
> The law prohibits arbitrary arrest and detention, and the government generally observed these prohibitions in practice. The law requires police to have a written warrant issued by a judge before making an arrest (except when police apprehend the accused during commission of a crime), and authorities generally respected this provision in practice. ...

---

5 To read more about the comparison of the two reports, see Poe, Carey and Vazquez (2001).

> In July the government passed a law including rules and guidelines for
> police procedures respecting human rights. There were no reports of
> impunity involving the security forces during the year. ...
> There were no reports of political prisoners or detainees.

The report describes the country as one in which the physical integrity rights of individuals are generally respected and protected. Therefore for 2007 Uruguay is coded as PTS Level 1, which indicates that the country was under secure rule of law.

The report on the United Kingdom for the same year was slightly less positive:

> There were no reports that the government or its agents committed any
> politically motivated killings; however, the Independent Police Complaints
> Commission (IPCC) reported that police shot and killed five persons in the
> performance of their duties. ...
> There were no reports of politically motivated disappearances. ...
> The law prohibits [torture and other cruel, inhuman, or degrading
> treatment or punishment]; however, there were allegations that
> individual members of the police occasionally abused detainees and
> allegations that guards under contract to immigration authorities abused
> deportees while returning them to their home countries. ...
> On April 30, a soldier pled guilty at a court-martial to inhumane
> treatment of Iraqi detainees in the trial of soldiers charged with
> killing Iraqi civilian Baha Musa in 2003. The soldier was sentenced
> to jail for one year and dismissed from the army. In connection with
> this case, the Law Lords ruled that detainees in military custody are
> covered under laws prohibiting torture and inhuman or degrading
> treatment. ...
> According to an October 5 article in the *Independent* newspaper,
> contractor escort teams assisting in the deportation of failed asylum
> seekers to their home countries beat or racially abused hundreds of them.
> The newspaper and an organization that defends failed asylum seekers
> compiled a dossier of 200 cases, some of which included allegations of
> physical and sexual assault. ...
> The law prohibits arbitrary arrest and detention, and the government
> generally observed these prohibitions, but critics charged that some
> procedures introduced to combat terrorism constituted preventative
> detention. ...
> There were no reports of political prisoners or detainees.

The report refers to some instances of torture, including one case that took place at a UK military base in Basra.[6] But overall, the physical integrity rights are largely respected, leading to a categorization of the Level 2 on the Political Terror Scale.

The next example is a description of the human rights conditions in the United States. This is based on the Amnesty International Report, since the United States State Department does not issue a report on the US itself. Amnesty summarizes the situation from 2007 as follows:

> The US authorities continued to hold hundreds of foreign nationals at the US Naval Base in Guantánamo Bay, Cuba, although more than 100 were transferred out of the facility during the year. Detainees in Guantánamo were held indefinitely, the vast majority of them without charge, and effectively without recourse to the US courts to challenge the legality of their detention. Most detainees in Guantánamo were held in isolation in maximum security facilities, heightening concerns for their physical and mental health. The Central Intelligence Agency (CIA) programme of secret detention and interrogation was re-authorized by President Bush in July. In December, the Director of the CIA revealed that the agency had destroyed videotapes of detainee interrogations.
>
> Soldiers refusing to serve in Iraq on grounds of conscience were imprisoned. Prisoners continued to experience ill-treatment at the hands of police officers and prison guards. Dozens of people died after police used tasers (electro-shock weapons) against them.

This degree of political brutality, political imprisonment and unlimited detention for political views is captured by Level 3 of the Political Terror Scale. In fact, the United States has been placed on the PTS Level 3 since 2004.

The summary report by the State Department on the human rights situation in India in 2007 paints a rather bleak picture, referring to extrajudicial killings and torture.

> Major problems included extrajudicial killings of persons in custody, disappearances, and torture and rape by police and other security forces.

---

6 The UK's highest court, the Appellate Committee of the House of Lords (the Law Lords), ruled in 2007 in *Al-Skeini and Others* v. *Secretary of Defence and Others* that the behaviour of UK soldiers in Iraq does not fall under the European Convention on Human Rights. Individuals affected by violence at the hands of British soldiers are only within UK jurisdiction, and are therefore protected by the European Convention on Human Rights if the individuals are at a UK-run detention facility at the time of the – alleged – violations.

A lack of accountability permeated the government and security forces throughout the country, creating an atmosphere of impunity ... In West Bengal, violence in the Nandigram district led to accusations of state government failure to control ruling Communist Party cadres, which were accused by human rights groups of killing more than 30 rural villagers and intimidating them through violence and rape. Although the country has numerous laws protecting human rights, enforcement was inadequate and convictions rare. Poor prison conditions, lengthy pretrial detention without charge, and prolonged detention while undergoing trial remained significant problems. Government officials used special antiterrorism legislation to justify the excessive use of force while combating terrorism and several regional insurgencies. While security officials who committed human rights abuses generally enjoyed impunity, there were investigations into individual abuse cases as well as legal punishment of some perpetrators ... Attacks against religious minorities and the promulgation of antireligious conversion laws were concerns. Social acceptance of caste-based discrimination often validated human rights violations against persons belonging to lower castes.

The violation of physical integrity rights is extended to large parts of the population, but still only affects certain elements within the population. This situation is classified as PTS Level 4, which indicates widespread violations of physical integrity rights, but where repression is not applied indiscriminately across the whole population. This most severe condition of physical integrity rights is highlighted in the State Department report on Sudan during 2007:

The government's human rights record remained poor, and there were numerous serious abuses, including: abridgement of citizens' rights to change their government; extrajudicial and other unlawful killings by government forces and other government-aligned groups throughout the country; torture, beatings, rape, and other cruel, inhumane treatment or punishment by security forces ... arbitrary arrest and detention, including incommunicado detention of suspected government opponents, and prolonged pre-trial detention ... harassment of internally displaced persons (IDPs) and of local and international human rights and humanitarian organizations; violence and discrimination against women, including the practice of female genital mutilation (FGM); child abuse, including sexual violence and recruitment of child soldiers, particularly in Darfur; trafficking in persons; discrimination and violence against ethnic minorities.

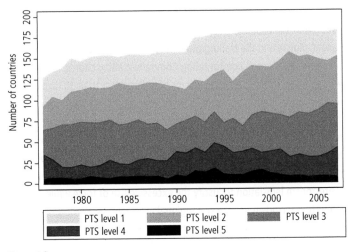

Figure 4.2
Political Terror Scale classification of countries over time
Source: Political Terror Scale, www.politicalterrorscale.org.

As this brief excerpt indicates, the population at large suffered from serious and widespread life integrity violations. This is reflected in the Political Terror Scale, which puts Sudan at Level 5, the worst level of life integrity violations.

In the following, we present the values of the Political Terror Scale that are based on the Amnesty International reports, but where these were not available for certain countries during specific years, we replaced them with the code derived from the State Department reports.

Figure 4.2 shows how many countries fell in each of the five categories of the Political Terror Scale between 1976 and 2007. The darker the colour in this figure, the more severe and widespread are the human rights violations. The good news is that the smallest category is PTS Level 5. Generally only a few countries experience widespread state terror and indiscriminate violation of physical integrity rights. In 2007 the Democratic Republic of the Congo, Somalia, Sudan, Iraq, Afghanistan, Myanmar and Sri Lanka were classified as suffering from such widespread forms of repression. But countries that are under the secure rule of law, where citizens do not have to live in fear of state terror and the violation of their physical integrity rights

Table 4.1 **Worst human rights offenders**					
1980–1989		**1990–1999**		**2000–2007**	
Country	Mean PTS score	Country	Mean PTS score	Country	Mean PTS score
El Salvador	4.8	Iraq	5.0	Sudan	4.9
Iran	4.7	Colombia	4.9	DRC	4.9
Guatemala	4.6	Rwanda	4.8	Colombia	4.9
Afghanistan	4.6	Burundi	4.6	Iraq	4.8
Syria	4.4	Sudan	4.5	Afghanistan	4.8
Iraq	4.4	Sri Lanka	4.5	Algeria	4.4
Colombia	4.4	Somalia	4.5		
		Afghanistan	4.5		
		Myanmar	4.4		

(indicated by PTS Level 1), made up only 17 per cent of all countries in 2007 – which is the next smallest category after PTS Level 5. Most countries (31 per cent) are categorized as PTS Level 2. In these countries, most individuals have their right to physical integrity fully respected – while a limited number of people suffer from political imprisonment and even torture. This group of countries has been getting bigger over time. Several Western countries with excellent human rights records in the past now find themselves in this category, mostly as a result of the 'war on terror'. Due to this campaign, many countries have used strategies of political imprisonment and forms of torture against alleged terrorists.

Table 4.1 provides a clearer idea of which countries had the worst records for protecting physical integrity rights. In this table, we list the top offenders for three different periods, 1980–9, 1990–9 and 2000–7, alongside the mean PTS score over these periods. Iraq, Colombia and Afghanistan are the only three countries that consistently scored an average of 4.4 or worse over these periods.

Figure 4.3 maps the degree of physical integrity rights violations around the globe in 2007. As in Figure 4.2, the darker the shade, the more common, widespread and severe state terror was in that year. Remember that the Political Terror Scale assigns only one value to each country, so regional variations of the level of terror within one country

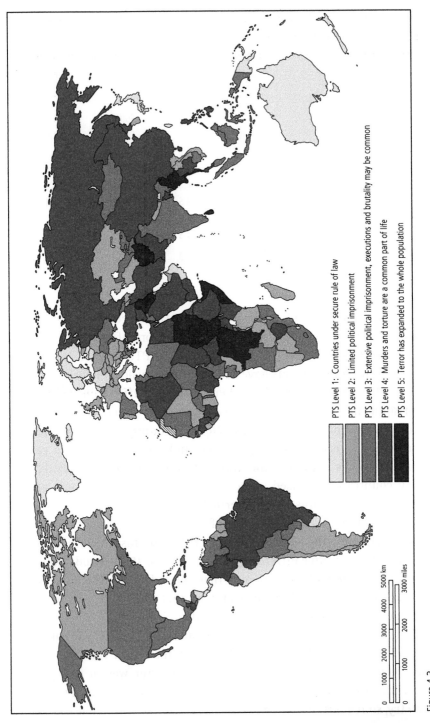

PTS Level 1: Countries under secure rule of law

PTS Level 2: Limited political imprisonment

PTS Level 3: Extensive political imprisonment, executions and brutality may be common

PTS Level 4: Murders and torture are a common part of life

PTS Level 5: Terror has expanded to the whole population

0   1000 2000 3000 4000 5000 km
0   1000   2000   3000 miles

Figure 4.3
A map of physical integrity violations in 2007

are not reflected in this map. Asia and Africa are the most insecure regions, where torture, disappearances, political imprisonment and even killings are more common than in other parts of the world. Countries that fully respect the right to physical integrity are quite rare – but are scattered across the globe, reaching from Bhutan, Brunei, and Oman to Croatia, Slovenia and Lithuania, to Costa Rica, Peru and Uruguay (in total thirty-one countries are coded as PTS Level 1 for 2007).

What causes some of these countries to have very good human rights records, while some of their neighbours suffer from state terror and repression? What characteristics are generally associated with higher rates of human rights abuse, and which ones are linked with higher levels of respect for these rights? We shall investigate these questions further in the next chapter. But before we turn to causes of human rights violations, we provide a brief overview of the violation of economic and social rights.

Box 4.2. **Press freedom**

Freedom House also measures the extent of press freedom across the world. The right to free media is incorporated in Article 19 of the Universal Declaration of Human Rights:

> Everyone has the right to freedom of opinion and expression; this right includes freedom to hold opinions without interference and to seek, receive, and impart information and ideas through any media regardless of frontiers.

Freedom House highlights the importance of this right in the following way:

> To deny that doctrine is to deny the universality of information freedom – a basic human right. We recognize that cultural distinctions or economic underdevelopment may limit the volume of news flows within a country, but these and other arguments are not acceptable explanations for outright centralized control of the content of news and information. Some poor countries allow for the exchange of diverse views, while some economically developed countries restrict content diversity.[7]

---

7 See Freedom House (2008), *Survey Methodology*.

The right to freedom of opinion and expression is an important right in itself, one that is crucial for allowing individuals to express themselves. It is part of their humanity. But the freedom of opinion and expression is also important with respect to the enjoyment of other rights, as human rights are generally interlinked and dependent on one another. If the press is allowed free reign in a country, if individuals are free to voice their opinion about their government and its policies, for example, then exercising this right to freedom of opinion and expression functions is an important check on rulers and how they use their authority and power. Leaders will be weary of allowing, or instructing, the ill-treatment of prisoners if there is a real risk that 'word gets out' and that this might have negative repercussions for the leaders, domestically and internationally. The importance of free speech and press freedom becomes clear when you consider just how much effort authoritarian governments put into restricting these rights, such as in Iran or China, for example.

The measure of the Freedom of the Press captures three dimensions: the legal environment (laws and regulations influencing the media), the political environment (the degree of political control over the content of the media) and the economic environment (including issues of ownership, subsidies, and corruption). After the evaluation of over 20 different questions by regional experts, countries are classified as free, partly free or not free. In 2007, 72 countries (37 per cent) were categorized as free, 59 (30 per cent) as partly free and 64 (33 per cent) as not free. The worst offenders of the Freedom of the Press in that year were North Korea, Burma, Turkmenistan, Libya, Eritrea and Cuba. As you can see in Table 4.2, almost all countries in western Europe are classified as free, with Turkey being the only country identified as having a 'partly free' press. The worst region for press freedom in 2007 was the Middle East and North Africa, where only Israel reached the status 'free'. Overall, Freedom House highlighted that the key trend in 2007 was a decline in the freedom of the press. Violence against journalists and attacks on the media while covering political unrest are given as two of the indicators for this downward trend.

Economic and social rights

The Covenant on Economic, Social and Cultural Rights is very complex and includes a large range of different rights, as already discussed earlier. The Covenant includes the right to self-determination

Table 4.2 Freedom of the press across the regions in 2007

	Free		Partly free		Not free		Total number of countries
	Number of countries	Percentage	Number of countries	Percentage	Number of countries	Percentage	
Sub-Saharan Africa	7	15	18	37	23	48	48
Americas	16	46	17	48	2	6	35
Asia–Pacific	16	40	10	25	14	35	40
Middle East & North Africa	1	5	3	16	15	79	19
Western Europe	24	96	1	4	0	0	25
Central & eastern Europe/ former Soviet Union	8	28	10	36	10	36	28

Source: Freedom House. 2008. *Global Press Freedom 2008: A Year of Global Decline*, available at http://www.freedomhouse.org/uploads/ffop08/FOTP2008Tables.pdf

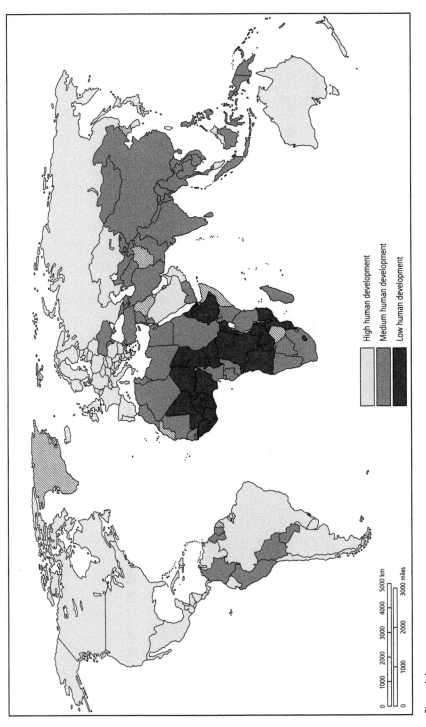

High human development

Medium human development

Low human development

Figure 4.4.
A map of the Human Development Index in 2006

for peoples (Art. 1), the right to work and various labour rights (Art. 6, 7 and 8), the right to an adequate standard of living, including the right to adequate food (Art. 11) and the right to the enjoyment of the highest attainable standard of physical and mental health (Art. 12).

In this section we show how one aspect of these rights has been implemented, or not, across the globe. To do this, we rely on the Human Development Index (HDI). This index is collected and generated by the UN Development Programme (UNDP). The HDI captures life expectancy, educational attainment and poverty.[8] As such, it focuses mainly on the economic right to an adequate standard of living, while also including the social right to an education.

Figure 4.4 shows the HDI in three categories, as classified by the UNDP: low development, medium development and high development. The darker the shade, the lower the HDI was in the country during 2006. The map clearly shows that the worst-off region is sub-Saharan Africa. On average, this region has the worst combination of life expectancy, education and poverty. South Asia and east Asia are in the middle category, while the OECD countries are overall in the highest category of development.

---

8 The home page of the Human Development Report contains additional information about their data; see http://hdr.undp.org/.

Conclusion

This chapter provided a brief overview of how certain human rights can be measured across the globe, and we have shown in which regions and countries civil liberties and political rights, physical integrity rights, and economic and social rights are most severely violated. The picture that has emerged is somewhat complicated and warrants further investigation. Comparing the map of physical integrity rights (Figure 4.3) with the map of the Human Development Index (Figure 4.4) already reveals that the connection between the respect for economic and social rights and the respect for physical integrity rights is not always straightforward. In general, countries that offer better protection of physical integrity rights also provide better for economic and social rights. Examples are countries in Europe, as well as Australia, Japan, Chile and Argentina. But there are also stark differences. Russia, Saudi Arabia and Brazil are identified as highly developed by the Human Development Index in 2006, but are classified as very repressive, at Level 4 on the Political Terror Scale, in 2007. Of these three countries, Saudi Arabia and Russia are identified by Freedom House as 'not free', both with respect to civil liberties and political rights, and with respect to press freedom. Brazil, however, is considered to have a partly free press and considered to be free in terms of respect for civil liberties and political rights. At the other end of the spectrum, Mali, Benin, Togo and Zambia score very well on the Political Terror Scale – that is, these states generally respect physical integrity rights – but are unable to provide economic and social rights as measured by the Human Development Index. Some countries manage to do very well in protecting some kinds of human rights, while severely violating others. So what causes countries to violate physical integrity rights, and what factors lead to poor performance with regard to development and education? Can we identify certain indicators that put a country at a heightened risk of certain types of human rights violations? We address these questions in the following chapter.

FURTHER READING

- Landman, Todd. 2005. *Protecting Human Rights: A Comparative Study.*
  Landman offers a very thorough, quantitative analysis to evaluate the gap between the *de jure* protection and *de facto* realization of human rights globally.

- Landman, Todd. 2006. *Studying Human Rights.*
  This is a highly accessible and interesting book that introduces students to the empirical analysis of human rights issues, including questions related to the measurement of human rights.

- Wood, Reed and Mark Gibney. 2010. 'The Political Terror Scale (PTS): A Re-introduction and Comparison to the CIRI Human Rights Database', *Human Rights Quarterly* 32: 367–400.
  This journal article describes and explains the Political Terror Scale and compares it with another widely used measure of physical integrity rights, the CIRI Human Rights Database.

Historical examples of human rights violations

- Weschler, Lawrence. 1990. *A Miracle, A Universe: Settling Accounts with Torturers.*
  Weschler's book is in two parts. The first is a political thriller documenting the clandestine efforts by Brazilian human rights organizations to publish *Brasil: Nunca Mais*, a national bestseller that uses the government's own documents to expose the human rights abuses carried out by the military regime in 1964–79. The second half of the book examines the determined efforts in Uruguay to escape from the clutches of the country's military dictatorship.

Genocide

- Power, Samantha. 2002. *"A Problem from Hell": America and the Age of Genocide.*
  Power has written an exhaustive study detailing how the US government has responded (or not responded) to the various genocides of the past century.

- Schabas, William. 2000. *Genocide in International Law: The Crime of Crimes.*
  Schabas' work remains the standard text on the drafting and meaning of the Genocide Convention.

RELATED WEBSITES

- The Political Terror Scale, http://www.politicalterrorscale.org.
- CIRI Human Rights Data Project, http://ciri.binghamton.edu/.
- Freedom House, http://www.freedomhouse.org/.
- US State Department Country Reports, http://www.state.gov/g/drl/rls/hrrpt/.

RELATED FILMS

War in Iraq and Afghanistan

- **Iraq in Fragments** (James Longley, 2006). This movie is a visually stunning kaleidoscope of what life is like for several Iraqi civilians, including the lives of two young boys, after the US invasion.

- **My Country, My Country** (Laura Poitras, 2006). The 2005 national elections in Iraq serve as the central grounding for this film. The protagonist is the remarkable Dr Riyadh, who is everywhere and everyman. Riyadh is a member of the Baghdad City Council and a fearless defender and protector of those caught up in the mayhem and violence of the war. Yet perhaps the most effective scenes are those filmed at his home, as we see a 'typical' Iraqi family attempting to maintain a 'normal' existence amidst the abnormality that surrounds them.

- **Pulled From the Rubble** (Margaret Loescher, 2004). This film is about a remarkably brave man, Gil Loescher, who was the only survivor of the bombing of the UN headquarters in Baghdad in 2003 that killed, among others, UN official Sergio Vieira de Mello, the UN Special Representative in Iraq. The film, directed by Loescher's daughter, focuses on his physical and mental rehabilitation. What helps to spur this double amputee on is his family, but also the decades of work he has done with refugees – people who have taught him the meaning of courage and perseverance.

AFGHAN FILMS

Kandahar (Mohsen Makhmalbaf, 2001). From the startling opening scene of prosthetic devices parachuting to the ground in the manner of dismembered body parts, this film about a Canadian-Afghan woman who returns to Afghanistan in search of her missing sister is not only able to convey the dire situation facing Afghan women, but also the horrors and hopes of the country's war. Made a decade ago at the onset of the war, the film has proven to be prescient in terms of its ambiguous stance regarding Western involvement, perhaps best summed up in the movie's last scene of a brilliant sunset as seen through the veil of a burka.

Jung (War) in the Land of the Mujaheddin (Alberto Vendemmiati and Fabrizio Lazzaretti, 2001). The hero of this documentary is Gino Strada, an Italian doctor who is bravely attempting to build a hospital near the front lines in northern Afghanistan. Playing out almost in the manner of *Mash*, but without the sex or the black humour, Strada and his co-workers face a daily onslaught brought on by war's work. Still, the story really is about the Afghan people, who continue to suffer through decades of endless conflict.

Enemies of Happiness (Eva Mulvad, 2006). This documentary follows Malalai Joya, a young Afghan women seeking political office in the newly 'liberated' Afghanistan. Harking back to such screen heroines as *Norma Rae* or perhaps even the real-life Joan of Arc, Joya squares off against all forms of societal prejudice that are intended to keep her, and her gender, in 'their place'. From the opening scene where Joya openly and publicly challenges the country's patriarchal leaders, the viewer is unreservedly caught up in this remarkable woman's life.

IRAQI FILMS

No End in Sight (Charles Ferguson, 2007). Although the viewer already knows much of the story of the advent of the Iraq war – the duplicity, the incompetence, the hubris, the enormous levels of human suffering, and so on – this film still makes the tragedy seem fresh and maddening all at the same time. Ferguson limits himself to the period between January and May 2003, when decisions were made (or not made) that led to the nightmare that has become post-war Iraq. We are all familiar with so many of the scenes shown in the film, from Donald Rumsfeld's glib response to the looting in Baghdad that 'stuff happens', to the repeated assurances that the insurgency was in its 'last throes'. Although many documentaries suffer from hosting too many 'talking heads', one of the more fascinating aspects of *No End in Sight* is the candour with which several members of the Bush administration speak out against former colleagues. All of this might be nothing more than an attempt to rewrite history or to settle old political scores, but the viewer comes to understand better how disposable the Iraqi people were for US policymakers.

The Hurt Locker (Kathryn Bigelow, 2008). Some of the most insightful and successful films on the Iraq War focus on the soldiers who have been called upon to fight. One of these is *The Hurt Locker*, which was given the 2010 Academy Award for Best Picture. An extraordinarily intense film, the viewer travels with a bomb detonation unit and what we are witness to are the physical and psychological wounds that these and other soldiers carry with them. Providing a soldier's view of the war, the film does not make a single reference to larger political events. But there simply is no need for this because the film is able to show so effectively at least one small segment of the human devastation from this war.

The Messenger (Oren Moverman, 2009). While *The Hurt Locker* takes place in Iraq, *The Messenger* is a stateside view of the war. Much in the nature of other buddy films, the viewer follows two soldiers – one who has served and been wounded in Iraq and the other who has missed his opportunity to fight – as they carry out their assignment, to notify the families of the deceased. Although the appearance of the two 'messengers' can only mean one thing, neither the family member nor the audience can properly brace itself for the inevitable news. Although the deceased remain off-screen, nothing says more about the humanity of these fallen soldiers than the devastation to those who have loved them.

chapter 5

Why are human rights violated? An examination of personal integrity rights

In the previous chapter we showed where certain rights are commonly violated. But what motivates governments to torture and to kill others? Why do peaceful forms of communication and negotiation collapse in favour of violence and destruction? Are acts of atrocity born out of rational calculations or are they the product of erratic and unpredictable behaviour? In this chapter we present a theoretical framework that helps us to understand the circumstances that give rise to such actions. We do not argue that we can accurately predict and explain every act of violence and repression. But we show empirically that this framework can help us to identify situations and characteristics of countries that make them more prone to experiencing the violation of personal integrity rights.

The state as perpetrator of human rights violations

The primary goal of governments is to protect the lives and well-being of their citizens. To fulfil this role, political leaders control the institutions that are designed to enforce law and order and to defend their people against foreign aggression. But this control over power can be misused and those institutions can be turned against their own citizens. A range of actors besides governments have violated the right to personal integrity in the past, such as guerrilla groups, rebels and terrorists. But governments are particularly powerful actors, as they have a range of tools at their disposal that they can use to imprison, torture and kill their citizens unlawfully. Donnelly argues that 'the modern state has emerged as both the principal threat to the enjoyment of human rights and the essential institution for their effective implementation and enforcement' (Donnelly 2003: 35). In addition to violations perpetrated by state actors, such as the military or the police, one could argue that governments should also be held responsible for the violent actions of groups that act independently or even against the government. The main goal of a government ought to be to protect its citizens. If rebel groups commit violent crimes, the government has failed to provide the necessary security to guarantee the respect of the life integrity rights of its citizens.

Under what conditions are governments most likely to choose repression, as opposed to dealing with a situation in a non-violent manner? We argue that a government employs repression when it feels *threatened* in its strength and power and when it has the *opportunity* and *will* to use violence against its citizens.[1] We now explain these concepts in more details.

As starting point we use the assumption that states are rational actors, which calculate their actions in order to increase, or at least to maintain, their political power and their strength. This is not to say that some actions reflect irrational behaviour by a country's

---

1 This decision-making model is based on a model first developed by Most and Starr (1989). It has been adapted to the context of repression by Poe (2004).

leader. But we argue that in general there is logic behind a government's actions, and the leader's goal is to maintain or to increase his or her political strength and power. Therefore, in situations when political leaders perceive their power to be threatened, they will take steps to minimize or eliminate this threat. As such, repression and human rights violations are employed by governments to deal with threats to their political power. For example, in China during May 1989 several hundred thousand students, workers, intellectuals and civil servants demonstrated in Tiananmen Square for democratic reform and equality according to socialist principles. The Chinese government responded with a declaration of martial law, but the demonstrations continued. In response, the People's Liberation Army violently ended the protests. The estimates of how many people were killed during the Tiananmen Square massacre range from 400 to over 7,000.

Applying our theoretical argument that governments use repression when they perceive their power to be threatened, the Tiananmen Square massacre can be explained as a response by Communist Party leaders and the government to the threat posed by the demonstrations. The large number of demonstrators was seen by the Chinese government as a threat to its political power; it felt its position and the political status quo to be in danger. As a response, it tried to reduce the threat and to increase its own strength. To do so, it chose a military solution and sent troops and tanks into the square. By injuring, imprisoning and killing, not only did it end the demonstration, the government also re-established its position of power and strength by sending a forceful signal to potential future protestors that such behaviour was not tolerated. The violent response of the Iranian government to protesters following the disputed elections in June 2009 follows a similar rationale.

The threat to which governments respond with the violation of personal integrity rights does not have to be as 'visible' as in the case of Tiananmen Square or the demonstrations in Iran. Repression can also be used as a preventive measure to strengthen the government and its regime by intimidating potential opponents. And the threat to the regime does not have to be real in order for a government to choose repression as a tool to increase its strength. Times of alarm also arise when the strength of the state is perceived to be in decline. Adolf

Hitler employed widespread terror to threaten what he perceived as the state's enemies in order to strengthen his power:

> I shall spread terror through the surprising application of all means. The sudden shock of a terrible fear of death is what matters. Why should I deal otherwise with all my political opponents? These so-called atrocities saved me hundreds of thousands of individual actions against the protesters and discontents. Each one of them will think twice to oppose us when he learns what is [awaiting] him in the [concentration] camp. (Hitler, quoted in Gurr 1986; 46–7)

But not all governments that feel the need to increase their strength and political power violate life integrity rights of their, or other, citizens. They could employ other strategies as well, such as co-opting opponents of the regime. So why do they choose violence during times of alarm?

According to the decision-making model of Most and Starr (1989), on which our theoretical model is based, two conditions have to be fulfilled. First, governments have to be *able* to use repression; in other words, without the opportunity to use violence, leaders have to look for other solutions to address the perceived threat or to increase the state's strength. If governments do not possess the necessary repressive apparatus, if they do not control the police, the military or other paramilitary groups that are equipped to carry out the life integrity violations, they are unable to choose repression as a policy tool. Second, governments have to be *willing* to apply violence and terror. This willingness to violate human rights is substantially influenced by whether, to what extent and by whom the actors, meaning the potential human rights violators, are held accountable for their actions. If leaders are likely to be held accountable for the repressive actions carried out by their security agents, they will be more hesitant in using repression to address a threat and will look for alternative ways. For example, a government in a democratic country is generally accountable to other state bodies, such as the judiciary and legislature, but also to its electorate. Hence, a democratically elected government in a country with a free press that effectively monitors the behaviour of the government and its agents might not want to use repression because the leaders would risk losing office. Violating life integrity rights on a grand scale could also result in the loss of international reputation and international trade. Therefore governments of democracies might be unwilling to use repression to confront a threat or to increase their strength and power.

Causes of human rights violations

A range of factors influences the perceived balance between the strength of and the threat to a state. The willingness and the opportunity to employ repression can also be shaped by a variety of characteristics. In this section we discuss how primarily political and economic factors can lead to the violation of personal integrity rights by the state. We explain each characteristic in the context of the above theoretical decision-making model and show empirically how it influences human rights violations.

Political regimes

The characteristics and nature of political regimes play a crucial role when we try to understand why human rights violations occur. A political regime can be defined as 'the formal and informal organization of the center of political power, and of its relations with the broader society. A regime determines who has access to political power, and how those who are in power deal with those who are not' (Lawson, 1993: 185). How access to power is regulated and how the interactions between those in power and those outside political power are regulated influences both the opportunity and the willingness of leaders to use repression. It also affects how leaders perceive threat within their own borders.

Democracy

Towards the end of the twentieth century, leaders of Western democracies have increased the promotion of democracy around the world through a variety of ways, for example by linking the receipt of foreign aid to certain democratic reforms or by making membership of international organizations conditional on some democratic characteristics. Governments have also used military force to topple undemocratic regimes in order to pave the way for democratic reforms. A range of reasons can be used to explain this behaviour by established democracies. The one that we are concerned with here is that it has been argued that democracy improves the protection of human rights.

Democratic political systems affect the risk that governments violate the personal integrity of their citizens in several ways, because democracy shapes the leaders' perception of threat as well as their opportunity and willingness to implement repressive policies and actions. Democratically elected governments are less willing to violate life integrity rights of their citizens because they are accountable for their actions. This adds an additional layer of accountability, where the executive is held accountable by the judiciary and the legislature. Therefore, in democracies leaders can expect to be held accountable for their actions, which makes using violence a risky strategy if they intend to stay in power.

Additionally, the behaviour of democratic governments is conditioned by democratic norms of non-violence and compromise. Democratic norms affect the willingness of political leaders to use repression as a policy tool. 'Democratic political norms emphasize compromise in conflict and participation and responsiveness in relations between rulers and ruled, traits that are inconsistent with reliance on violence as an instrument of rule or oppression' (Gurr 1986: 58). Therefore, even when a government perceives its strength to be in decline compared with an alleged threat, it is less likely to use the security apparatus to inflict violence on its citizens in comparison with a non-democratic government. The norms that are associated with a democratic regime facilitate the peaceful solution of conflicts. 'Democracy promotes a culture of negotiation, bargaining, compromise, concession, the tolerance of differences, and even the acceptance of defeat' (Rummel 1997: 101). This democratic culture reduces the willingness of a government to use torture and other forms of life integrity violations.

Democratically elected governments are less susceptible to perceiving certain events or constraints as threatening. Democratic leaders have been voted into office by some form of majority of the electorate. This means that, in general, they can rely on substantial popular support. This support and the legitimacy gained by popular elections strengthen governments, which makes them less vulnerable to potential threats. For example, democracies are less likely to feel severely threatened by signs of popular opposition and resistance. As a result, when democratic governments are faced with demonstrations and strikes they are less likely to respond with violence to these activities compared with non-democratic governments because democratic institutions influence the perception of potential threats to the government. If conflict occurs, then a democracy provides peaceful strategies for handling this conflict, as the democratic system facilitates co-operation and the accommodation of opposing demands. Democracy 'institutionalizes a way of solving without violence disagreements over fundamental questions' (Rummel 1997: 101).

By institutionalizing channels for expressing discontent without resorting to violence, the behaviour of the opposition is more predictable and less threatening to those in power. Democracy 'offers a meaningful alternative for handling conflict if leaders choose to use it. Democracy should not be viewed as an idealistic process, but as a realistic way to accommodate demands with a minimum of conflict ... With a large measure of democracy, conflict should not grow so sharp as to invite repression' (Henderson 1991: 123–4). Within our theoretical model, democracy reduces the perception of threat and therefore lowers the risk of life integrity violations.

Finally, democratic institutions influence the opportunity leaders have to use violence. In elections the electorate can vote leaders out of office before they can implement repressive strategies, as '[e]ffective democracy ... provides citizens (at least those with political resources) the tools to oust potentially abusive leaders from office before they are able to become a serious threat' (Poe and Tate 1994: 855). In Chapter 4 we briefly discussed the impact of press freedom on the respect for other types of human rights. Democracies (generally) have a free and critical press that is able to report on the behaviour of the executive and its agencies. Such controls make the secret use of state violence more difficult and more dangerous. This form of external monitoring that is commonly found in democracies therefore reduces the opportunity of leaders to resort to repression.

Semi-democracy

Some argue that although democracies are generally very good in protecting human rights, and in particular life integrity rights, countries that are classified as semi-democracies, meaning regimes that combine democratic and authoritarian characteristics, are particularly at risk of experiencing repression.[2] Such mixed regimes in particular might be likely to perceive potential threats, as '[t]he extension of democracy should give formerly excluded groups and suppressed class challengers the possibility to change the political and distributive order by mobilization of numbers' (Fein 1995: 173). Authoritarian regimes allow for very little political activity. Their internal strength partly rests on projecting fear and thus preventing people from expressing open dissent. The threat posed by an authoritarian regime inhibits people from displaying activities that might invite a government to employ repression. But as political restrictions disappear and the power of the government is limited and subjected to checks and balances, opponents of the regime 'may regard civil disobedience and violence as both feasible and necessary strategy for pressing their claims for a share of influence over political decisions' (Muller 1985: 48). Such mixed regimes are likely to be particularly sensitive to any form of dissent, which means that they might violate life integrity rights as a reaction to a perceived threat. In short, if political regimes adopt only some democratic features and do not fully implement a democratic system, people might be at an increased risk of suffering from torture, political imprisonment and extrajudicial killings.

Figure 5.1 shows the average value of the Political Terror Scale between 1976 and 2007 for different levels of democracy. For each degree of democracy, the mean value for the Political Terror Scale over this period is calculated. Regime type is measured by a variable that captures the restrictions on the executive, the competitiveness of executive recruitment and the competitiveness of political participation.[3] Thus this measure focuses on the nature of political institutions and procedural elements of democracy. The higher the value is on this scale, the more democratic is the country. A country that is

---

2 See, e.g., Fein (1995) and Muller (1985)

3 The data on regime type are taken from the Polity IV data set. You can find more details about these data at www.systemicpeace.org/polity/polity4.htm.

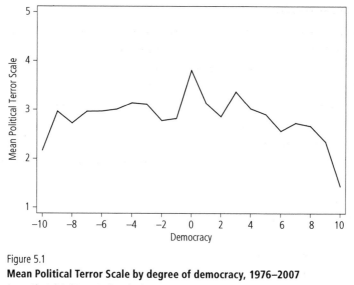

Figure 5.1
Mean Political Terror Scale by degree of democracy, 1976–2007
Source: The Political Terror Scale and Polity IV

classified as minus 10 on this scale is an autocratic regime that suppresses political participation and where the executive is selected in a closed process and possesses unlimited power. A country at the other end of the spectrum is a full democracy with competitive political participation and an elected executive whose powers are constrained by institutional checks and balances, while a country in the middle of the scale combines features of both a democracy and an autocracy. The graph indicates that those mixed regimes have the worst record of life integrity violations. On average, they are classified as countries with widespread state violence and repression. Well-established democracies provide the best protection of life integrity rights. As we have outlined above, democratic institutions make governments less likely to perceive domestic opposition as a threat and combined with democratic norms they generally use negotiations, bargaining and compromise to solve conflicts peacefully.

At the very extremes of the democracy scale, the mean value of the Political Terror Scale drops sharply. The most authoritarian regimes, which do not allow for competition or participation and where the leader is not subject to any effective constraints, have, on average, a better human rights record than countries that have at least some democratic features. For example, Qatar, a small peninsula bordering Saudi Arabia, has been coded as -10 on the polity scale, indicating a full autocracy, but is also placed on Level 1 of the Political Terror Scale, to reflect that almost no life integrity violations occurred, for most years since 1976. Qatar is a hereditary emirate, in which the emir has absolute power and political parties are banned. At the same time, there have been almost no reports of life integrity violations. However, the country benefits from other characteristics that, in general, make governments less likely to violate the life integrity rights of their citizens. Due to significant oil and natural gas revenues, Qatar is one of the richest countries, achieving the highest per capita income in the world in 2007. Qatar is also a very small country. As we discuss in more detail below, economic wealth and small populations are generally associated with better respect for human rights. Bhutan is another country that until 2005 was classified as a full autocracy and had a very good record for protecting life integrity rights for most years since the late 1970s. Like Qatar, Bhutan is one of the smallest countries, sandwiched between China and India, but unlike Qatar, is one of the poorest.

At the other end of the democracy spectrum we can observe a similar pattern. Although the average level of life integrity violations generally decreases slowly as countries become more democratic, there is a rather sharp drop in the mean PTS value at the very top end of the democracy scale. Fully established democracies have, on average, far better human rights records than countries with institutions that retain some element of limited participation or limited competition or do not effectively constrain their executives. Davenport and Armstrong explain this in the following way:

> [I]t does not make much sense to talk about the legislature's ability to sanction political authorities if the people have no power to remove individuals from office. Similarly, it would be equally ineffective for citizens to have the power to remove the president through the vote in periodic elections without some other institutional constraints on the chief executive's behavior. Indeed, it seems to make the most sense to think about a combination or mutual reinforcement of democratic elements when one talks about the conditions under which government leaders will and will not use repressive activity. (Davenport and Armstrong 2004: 542)

Protest, rebellion and civil war

Governments often use violent tactics in order to tackle violent opposition. The examples of Tiananmen Square and Iran given earlier are two instances where a government ordered its security forces to use violence to disperse protesters, to end this show of discontent with the regime and to send a strong message to potential future protesters. Examples of governments violating physical integrity rights in the face of anti-government demonstrations or riots can be found on all continents. Police forces often used violence against African American civil rights activists in the United States during the 1960s. On 7 March 1965, known as 'Bloody Sunday', several hundred civil rights marchers were attacked and beaten by state and local police in Alabama during the Selma to Montgomery marches. During the Vietnam War, anti-war demonstrations were also often met with police violence. In the United Kingdom, the most widely known instances of violent police response to demonstrations and riots occurred in Northern Ireland during the 1960s and 1970s. Again, one event is called 'Bloody Sunday': on 30 January 1972, fourteen people were shot dead by the British army during a demonstration. In Chile, Pinochet acted heavy-handedly against protests by shantytown dwellers. In many countries, such as Kenya and Zimbabwe, government forces have used severe violence against demonstrations by opposition supporters in the run-up to elections.

Applying the theoretical model we have introduced above, it is easy to see why display of dissent is one of the main reasons for life integrity violations. When people go out into the streets to protest against their government or specific government policies, the government is likely to feel, at least in some way, threatened by this show of opposition. Governments are even more likely to use repression as a response to protest when there are no well-developed institutional mechanisms in place that can facilitate the accommodation of popular grievances (Mason 2004). Popular protest questions and undermines the expertise and authority of the government and makes it look unpopular, weak and vulnerable. Under such conditions it is not surprising that the government will take action to restore its strength and try to regain control (Davenport 1995). Using violence and intimidation forms one option in a government's toolkit to achieve this goal. Depending on the nature of the protest activities, the likelihood of life integrity violations, and the risk of their being more severe and widespread, increases. Violent riots are perceived to be more threatening than peaceful anti-government demonstrations, while attacks by guerrilla groups and a violent rebellion against a president pose an even greater threat – and are therefore more likely to be countered with severe government violence and severe human rights violations.

A particularly threatening experience for a government is a civil war. In a civil war government troops and rebel groups violently contest the political structure of a country, the distribution of power and the way in which the country is governed. The outbreak of a civil war signals that the authority of the current government and its control over the country have suffered significant damage. A civil war has dramatic effects on a country; it destabilizes its political, economic and social foundations. A civil war poses the most serious threat to a government.

During a civil war, governments attempt to re-establish some of their power and control by eliminating members of the group that challenges their position. Military or police forces that are loyal to the government, or forces especially trained to torture and kill, are used to increase the strength of the regime by using violence against people or groups of people that are deemed to be a threat. Widespread terror is also often employed to intimidate ordinary people and to weaken their support for the rebels.

Clearly, domestic dissent poses a threat to governments. When government opponents participate in protest activities, in particular when the protest turns violent, governments are more likely to violate the human rights of their citizens because they see this action as justified. So while the level of threat as perceived by a government increases during times of popular dissent, so does the government's willingness to use harsh measures to end such protest.

Figure 5.2 shows the mean values of the Political Terror Scale for the different degrees of dissent. The dissent categories, apart from civil war, are measured using data from the Cross-National Time-Series Data Archive.[4] Peaceful dissent identifies non-violent strikes or non-violent

---

4 See www.databanksinternational.com/ for more details about these data.

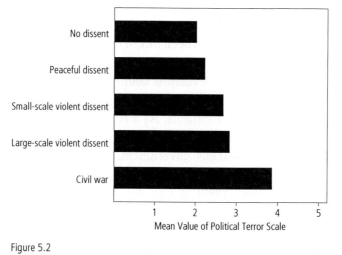

Figure 5.2
Mean values of the Political Terror Scale by dissent type, 1976–2007
Source: Political Terror Scale, Cross-National Time-Series Data Archive, UCDP/PRIO Armed Conflict Dataset

anti-government demonstrations, small-scale violent dissent captures violent demonstrations or riots involving the use of physical force, and large-scale violent dissent measures guerrilla warfare, such as bombings and armed rebellion against the government. Civil war is measured with the UCDP/PRIO Armed Conflict Dataset (Gleditsch *et al.* 2002), which codes intra-state conflict that results in at least twenty-five deaths per year. For each country and each year between 1976 and 2007, we identified the most severe form of dissent that took place. Then we calculated the mean value of the Political Terror Scale for all these country-years, separately for the different degrees of dissent.

Figure 5.2 shows that as dissent becomes more violent, so does the government's response in terms of life integrity violations. In countries during years in which no protest takes place, the PTS mean value is 2.02, and it increases to 2.84 for those that experience large-scale violent dissent, and further increases to 3.86 for those country-years during which a civil war occurs. A country without any dissent is, on average, likely to see limited imprisonment for non-violent political activity, but is unlikely to suffer from state violence. During a civil war, however, political imprisonment and political murder generally become a common part of life.

Economic development

Economic development has often been linked to repression and the violation of life integrity rights. Poorer countries have, on average, worse human rights records than developed countries. Economic scarcity puts governments under pressure as it hinders their ability to provide goods and services for their citizens. As a result, governments often lose trust and support from the electorate when the economy is doing badly. Hence poverty weakens governments. Governments in poor countries are also more vulnerable to social and political instability (Mitchell and McCormick 1988). In least developed countries the constraints on governments are substantial. They are often unable to provide even the most basic commodities, such as food, a working health system, housing or free education. Under such precarious conditions, when economic rights are already widely violated, governments are highly likely to perceive of potential threats, therefore making it more likely that they will use violence to maintain or strengthen their own position in power.

Figure 5.3 shows the average score on the Political Terror Scale by income group for 2007. The income group classifications are taken from the World Bank. This categorization is based on the gross national income (GNI) per capita. Countries with an average of US$935 per capita or less are classified as low income, countries between US$936 and US$3,705 as lower middle income, between US$3,706 and US$11,455 as upper middle income and countries above US$11,455 income per capita are placed in the high income group. Figure 5.3 shows a clear relationship between income and life integrity violations. The higher the income group, the lower is the group's average value on the Political Terror Scale. Countries in the low income group are, on average, placed on Level 3 of the Political Terror Scale, indicating that political imprisonment is widespread and that political murders and brutality may be common. Countries in this category include Rwanda, Laos, Mozambique and Tajikistan.

Figure 5.3 also shows that there is barely a difference between the mean PTS value of the low income group compared with that of the lower middle income groups. For the former the mean PTS value in 2007 was 3.18, while for the latter it was 2.96. There is a far bigger gap between the lower middle income group and the upper

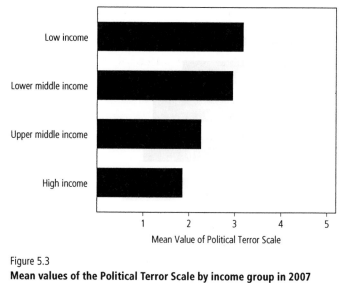

Figure 5.3
Mean values of the Political Terror Scale by income group in 2007
Source: Political Terror Scale and World Bank

middle income group, which has a PTS mean value of 2.26. This suggests that only past a certain threshold is higher income linked with better life integrity rights. Lower middle income countries, such as Indonesia, Cameroon and Paraguay, generally have human rights records very similar to those of low income countries. Only countries in the upper middle income group, such as Argentina, Poland and Botswana, benefit from improved protection of physical integrity rights. In general, however, governments in richer countries have better human rights records than governments in poorer countries. Poverty places a strain on governments, which makes it more likely that governments feel threatened and, as a result, use violence, such as torture and political imprisonment, to strengthen and secure their position in power.

Population size and growth

Quantitative human rights research has found that more populous countries are more susceptible to life integrity violations compared with countries with smaller populations. In countries with large populations, more people compete for food, land and housing, jobs,

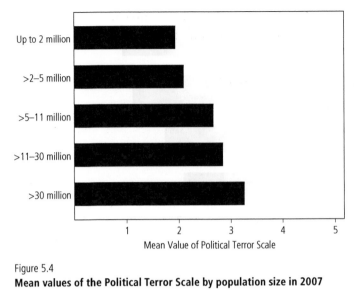

Figure 5.4
Mean values of the Political Terror Scale by population size in 2007
Source: Political Terror Scale and World Bank development indicators

health care, government support and so on. This means that larger populations tend to put a greater stress on finite resources compared with smaller populations. This higher level of demand placed on finite resources can be perceived by the government as a threat to its ability to provide for its people and to be seen as competent. Therefore, on average, larger countries have a higher risk of repression than countries with a smaller population.

Figure 5.4 graphically displays this relationship between the size of a country's population and its position on the Political Terror Scale for 2007. For this graph 173 countries are divided into five categories, so that each category contains roughly the same number of countries. Then the average value of the Political Terror Scale in 2007 is calculated for each of the five groups. The graph shows that the countries with populations of up to two million have the best human rights records. Such small countries that scored best on the Political Terror Scale in 2007 include Luxembourg, Iceland, the Seychelles, Bhutan and Samoa. On the other end of the spectrum, countries with more than 30 million people have the worst record, with an average PTS score of just over three, indicating that in such countries political imprisonment, as well as political brutality, is common. Examples of such large countries with a PTS score of three in 2007 include Mexico, South Africa, Morocco and Indonesia.

British colonial heritage

As with those on population size, quantitative studies on life integrity violations have found that countries that had been colonized by the British have, on average, a better human rights record than other countries. Cultural experiences shape political culture and the framework of what kinds of behaviour are more or less legitimate and justified. Therefore certain colonial experiences in the past can affect the use of repression in the present. Particularly violent colonial rule might be associated with higher levels of life integrity violations today, compared with countries in which their colonizers used less violent measures. Comparing the mean values of the Political Terror Scale for former British colonies and other countries shows only rather small differences. However, we shall continue investigating this argument about the impact of British colonial heritage on life integrity violations in the next section.

Previous life integrity violations

Empirical research has found overwhelming evidence that the level of human rights violations in a particular country does not change overnight, at least not in most cases. This is not particularly surprising. Once a government has decided to employ repressive tactics, and has taken the necessary steps to put this decision into practice, repression is likely to continue for some time. Policy inertia makes radical changes of government policies unlikely. Additionally, like other organizations, the security apparatus that carries out the violence is likely to try to perpetuate and justify its own existence. It will be in its self-interest to continue with its repressive strategies in order to maintain the group's status, position and income. Therefore, when we compare levels of life integrity violations from one year with the next, we do not expect to see much change.

Figure 5.5 graphically shows the close link between the level of life integrity violations in a particular year t and the level of life integrity violations in the previous year t-1. Each bar represents one level of the

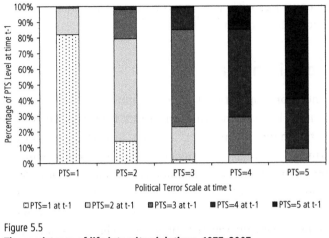

Figure 5.5
The persistence of life integrity violations, 1977–2007
Source: Political Terror Scale

Political Terror Scale. Each bar is broken down into the percentage of country-years that were placed on the different levels of the PTS in the previous year. For example, the first bar represents all country-years between 1977 and 2007 that were coded as Level 1 on the PTS. The dotted area shows that 82 per cent of these country-years had also scored a one on the Political Terror Scale in the previous year, while 17 per cent had been coded as PTS Level 2 and 1 per cent as PTS Level 3, none being worse than that. Of countries that were placed on Level 2 of the PTS in a particular year 66 per cent had also been placed on Level 2 in the preceding year. For PTS Level 3 this percentage is 62 per cent, for Level 4 56 per cent and 60 per cent of countries in the worst PTS category also scored 5 in the preceding year. Figure 5.5 clearly visualizes that the level of life integrity violations in the current year is generally a very good indicator of the level of life integrity violations to be expected in the next year. The more repressive the present is, the more repressive the immediate future is likely to be.[5]

---

5 The factors that we have discussed above are probably the most widely and thoroughly studied in the empirical literature on the violation of physical integrity rights – but they are by no means the only ones. Recent studies suggest that as countries become more integrated into the global economic or financial markets, for example captured with foreign direct investments or trade flows, they improve their human rights records (Hafner-Burton 2005; Richards, Gelleny and Sacko 2001). Another factor often argued to be related to human rights violations is ethnic diversity. Recent studies find that countries that are more ethnically or culturally diverse suffer from fewer, and not more, human rights violations (Lee et al. 2004; Walker and Poe 2002).

A more complete picture

To understand better why human rights are violated, it is helpful to look at the bigger picture. Above, we have introduced and discussed the main factors that have consistently been linked with the violation of the right to physical integrity. In this section, we consider the impact of these indicators simultaneously, in order to find out how one specific indicator affects physical integrity rights, while taking into account the impact of other factors. As mentioned above, some countries are both small and rich, such as Qatar, and have a very good PTS score, despite being non-democratic. The question is how these factors impact on the risk of human rights violations, taking into consideration the impact of the other factors at the same time. To do this, we utilize the tools of multivariate analysis. This means that we can evaluate the impact of several factors on the respect for physical integrity rights simultaneously. Table 5.1 shows the results of this analysis.[6]

For this analysis we have used the same data sources as the ones we have relied on in the discussion above. Due to data constraints, this table is based on the analyses of data from 1980 to 2007. All variables are highly statistically significant, which means that we can be highly confident that we did not receive these values by chance. First, the model includes four different variables (PTS level 2_{t-1} to PTS level 5_{t-1}) which measure whether or not a country was coded at a particular PTS Level during the previous year t-1. The results show that whenever a country was coded on PTS Level 2, 3, 4, or 5 at time t-1, the level of human rights violations at time t was higher compared with a country that was coded at PTS Level 1 at time t-1. This confirms what we have already seen in Figure 5.5 above, which is that higher life integrity violations in the previous year increases life integrity violations in the current year.

The next two variables in the model measure the impact of democracy on the violation of physical integrity rights. We have included

---

6 We have used an ordered logit model to analyse statistically how the factors we have discussed above impact upon physical integrity rights, because the variable whose variations we are trying to explain, the Political Terror Scale, consists of five categories which are ordered from 1 (almost no physical integrity rights violations) to 5 (widespread and indiscriminate physical integrity rights violations).

Table 5.1 **A multivariate model of the violation of physical integrity rights**

	Coefficient	(Robust std. err.)
PTS level 2_{t-1}	1.566***	(0.078)
PTS level 3_{t-1}	2.570***	(0.094)
PTS level 4_{t-1}	3.595***	(0.114)
PTS level 5_{t-1}	4.552***	(0.157)
Democracy	0.061***	(0.016)
Democracy^2	−0.004***	(0.001)
Peaceful dissent	0.169*	(0.066)
Small-scale violent dissent	0.421***	(0.070)
Large-scale violent dissent	0.445***	(0.067)
Civil war	0.712***	(0.074)
GNI per capita^a	−0.047**	(0.018)
Population^a	0.089***	(0.014)
Former British colony	−0.085*	(0.043)
τ_1	1.132	(0.273)
τ_2	3.047	(0.285)
τ_3	4.710	(0.289)
τ_4	6.349	(0.299)
Log pseudolikelihood	−3085.307	
χ^2	2287.34***	
Pseudo R^2	0.416	
N	3570	

^{a} Variable log-transformed due to skewed distribution.

* $p < 0.05$, ** $p < 0.01$, *** $p < 0.001$, two-tailed tests.

one linear measure of democracy, which has been recoded to range from 0 (no democratic features, full autocracy) to 20 (fully established democracy). To account for a possible non-linear impact of democracy on human rights violations, as discussed above, we have also included a squared term of this democracy scale. The results suggest that there is indeed a non-linear impact of democracy on human rights violations, which we will explore further below. The table also shows that all dissent variables have a positive impact on the Political Terror Scale, which means that when any of these types of protest or civil war are present in a country, then the risk of human rights violations increases, while all the other characteristics of the

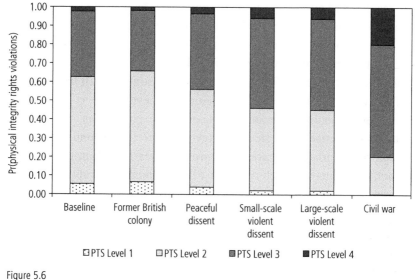

Figure 5.6
Predicted probabilities of physical integrity rights violations

countries that we have accounted for remain the same. The measure for economic development, GNI per capita, has a negative sign. This indicates that as economic development increases, the risk of physical integrity rights violations decreases. The coefficient for population size is, as expected, positive, confirming our argument that countries with larger populations are at a higher risk of human rights violations. Finally, the negative coefficient for former British colonies shows that, on average, former British colonies have lower human rights violations than other countries. In the following, we graphically explore the impact of these indicators on the level of human rights violations.

Figure 5.6 shows how likely a particular country is to receive a certain PTS score. The first bar shows the predicted probabilities of the different PTS Levels for an 'average' country, meaning a country with an average level of economic development, an average population size, no dissent or civil war and not having been a former British colony. The dotted area indicates that in such a country, there is a 0.06 probability, or a 6 per cent chance that this country has almost no human rights violations (PTS Level 1). But there is a 57 per cent chance that this country reaches a PTS score of 2, a 35 per cent chance to reach PTS Level 3, a 2 per cent chance to be placed at PTS Level 4 and a less than 0.01 per cent risk of experiencing full-scale repression (PTS Level 5). Since the risk of this most severe from of repression is generally very small, we have excluded this category from this and the following figures. So on average, most countries will be placed on PTS Level 2, but many will also be on PTS Level 3.

But how do these probabilities, or risks, change as the circumstances and conditions in a country change? The second bar in this graph re-calculates the predicted probabilities for a country that has exactly the same characteristics on all the dimensions captured in this model, with the one difference that it had been colonized by Britain. The graph shows that the human rights conditions improve only very slightly. The chances of PTS Level 2 increase by about two percentage points, while the risk of PTS Level 3 declines about roughly the same amount.

The third bar in Figure 5.6 represents the predicted probabilities of physical integrity rights violations in a country that has all the same characteristics as the baseline model, but where people undertake peaceful dissent, such as strikes or anti-government demonstrations. The fourth bar models a country with small-scale violent dissent, such as violent, spontaneous riots, and the next one represents a country where large-scale violent dissent, such as guerrilla warfare or rebellion, takes place. The last bar represents a country where large-scale violent dissent has escalated into civil war. Figure 5.6 shows that, in general, as dissent becomes more violent, the dark-shared areas of the bars get larger – meaning that more severe human rights violations become more likely. Even peaceful forms of dissent reduce the chance of PTS Level 1 from 6 per cent to 4 per cent, and the risk of PTS Level 3 increases from 35 to 40 per cent.

Unsurprisingly, governments feel more threatened by violent than by peaceful protest, and are therefore more likely to use violence when faced with violent opposition. For example, when riots take place, the risk of PTS Level 3 increases to 48 per cent, which is significantly higher than the 35 per cent of the baseline model or the 40 per cent in the scenario of peaceful dissent. Governments do not seem to distinguish small-scale from large-scale violent dissent when calculating their response. The predicted probabilities of physical integrity rights violations are almost the same under both scenarios. Civil war,

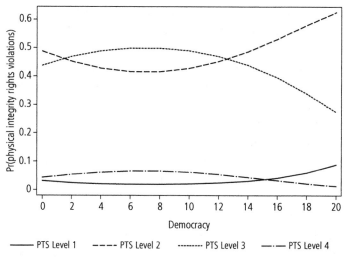

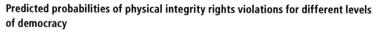

Figure 5.7
Predicted probabilities of physical integrity rights violations for different levels of democracy

however, presents a different situation. During a civil war there is a 60 per cent risk that human rights violations occur at PTS Level 3, and even the risk of PTS Level 4 increases to 20 per cent – this is ten times higher compared with the baseline model, and almost four times as high as during violent dissent!

Figure 5.7 shows how the risk of countries achieving a particular PTS Level changes depending on their degree of democracy. The vertical y-axis shows the predicted probabilities of a certain PTS score. The horizontal x-axis represents the democracy scale, ranging from 0 (full autocracy) to 20 (full democracy). The solid line plots the predicted probabilities of a country receiving a PTS score of 1, the dashed line the predicted probabilities of a country receiving a PTS score of 2, the dotted line represents the PTS score 3 and the dotted–dashed line stands for the predicted probabilities for PTS score 4. Since there is generally a very low predicted probability that a country reaches PTS Level 5 (less than 0.001), we have again omitted this category from the graph. The figure shows that the most non-democratic countries (democracy = 0) have an almost 50 per cent chance of being placed at PTS Level 2, with the predicted probabilities for achieving this level being 0.49; but there is also a 44 per cent chance that such a country is placed at PTS Level 3. However, for countries that have some democratic features, without being a fully consolidated democracy, physical integrity rights violations at PTS Level 3 are the most likely outcome. The graph also shows that, for these countries, it is more likely that they experience widespread human rights violations (PTS Level 4) than almost no violations at all (PTS Level 1). Both have very low predicted probabilities, but the predicted probabilities of PTS Level 4 are still higher than for PTS Level 1 for these countries in the middle of the democracy scale. However, as countries become more fully consolidated democracies, the risk of more widespread human rights violations (indicated by PTS Levels 3 and 4) drops significantly. At the same time, it becomes more likely that a country receives a PTS score of either 1 or 2. But even for the most democratic countries, there is only a 9 per cent chance that it receives a PTS score of 1, but there is a 63 per cent chance that it is placed on the PTS Level 2. Taking into consideration that the average value of the Political Terror Scale for this sample is 2.5, being a consolidated democracy substantially improves the human rights record, all other factors held constant.

Next, we look more closely at how the level of economic development influences physical integrity rights in this model. Figure 5.8

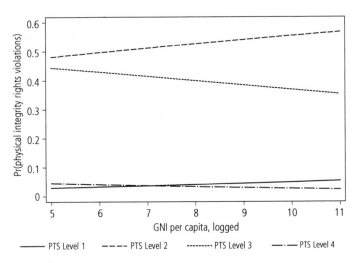

Figure 5.8
Predicted probabilities of physical integrity rights violations for different levels of economic development

graphs the predicted probabilities for each of the PTS scores, depending on the level of economic development, which is measured using per capita gross national income (GNI).[7] Figure 5.8 shows that PTS Level 2, meaning limited physical integrity rights violations, represented by the dashed line, is the most likely scenario for an average country. For very poor countries, however, the risk of more severe violations at PTS Level 3 is almost just as likely. But as countries move up on the economic development scale, the risk of being at PTS Level 3 declines to 0.35, while at the same time the probability of more limited violations at PTS Level 2 increases to 0.57. The graph also shows that whereas the level of democracy has a non-linear effect on the risk of human rights violations, where not every step towards 'more' democracy decreases the risk of human rights violations by the same amount, economic development is related to human rights violations in a linear way. Each increase in economic development decreases the risk of physical integrity rights violations, irrespective of where a country is on the development-scale.

In this section we have shown how certain indicators affect the risk of human rights violations, using data from around the globe over a period of almost thirty years. We were able to draw general conclusions about the impact of past repression, regime type, protest, civil war, economic development, population and the experience of having been a former British colony on the human rights situation. The conclusions have provided us with a broad picture of why human rights are violated, a picture that represents all continents, rich and poor countries and countries with different cultures and historical experiences. The advantage of this general picture is also its downside, which is that summarizing trends across all countries tells us very little about the situation in a specific country. In the final part of this chapter we show how the human rights conditions in one particular state have changed over time, and how the government's perception of threat influenced its use of violent policies.

---

7 Since this variable is highly skewed, as a small number of countries have extremely high levels of income compared with the majority of countries, we have taken the natural log of this variable.

A case study: Nigeria

Nigeria provides a good example of the arguments we have outlined above, since it underwent various regime transitions, an unsuccessful war of secession, oil crises and high levels of regional violence. Since 1976, when the first Amnesty International reports were available to code the level of physical integrity abuse, Nigeria moved up and down the Political Terror Scale, ranging from Level 1 in 1976 to Level 4 in 2007, when torture, killings and disappearances were a common part of life. With this brief case study, we highlight how some of the general trends and causes of human rights violations have played out in one particular country.

During the first six years of independence, from 1960 until 1966, Nigeria was ruled by a federal government, which gave substantial autonomy to the three regions, the North, East and West. After a coup in January 1966, the army's commander-in-chief, General Ironsi from the East, formed a military government and abolished the federation. In July the same year army units from the North staged a countercoup, which led to the massacre of thousands of Igbo in the northern states. Hundreds of thousands of Igbos fled to the south-east, where a strong secessionist movement developed and culminated in the declaration of the Republic of Biafra in 1967. What followed was a bloody civil war that ended in 1970 with the defeat of Biafra.

The military coup in 1966 started a process of rapid deterioration of the political and humanitarian situation. Political institutions were weak and unable to balance power politically between the three most powerful groups. This posed a precarious situation in which the fear of coups and countercoups was high. The level of threat was perceived by the military regime as very high, which resulted in widespread human rights violations.

Figure 5.9 traces the ups and downs of the Political Terror Scale in Nigeria from 1976 to 2007. It points out certain high and low points in the country's respect for physical integrity rights. In 1979, Nigeria returned to civilian rule. The Second Republic under President Shagari was characterized as a full democracy by the Polity IV scale. Consistent with our argument about the link between democracy and human rights, during that time only limited forms of life integrity

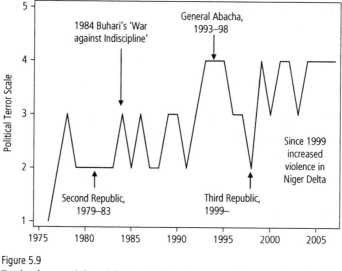

Figure 5.9
Tracing human rights violations in Nigeria

violations were recorded. Between 1979 and 1983, Nigeria was placed on the PTS Level 2, based on the Amnesty International reports. Overall, the democratic regime of the Second Republic provided substantially better protection of human rights than did the preceding military regimes.

But the Second Republic faced multiple severe problems, such as economic crisis, mismanagement and claims of corruption. The oil boom, which had fostered the expectation of unlimited development in Nigeria during the 1970s with annual growth rates of up to 14 per cent, came to an end in 1980, when GNP per capita fell by 15 per cent (source: World Bank World Development Indicators). The general election in 1983 took place amidst high levels of corruption, tension between different political camps, increased violence and allegations of vote rigging. This turbulence led again to a coup, on 31 December 1983, this time led by Major-General Muhammad Buhari. His rule was particularly repressive. He launched a 'war against indiscipline' and issued a number of decrees that enabled him to implement a rather heavy-handed approach, including detaining people without charge for long periods of time. This increase in human rights violations is reflected in the PTS score moving from Level 2 in 1983 to the worse Level 3 in 1984.

The public outcry in response to Buhari's policies, coupled with continuing economic decline, led to another bloodless coup on 27 August 1985 by Major General Ibrahim Babangida. Among his promises was greater respect for human rights. But the combination of the continuing economic crisis, corruption and abuse of power caused people to take to the streets in widespread public protests, initially against the structural adjustment programme imposed by the IMF. But at the beginning of the 1990s the targets of the protests changed to government policies and its abuses of human rights. Between 1985 and 1992, Nigeria moved between PTS Levels 2 and 3. As we have shown with the general analysis above, poverty and protest put governments under severe strain, increase their perception of threat and therefore make it more likely for them to use violence against their citizens. This was the case in Nigeria.

On 12 June 1993 Nigeria held presidential elections, which were won by a businessman, Chief Moshood Abiola. Although the elections were seen as the country's fairest elections to date, Babangida's military regime annulled the result two weeks later. This move by the military leaders triggered the most widespread protest by civil society, which was again countered by a mix of repression and co-optation by the regime. In August 1993 General Babangida resigned. An Interim National Government was put in charge, led by Chief Ernest Shonekan and with General Sani Abacha as defence minister. But as the economy continued to decline, protest and strikes continued and Abacha ended Shonekan's rule with a military coup in November 1993. During this highly turbulent year, during which large and diverse masses took to the streets to protest against their rulers, Nigeria moved from PTS Level 3 to PTS Level 4 and remained there for the next two years. As before, the combination of poverty and protest had led to repression. But this time the level of threats was far higher. As internal dissent was more widespread and sustained for longer periods, the response by the government was even more violent and affected larger parts of the population.

Under the regime of General Sani Abacha, from 1993 to 1998 the respect for human rights drastically deteriorated. Detention without trial, and torture and killings of political opponents and human rights activists were commonplace. The most prominent incident was the execution of the author and Ogoni activist Ken

Saro-Wiwa in 1995. Most political detainees who were not executed remained in prison until Abacha's death in 1998. On the basis of the decision-making model introduced above, General Abacha was highly susceptible to potential threats to his rule and responded with severe and widespread violence to any real or perceived challenges. According to the US State Department, all elements of the security apparatus committed serious human right violations under Abacha's rule.

Since Nigeria's return to civilian rule in 1999 with President Olusegun Obasanjo, the country has been classified as a semi-democracy that shows signs of a democratic system, such as substantial constraints of the executive by the legislative branch and the judiciary, but also includes elements of a more authoritarian system such as alleged election rigging and limited political competition. Although respect for human rights has improved since the end of the military regime, human rights reports still point to political imprisonment, police brutality and murders. From 1999 until 2007 Nigeria was placed on PTS Level 4, with the exception of 2000 and 2003, when it was classified as PTS Level 3.

The period since 1999 is characterized by the mobilization and radicalization of youths, particularly in the Niger Delta. The Niger Delta is extremely important to the Nigerian government, as the oil resources from this region provide the country with its most essential export earnings. Since the 1970s, ethnic minorities living in the Niger Delta have repeatedly protested against the exploitation of their land and demanded better economic conditions and political influence. These protest activities have become very violent, and often led to conflict between militant groups under the Fourth Republic. The Niger Delta has become a 'region of insurrection, because of the scale of protests, frequency of occupation and disruption of oil production and violent confrontations with the state' (Ikelegbe 2001: 463). Due to the vital role that the Niger Delta plays for the government and the country as a whole, any disturbances in this region will be observed very carefully by the government – and be perceived as highly threatening, and therefore to be eliminated, at high cost if necessary. Ikelegbe argues that 'the manner of conduct of the struggle and resistance of the ND [Niger Delta] people represents the greatest challenge to state authority since the Nigerian civil war, as well as the greatest manifestation of state repression in response to civil challenge to its authority' (Ikelegbe 2001: 438).

The decision model introduced earlier helps us to understand why there are such extensive violations of the right to physical integrity in Nigeria. The severe forms of dissent and violent mobilization of groups against the government pose substantial threats to the authorities. In order to eliminate, or minimize, the threat, the government uses violence and intimidation. Under the political regime, which is classified as a semi-democracy by the Polity IV scale, the government is even more susceptible to the perception of threat. Although there have been presidential elections in 1999, 2003 and 2007, they have been marred by problems and accompanied by political violence and intimidation. The presidential elections in 2003 and 2007 suffered from serious breaches of the electoral process and in both years the opposition disputed the election result. As discussed above, regimes that carry out multiparty elections but are missing other important elements of an institutional democracy, such as a professional bureaucracy, effective government control of the country, strong and independent political institutions and an independent, engaged and non-violent civil society, are more likely to experience internal dissent, which leads to human rights violations. At the same time, they are also more likely to feel threatened by the display of protest, for example by peaceful demonstrations and strikes, and as a result respond with violence to these actions, where other regimes would choose non-violent methods of response. Finally, widespread poverty in the country increases the pressure on the government and further increases the risk of human rights violations, as we have seen in the example of Nigeria.

Summary and conclusion

In this chapter we have presented a decision-making model that enables us to understand why and under what conditions governments are likely to violate human rights. We assumed that governments are rational actors that want to remain in power and want to minimize, or eradicate, threats to their power. But if governments perceive themselves to be under threat, they do not automatically employ violence. Governments also need to be willing and able to implement violent strategies. The more transparent government actions are, and the more likely it is that perpetrators will be held accountable for human rights violations, the less likely it is that governments will choose violence to counter a potential, or real, threat to their rule.

In our discussion above we have focused on six factors that help us identify countries and situations that are particularly prone to experiencing the violation of physical integrity rights. First, in general, more democratic countries are less likely to violate human rights. The institutions, procedures and norms that characterize democratic political systems make governments less susceptible to threats. At the same time, these democratic features also provide incentives to manage such threats and conflicts in a peaceful way and discourage the use of violence by holding governments and their agents accountable for their actions. But our empirical analysis has also shown that only fully established democracies have a substantially lower risk of human rights violations, while semi-democracies are more likely to experience the violation of physical integrity rights.

Second, we have shown that any form of protest increases the risk that governments violate the right to physical integrity and employ political imprisonment, torture or even extrajudicial killings. The more violent and widespread the protest is, the higher the risk of more severe human rights violations. In general, governments feel threatened by anti-government demonstrations, riots and, particularly, more violent acts of dissent, such as rebellions and civil war, and therefore will likely use extreme measures to counter this threat.

Third, governments in poorer countries feel more vulnerable, hence we have seen that, in general, the poorer a country is, the higher the risk that it will experience human rights violations. Fourth, larger populations put more strain on limited resources and therefore make governments more vulnerable to threat, and, in turn, more likely to violate human rights. Fifth, historical experiences shape the risk of human rights violations. In this chapter we have focused on one factor, namely on having a certain colonial past. Comparing the experience of having been a British colony to the experience of having had a different colonizer (or no colonizer at all) has shown that former British colonies have, on average, developed a greater respect for human rights than other countries, even if one takes into account the role of economic development, regime type and size of population. Finally, one of the most important reasons why countries suffer from human rights violations is their past experience with such violations. Once human rights violations take place, it is very difficult to end these practices. Clearly, in terms of human rights violations, prevention is the best cure.

In this chapter we have concentrated on how structural factors influence human rights violations. Yet one could also focus on the individuals who are responsible for the violations. Neil Mitchell (2004) argues that individuals have three motives for violating human rights: the desire to get and hold on to power, a dogmatic belief system, which drives them to inflict violence on those with the 'wrong' belief system, or the personal interests of those actually carrying out the violence (e.g. revenge, loot). In particular, the way in which leaders choose to control (or not) the actions of their soldiers and police, or the extent to which the leaders hold their agents accountable for their behaviours, substantially influences whether or not these agents will violate the rights of individuals.

Using such a quantitatively based approach to explain why life integrity violations occur has both strengths and weaknesses. Using the Political Terror Scale to capture human rights violations has the disadvantage that we have only one single measure for a whole country over a whole year. If there are drastic changes within a particular year, these cannot be captured with these data. Similarly, it does not account for intra-state variations, such as highlighting particular areas within a country that experience more human rights violations than other parts of the country.

Another weakness of this approach is that it reveals only general trends, without providing any details about specific countries or instances of human rights violations. But, at the same time, this weakness is also one of the main strengths of this method. The results that come out of the analysis are not driven by the characteristics and perhaps peculiarities of one particular region, but instead allow us to uncover general patterns of human rights violations. We are therefore able to generalize widely from our results. We are also able to test a large number of competing hypotheses and evaluate their effectiveness in explaining human rights violations against each other. In the brief case study of Nigeria, we have shown how these different factors have led to physical integrity rights violations in specific circumstances. But one problem is shared by all empirical approaches that strive to provide us with a better understanding of why human rights violations occur. We can never be completely sure that the information we have and rely on to evaluate this phenomenon, whatever form it takes or wherever it comes from, represents the full picture. Where human rights are violated, the perpetrators will try to keep their actions secret. Yet this certainly does not mean that we could not or should not attempt to put the pieces we do have together in order to get a better understanding of why human rights are violated, as without this understanding it will be impossible to work towards improving the protection and guarantee of these rights in the future.

FURTHER READING

Causes of repression

- Carey, Sabine C. and Steven C. Poe (eds.). 2004. *Understanding Human Rights Violations.*
  This volume tackles the question of why human rights are violated from a range of different angles, including the individual perpetrator, security organizations, the role of legal instruments, foreign policy and economic development.

- Mitchell, Neil J. 2004. *Agents of Atrocity: Leaders, Followers, and the Violation of Human Rights in Civil War.*
  This is an extremely readable book that moves away from focusing on structural conditions as causes of human rights violations and concentrates instead on the role of the agents of violence and their principals. It analyses why there is so much repression during civil wars and offers suggestions on what could be done about it.

Human rights and democracy

- Carey, Sabine C. 2009. *Protest, Repression and Political Regimes: An Empirical Analysis of Latin America and Sub-Saharan Africa.*
  Carey uses a multi-method approach to investigate how political regimes shape the dynamic interaction between popular protest and regime repression.

- Davenport, Christian. 2007. *State Repression and the Domestic Democratic Peace.*
  This book uses quantitative analyses to investigate the influence of various aspects of democracy on the use of state repression.

Human rights and the global economy

- Abouharb, M. Rodwan and David Cingranelli. 2007. *Human Rights and Structural Adjustment.*
  Abouharb and Cingranelli provide a theoretical and empirical analysis of structural adjustment programmes and show how such policies impact on the protection of human rights.

- Hafner-Burton, Emilie. 2009. *Forced to Be Good: Why Trade Agreements Boost Human Rights.*
  Using quantitative analyses, Hafner-Burton investigates why more and more trade agreements contain human rights clauses and how these influence the protection of human rights.

RELATED FILMS

Civil and political rights

- **Standard Operating Procedure** (Errol Morris, 2008). By the director of *The Thin Blue Line* and *Fog of War*, this video challenges the viewer to re-think whether the infamous pictures at Abu Ghraib tell us the 'true' story about what happened there. The interviews with those who carried out the 'torture' are marvelously revealing, whether intentionally or not.

- **Battle of Algiers** (Gillo Pontecorvo, 1966). This documentary-style film tells the story of the fight for Algerian independence from the perspective of those fighting to gain freedom from French rule.

- **The Official Story** (Luis Poenzo, 1985). This film, made a short time after the fall of the military regime in Argentina, focuses on an adoption in which the young child in question may be the victim of a 'disappearance' from the country's 'Dirty War'.

- **Missing** (Costa Gavras, 1982). This film, starring Jack Lemmon and Sissy Spacek, is based on the true story of the 'disappearance' of Charles Horman following the overthrow of the Allende regime in Chile. In one of the best performances of his brilliant career, Lemmon slowly comes to the realization of the US involvement in the coup, and indirectly in the death of his son.

Israeli–Palestinian issues

- **Arna's Children** (Juliano Mer Khamis and Danniel Danniel, 2003). Arna is an Israeli woman who started a Palestinian theater group a number of years ago. These children have now grown into young adults and the viewer witnesses the transformation as several become 'terrorists'.

- **To See if I'm Smiling** (Tamar Yarom, 2007). This sombre and effective film interviews several female Israeli soldiers as they recount their actions while patrolling the Occupied Territories. The movie makes no pretence that these soldiers speak for all women (or all soldiers) who served in the Israeli Defense Force. On the other hand, the shame they feel at some of the things that they did is quite palpable.

- **Waltz with Bashir** (Ari Folman, 2008). *Waltz with Bashir* is an animation that centres on a group of Israeli soldiers and the war in Lebanon and what they did – and what they remember about what they did – during the 1982 massacre of Palestinians at the Sabra and Shatila refugee camps.

- **Paradise Now** (Hany Abu-Assad, 2005). Many would object to this film being listed as a 'human rights' film, but it offers a tremendously engaging and even-handed discussion of the morality and usefulness of suicide bombing – set against the backdrop of an ill-fated love story. The film is able to poke fun at the missionary zeal of Palestinian suicide bombers, while at the same time depicting the social and economic forces that compel so many young men to carry out such acts.

part III

Intervening and rebuilding in the wake of repression

chapter **6**

Intervening to protect human rights

In the preceding two chapters we have shown where and why human rights have been violated, focusing in particular on the right to physical integrity. We have seen that human rights continue to be violated around the globe, and that the risk of such violations increases when governments face a real, or perceived, threat and when they assume that they won't be held accountable for their actions. In the third part of this book, we focus our attention on how human rights violations might be halted once they are under way, and what challenges lie in dealing with the aftermath of gross human rights violations.

The first chapter in Part III focuses on military intervention as a means of ending widespread human rights violations, while the second chapter examines attempts to rebuild society and to establish transitional justice in the wake of repression. There are, of course, other measures that states undertake in an effort to put an end to continuing atrocities in other lands, including economic sanctions and diplomatic negotiation. However, military intervention represents the most serious and committed response, and it is for this reason that we focus on this practice. On the other hand, there have been a number of problems associated with humanitarian intervention, and in the second half of this chapter we examine the Responsibility to Protect (R2P) initiative that places military intervention in a much broader context of state responsibility. The second chapter in Part III focuses on transitional justice and asks how victims, perpetrators and (international) bystanders can try to move forward after the experience of gross human rights violations.

Humanitarian intervention

Humanitarian intervention can be defined as coercive action by one or more states involving the use of armed force in another state without the consent of its authorities, and with the purpose of preventing widespread suffering or death among the inhabitants (Roberts 2002). To avoid confusion, humanitarian intervention needs to be differentiated from what are generally termed peacekeeping missions or operations, which are often carried out under the aegis of the United Nations. The first difference involves the issue of consent. Humanitarian interventions are carried out against the expressed wishes of a state, while peacekeeping missions are undertaken with the consent of the government (or governments) involved. The second difference relates to the use of force. Humanitarian intervention is premised on the idea that there are times when force needs to be used in order to eliminate the causes of human suffering. Peacekeeping missions, as the name suggests, are intended to maintain peace in order to allow political negotiations to go forward, and force is generally limited to self-defence measures (Weiss 2007). Although this represents the basic distinction between military interventions and peacekeeping operations, there are times when distinctions between these two categories tend to blur.

Notwithstanding the longstanding recognition of humanitarian intervention in international affairs, there are several issues that remain problematic. The first is whether humanitarian intervention constitutes an infringement of state sovereignty. The strongest legal basis for this position is Article 2(4) of the UN Charter, which provides, 'All Members shall refrain in their international relations from the threat or use of force against the territorial integrity or political independence of any state.' However, the Charter does allow for humanitarian intervention – but only under certain conditions and by specified means. First, the Security Council must determine that massive levels of human rights violations are occurring or are likely to take place. Second, the Council must conclude that this constitutes a threat to international peace and security, although this standard has generally been given a liberal interpretation. The third requirement is that the Council must authorize an enforcement action to halt or prevent such violations. In the view of some international lawyers, any intervention without specific Security Council authorization is illegal. While this is questionable, it is clear that the Security Council was designed to play a central role in all military interventions. This, however, has not occurred with any degree of consistency, thereby leaving the door open to action by individual states – but also inaction on the part of the international community.

A second issue that arises is whether an intervention is being carried out to alleviate human suffering, or whether the intervening state (or states) is engaging in an unlawful invasion in the pursuit of its own political ends, but is espousing humanitarian principles as cover. One of the most important considerations in determining whether an intervention is 'humanitarian' or not is the previous relationship between the states involved. The rationale, quite simply, is that states do not invade enemy countries for humanitarian reasons. Rather, the working premise seems to be that they only do so as a means of weakening their enemy. Of course, what seldom seems to be considered is that states might intervene for a number of different and perhaps even conflicting reasons.

Humanitarian interventions are often contested, but what is also contested is the refusal to act: situations of enormous levels of human suffering, where the international community essentially turns a blind eye. To explore the issue of humanitarian intervention more fully, we shall examine both interventions and what we term 'non-interventions' since the 1970s. Our approach here is in large part chronological and the reason for proceeding this way is to help capture the manner in which interventions and non-interventions have often been related to one another. Thus, the 'failed' intervention in Somalia led directly to the non-intervention in Rwanda a short time later. On the other hand, the failure to intervene in Bosnia in a timely manner had a strong influence on the decision to intervene immediately in Kosovo several years later. We have traced the development of interventions and non-interventions over time in Figure 6.1.

We treat separately a group of states that have experienced years of gross and systematic human rights violations, but where the response of the international community has been slow, ineffective or non-existent. Furthermore, with the exception of Sudan, there is no readily identifiable constituency to halt massive human rights violations

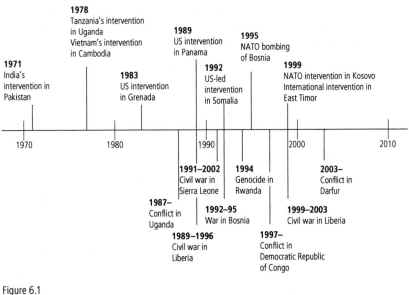

Figure 6.1
Timeline of interventions and non-interventions

in countries such as the Democratic Republic of the Congo, Liberia, Sierra Leone and Uganda. In certain respects these states (and the people who live in these states) seem almost to live (and die) in their own separate world. But not all the news is dire. In Liberia and Sierra Leone, small-scale humanitarian interventions helped to lead both countries to achieve some stability and peace.

The larger point is that there has been a great deal of disagreement, confusion and (deserved) criticism directed at the practice of humanitarian intervention. One of the main reasons for this is that there are no readily accepted governing standards in terms of when intervention is warranted, how it should be carried out, and what the international community must do after the intervention has taken place. This leads directly to our discussion of the Responsibility to Protect, R2P, in the second part of this chapter, which addresses these and other related issues.

The 1970s: three (humanitarian) interventions

Depending on one's point of view, the 1970s witnessed some of the most compelling examples of humanitarian intervention in human history – or, from the opposite perspective, several notable examples where states unlawfully invaded an enemy country under the pretence of humanitarian purpose. India's 1971 invasion of Pakistan serves as our starting point. According to the Indian government, this military intervention was carried out in response to the massive slaughter, taking place in what was then East Pakistan, that had caused millions of Pakistani refugees to flee to India. What complicates this matter is the fact that India and Pakistan were longstanding enemies that by this time had already engaged in various violent conflicts. Thus what remains unanswered is whether India intervened to help stop human rights violations from taking place (which the intervention apparently did help accomplish), or whether its primary goal was to weaken its enemy (which the intervention also did) – or was it some combination of these two? The UN General Assembly overwhelmingly disapproved of India's intervention, although this has no bearing on whether the intervention was 'humanitarian' or not.

The two interventions that began in 1978 raise the same issue. The first was Tanzania's intervention in Uganda after upwards of 300,000 people had perished under Idi Amin's brutal dictatorship. The second was Vietnam's intervention in Cambodia, which resulted in the removal from power of the Khmer Rouge regime. In both cases there had previously been enmity between the states involved. What is also problematic is the unilateral nature of these interventions. On the other hand, one cannot deny that when these actions occurred, both countries were experiencing massive human rights violations, and in the case of Cambodia, genocide of epic proportions. What also seems beyond question is that both interventions resulted in greatly reduced levels of violence. Finally, although these countries have been criticized for acting on their own, in neither case was there any indication that the rest of the international community was at all willing to intervene. Still, most governments viewed the actions of Tanzania and Vietnam as unlawful invasions – although in the case of Vietnam it is impossible to remove Cold War politics from the equation, best evidenced by the manner in which the United States and other Western states continued to recognize the Khmer Rouge as the 'lawful' government of Cambodia even after the genocidal nature of this regime became widely known.

The 1980s: two (non-humanitarian) interventions

It is impossible to prove whether the three interventions in the 1970s mentioned above were carried out for primarily humanitarian purposes or not. In at least two of the cases, the intervening states were able to achieve noteworthy political ends. In the case of India, its intervention helped lead to the dissolution of Pakistan as it was then constituted and the creation of the new independent state of Bangladesh from what had been East Pakistan. In the Cambodia situation, Vietnam's intervention resulted in governments that were much friendlier towards it.

However, as mentioned before, in both instances the intervention did lead to humanitarian results. Contrast this with the two interventions carried out by the United States in the 1980s. The first was the 1983 US invasion of Grenada, which resulted in the removal of what the Reagan administration termed a Marxist dictatorship. There were two problematic features of this intervention. The first involved timing. The invasion took place only a few days after scores of US Marines had been killed in a terrorist bombing incident in Lebanon, resulting in the removal of US troops from that country. Thus the United States has frequently been charged with using the intervention to 'save face' in the eyes of the international community. The fact that human rights conditions on the ground were quite good at the time the intervention/invasion took place supports this argument. The US government insisted that it was responding to an 'urgent, formal request' from the five-member Organization of East Caribbean states 'to assist in a joint effort to restore order and democracy'. The UN General Assembly certainly did not interpret the intervention in this way and it voted 189–9 to condemn the action of the United States.

The second problematic US intervention took place on 20 December 1989, when 24,000 US troops landed in Panama. The position of the US government was that the country's military dictator, Manuel Noriega, had declared a state of war against the United States. In addition, the first Bush administration relied on four 'humanitarian' rationales as justification for the invasion: to safeguard the lives of US citizens (approximately 35,000 lived in the Canal Zone); to help restore democracy; to protect the integrity of the Panama Canal treaties; and to bring Noriega to justice (he was eventually convicted of drug charges in a US court). One of the most important considerations in evaluating these military actions is the humanitarian imperative at the time of intervention. In this case, the loss of life before the onset of the invasion was virtually non-existent, which raises the question whether there was really any humanitarian purpose behind the intervention in the first place. Furthermore, the invasion resulted in the deaths of somewhere between several hundred and several thousand civilians (the data here remain unclear).

We argue that neither of these actions comes close to constituting a humanitarian intervention for two reasons. First, the wider circumstances under which the interventions occurred put a question mark on the intentions of the intervening state. Second, the human rights conditions on the ground were not characterized by widespread and gross human rights violations at the time of the interventions. They even significantly deteriorated after the intervention in the case of Panama. But it is not simply a matter of determining whether a particular intervention is humanitarian or not. What also has to be considered is the enormous damage that a false claim of humanitarian intervention will have on the principle of humanitarian intervention itself, thereby creating a cynicism towards this practice that ultimately ends by endangering the lives of countless numbers of people.

The 1990s: a cycle of interventions and non-interventions

During the 1990s the international community staggered between intervention and non-intervention. What often seemed to dictate the policy of the moment were the actions, or inactions, of the past. We explore this relationship in this section. Following that, we examine a group of largely 'forgotten states'.

Somalia, 1992

We begin with a humanitarian intervention that has come to be perceived as a failure: the US-led humanitarian intervention in Somalia in December 1992 in the wake of massive levels of deaths caused by starvation and disease. Few would question whether Operation Restore Hope, as it was termed, constituted a humanitarian intervention. The desperation was brutally evident, captured in a stream of images of reed-like figures and children on the edge of starvation. In addition, the operation had received full Security Council backing. Finally, the country that initially led the operation, the United States, had little, if anything, to gain by engaging in this operation, at least from a geopolitical perspective. Instead, it can be argued that it was the desire of the first Bush administration to leave office on a 'humanitarian high' that drove US involvement in Somalia.

However, problems began to arise in 1993, when the operation became more military in nature, as efforts were undertaken to disarm various warlord groups. In June 1993, twenty-four Pakistani soldiers were killed and their bodies mutilated, and later that year eighteen US soldiers were killed and the body of one of the soldiers was gruesomely dragged through the streets of Mogadishu. These events not only contributed to a change in public and government sentiments towards the operation in Somalia specifically but, at least for some time, it apparently dissuaded countries from intervening altogether, as we will see in a moment.

Was the intervention in Somalia a failure? Operation Restore Hope did save the lives of a large number of people (estimates go as high as a million). This is not to say that there were no failures – but, in our view at least, not those that are usually attributed to this intervention. The first failure was allowing the humanitarian disaster to arise in the first place. This seldom, if ever, gets mentioned, and it is an issue to which we return in the latter part of this chapter. Another failure was the unwillingness of political leaders of the intervening states to prepare their populations for the very real possibility that humanitarian interventions will entail the loss of life. Because this was not done, after the death of a relatively small number of military personnel, political leaders concluded that the public did not have the stomach for continued fighting and efforts began to shut down the Somalia operation. This leads to a third and final failure, which has been the abandonment of Somalia – a failure that continues to afflict that country to this day.

Bosnia and Herzegovina, 1992–5

Another humanitarian disaster occurred at about the same time as Somalia and involved the break-up of Yugoslavia, as constituent republics sought to form their own independent countries but were resisted by the central Serbian state. The fighting lasted from 1992 until late

1995, during which time approximately 250,000 people died and 2.5 million were left homeless. The most egregious human rights violations occurred in the war between Bosnian Muslims, who were seeking an independent Bosnian state, and Bosnian Serb groups that were closely aligned with the Serbian government fighting against this.

Although the international community's response was both tragically slow and at times brutally ineffective, it would be a mistake to accuse the international community of not doing anything. One policy enacted by the United Nations at the outset of the conflict was an arms embargo directed against all sides. Unfortunately, the policy had the effect of placing the outmanned and outgunned Bosnian Muslim forces at an even worse disadvantage, as Serbia simply ignored this policy and continued to provide massive amounts of arms and equipment to its Bosnian Serb allies throughout the course of the war. On the other hand, the UN's 'no fly' policy (Operation Deny Flight) was instrumental in limiting Serbian operations, and it resulted in the shooting down of several Serbian aircraft.

Another questionable policy was the establishment of what the UN termed 'safe areas'. The problem was that at least some of these areas were not safe at all. The most gruesome evidence of this was the overrunning of the 'safe area' at Srebrenica in July 1995, as UN peacekeepers could only stand by and watch as Bosnian Serb forces carried out an ethnic cleansing against 7,000–8,000 Muslim boys and men.

The embarrassment and recriminations caused by this event resulted in the London Conference, when the NATO command was given the authority to bomb without previous UN approval. Then, on 28 August 1995, Serb forces engaged in a mortar attack on a street market in Sarajevo that resulted in the killing of thirty-seven civilians. The video images of this attack were broadcast throughout the world, and two days later NATO commenced Operation Deliberate Force, a massive bombing campaign that lasted three weeks. In large part as a consequence of this intervention, the warring parties then met in Dayton, Ohio, where the Dayton Peace Accords were signed. At that time the UN committed itself to an Implementation Force (IFOR) of 60,000 peacekeepers, and one of the most remarkable things has been the continued UN involvement and presence in this area since then.

On balance, Bosnia was a qualified disaster. For three years, the efforts of the international community were marginal at best and ineffective at worst, while the human toll continued to grow. On the other hand, when the humanitarian intervention finally did take place it was as certain as it was effective. One last thing that could be said of the Bosnian intervention – and perhaps its most lasting legacy – is that it resulted in the creation of the International Criminal Tribunal for the former Yugoslavia, and not only has it prosecuted a number of war criminals (including former Serbian president, Slobodan Milošević), but the success of this body helped set the stage for further international justice proceedings, including both the International Criminal Tribunal for Rwanda and the creation of the International Criminal Court itself, which we discuss in Chapter 7.

Rwanda, 1994

Although the international response to the conflict in Bosnia and Herzegovina developed extremely slowly, Rwanda remains the most visible and arguably the gravest example of the refusal to intervene. In spring 1994, upwards of 800,000 Tutsis and moderate Hutus were butchered to death, in many instances by machete. Western states not only did nothing themselves to stop this, but they took measures to prevent African states themselves from doing so. In his stunning book *We Wish to Inform You that Tomorrow We will be Killed with our Families*, Philip Gourevitch (1998) describes how the international community cruelly disengaged itself from the minority Tutsi population in Rwanda – at the same time as Hutu genocidal rage was beginning to explode. Thus, in the aftermath of the killing of ten Belgian peacekeepers, the Security Council voted to *decrease* the size of the peacekeeping force that had been in the country from 2,500 to 270. In addition, the Security Council continually turned a deaf ear to the pleas of Major-General Dallaire, the head of the UN peacekeeping mission, who argued that with a force of 5,000 well-trained soldiers genocide could be averted.

In Gourevitch's view, the blame rests on the United States, highlighting the continuing impact of past humanitarian interventions:

> The desertion of Rwanda by the UN force was Hutu Power's greatest
> diplomatic victory to date, and can be credited almost single-handedly
> to the United States. With the memory of the Somalia debacle still very
> fresh, the White House had just finished drafting a document called
> Presidential Decision Directive [PDD] 25, which amounted to a checklist

of reasons to avoid American involvement in UN peacekeeping missions. (Gourevitch 1998: 150)

Gourevitch continues,

It hardly mattered that Dallaire's call for an expanded force and mandate would not have required American troops, or that the mission was not properly peacekeeping, but genocide prevention. PDD 25 also contained what Washington policymakers call 'language' urging that the United States should persuade others not to undertake the missions that it wished to avoid. In fact, the Clinton administration's ambassador to the UN, Madeleine Albright, opposed leaving even the skeleton crew of two hundred seventy in Rwanda. (Gourevitch 1998: 150)

Box 6.1. **Is it genocide – yet?**

Throughout the Rwanda crisis, the line taken by the Clinton White House was to acknowledge that 'acts of genocide' had occurred, while at the same time forbidding the unqualified use of the word 'genocide'. Gourevitch provides the following exchange between Christine Shelley, a State Department spokeswoman, and a reporter:

Q: So you say genocide happens when certain acts happen, and you say that those acts have happened in Rwanda. So why can't you say that genocide has happened?

Ms.Shelley: Because, Alan, there is a reason for the selection of words that we have made, and I have – perhaps I have – I'm not a lawyer. I don't approach this from the international legal and scholarly point of view. We try, best as we can, to accurately reflect a description in particularly addressing that issue. It's – the issue is out there. People have obviously been looking at it.

Gourevitch continues,

Shelley was a bit more to the point when she rejected the denomination of genocide, because, she said, 'there are obligations which arise in connection with the use of the term'. She meant that if it was a genocide, the Convention of 1948 required the contracting parties to act. Washington didn't want to act. So Washington pretended that it wasn't genocide. (Gourevitch 1998: 153)

Yet if the United States is largely responsible for the initial non-intervention, what is equally stunning is that when one of the Western states, France, finally did act in Operation Turquoise, it intervened on the side of its Hutu allies, namely, those responsible for carrying out the genocide. In 2008, the Rwandan government issued a report that was the result of a three-year study carried out by an independent commission. The report accused French government officials and the French military of participating in political assassinations, rapes of Tutsi women and active assistance to Hutu *genocidaires* as they escaped the advancing Tutsi armies in the final days of the genocide. In response, the French government claimed that the report's findings constituted 'unacceptable allegations' against the French state and its officials.

Box 6.2. **Responsibility for the Rwandan genocide**

The genocide in Rwanda constitutes one of the greatest human tragedies, at least of the past half century. It also shows, although this issue might be more contentious, how a number of different states contributed to this outcome, from arms sales to the initial refusal by Western states to intervene and finally to the manner of the French intervention. The question is whether any actors will be held accountable or responsible. Consider the various possibilities: The first is the International Criminal Tribunal for Rwanda. To date, this Court has only undertaken the prosecution of Rwandans, and there seems to be no interest in going beyond this. A second option might be for Rwanda to bring an action before the International Court of Justice. However, recall from Chapter 2 the ICJ's ruling in *Bosnia* v. *Serbia*, which concluded that Serbia was not responsible for committing genocide by providing wide-ranging support to Bosnian Serb paramilitary forces. Even if all the accusations that Rwanda has made are true, there would still be the difficulty of establishing French responsibility for committing genocide and/or for complicity in genocide (Schmitt 2009). Finally, the Rwandan government might seek to have certain French officials extradited to face charges before domestic Rwandan courts. However, it is not likely that the French government would co-operate. In short, one might conclude that although international human rights law is intended to hold states responsible for violating human rights standards, very little of this occurs in practice.

As noted earlier, throughout the 1990s humanitarian intervention appeared to be going in cycles. The response to massive starvation in Somalia was relatively quick. However, the decision to walk away from Somalia had implications for both Bosnia and Rwanda. Yet the pendulum seemed to swing the opposite way following the popular revulsion at the failure to act in Rwanda, which helped lead to two successful humanitarian interventions at the close of the century.

Kosovo, 1999

The first intervention took place in the Balkans once again, only this time involving Kosovo, a region (not a republic) in Serbia that is 90 per cent ethnic Albanian. Kosovo had long suffered severe repression under the rule of Serbian President Slobodan Milošević, including the abolishment of its regional government, the imposition of Serbo-Croat as the official language, the banning of Albanian-language media and the firing of thousands of teachers in Albanian-language schools (Donnelly 2007: 172). Throughout the 1990s, the Kosovo Liberation Army carried out a series of guerrilla operations, to little effect. However, the Serbian government responded quite harshly to these small-scale attacks, resulting in the killing of several hundred civilians, but also the displacement of more than 400,000 people from their homes.

In recognition of the danger of reacting too slowly, as embodied in Bosnia and Rwanda (or perhaps as an overreaction to these events), Western democracies took almost immediate action. There are, however, two major concerns with the 1999 Kosovo intervention. The first is the manner in which the UN Security Council was bypassed altogether and the matter was taken over by NATO. This raised questions of the legality of this particular intervention, but also of the vitality of the United Nations in such matters. A second issue is the way in which the intervention was carried out. In order to constitute a humanitarian intervention, not only must the intervention be based on humanitarian considerations, but the military action itself must also be conducted in a humanitarian fashion. Yet, rather than committing ground forces and carrying out the campaign in this fashion, the NATO intervention was conducted solely through aerial bombardment. NATO's position was that only military targets were hit; Serbia has taken sharp issue with this. But it has been established with some certainty that Serbia responded immediately to the bombing campaign by unleashing a massive ethnic cleansing campaign that resulted in the deaths of some 10,000 people and the forced displacement of some 1.5 million civilians. However, after the initial fury, peace in the region has generally prevailed. In this way, Kosovo provides us with an example of a successful humanitarian intervention, but which was not without its own problems.

East Timor, 1999

The other intervention in 1999 occurred in East Timor. In the colonial era, the South Pacific island of Timor was divided into East Timor and West Timor, the former under the rule of Portugal and the latter under the rule of the Netherlands. When Indonesia achieved independence, it received the Dutch holdings in West Timor. After a 1974 military coup in Portugal, East Timor declared its independence from that country. However, Indonesia used this opportunity to invade East Timor on 16 October 1975 and its occupation lasted for nearly a quarter century. A conservative estimate is that during this time at least 100,000 people were killed, representing one person in eight among the East Timor population (Donnelly 2007: 185).

Box 6.3. The Dili massacre

There are times when a particular event comes to symbolize the brutality of a government. In Nazi Germany it was the Kristellnacht, in South Africa the Sharpeville Massacre, in the United States the beatings administered at Selma, Alabama, in China Tiananmen Square and in East Timor the Dili Massacre. The Dili Massacre refers to the pro-independence march that took place in November 1991, when Indonesian security forces opened fire, killing upwards of 500 people and wounding at least 270 more. Graphic video images of the violence that appeared in a British television documentary that was shown in January 1992 helped attract world popular attention.

After years of international pressure, Indonesia finally agreed to allow a UN-sponsored referendum on independence, which was held on 30 August 1999. Over 75 per cent of the people of East Timor voted in favour of independence. However, Indonesia responded by unleashing affiliated militia forces. Thousands of people were killed and more than a quarter of the population had to flee from their homes. On 15 September 1999, the Security Council created the Australian-led International Force for East Timor, which quickly restored order and helped remove Indonesian forces by 1 November 1999. East Timor achieved full independence on 20 May 2002. The case of East Timor represents humanitarian intervention at its best in the sense that swift and effective military action by states operating on behalf of the international community prevented further atrocities from taking place. Yet why was a host of other humanitarian disasters unable to command an international response, when it was possible in the case of East Timor? We now turn to some of these 'forgotten countries'.

Box 6.4. **The wars in Afghanistan and Iraq – humanitarian interventions?**

One of the most disturbing aspects of the US-led wars in Afghanistan and Iraq is the manner in which the Bush administration attempted to put a 'humanitarian spin' on its actions. Afghanistan was a lawful self-defence measure undertaken against a state that had provided a safe haven to the al Qaeda forces that had attacked the United States. Thus there was no need to try to couch it as a humanitarian venture, including the idea that the war was also being fought to 'liberate' Afghan women.

In terms of Iraq, the three-step justification for the war (Sadam Hussein had weapons of mass destruction (WMDs); he was in league with al Qaeda; and he had already committed genocide against his own people) was based on 'humanitarian considerations' in the sense of protecting the world community from the harm that could be meted out by this individual.

Of course, what is now known is that Hussein never possessed WMDs and that he was never allied with al Qaeda forces. The only part of this trilogy that happens to be true is that Hussein did carry out genocide against his own people (and the Iranian people as well) when in 1987–8 his forces destroyed several thousand Iraqi Kurdish villages and killed close to 100,000 Iraqi Kurdish citizens. However, the US government responded to these acts at the time by increasing US agricultural supports (Power 2002: 173). As we said earlier, the false claims not only brought about massive levels of carnage in Iraq itself (and had a decidedly negative impact on neighbouring states as well), but this unlawful invasion will have a deeply chilling effect on humanitarian intervention more generally.

The 'forgotten countries'

In this section we turn to several countries that experienced massive levels of human rights violations for extended periods and where the international community's response to those violations has either been very slow or non-existent.

Sudan, 1956–present

We begin with a country that has attracted a great deal of international attention: Sudan. What is generally known about this country relates to the conflict in the Darfur region. However, less well known is the fact that Sudan has experienced almost uninterrupted warfare for more than a half century. First, from 1956 to 2005 (with an interlude in the early 1970s) a civil war took place between the northern and southern regions of the country. During this time more than 2.5 million people were killed and another 4.6 million were either displaced from their homes or became refugees in another country. No humanitarian intervention was undertaken in an attempt to halt this violence.

More present in people's minds is the ongoing conflict in the Darfur region, which began in 2003. This fighting involves two main rebel groups (Sudan Liberation Movement/Army and Justice and Equality Movement) on one side against the Sudanese government, along with their 'civilian' operatives, the Janjaweed, which loosely translates into 'man with a gun on a horse'. Unlike the earlier civil war, the present conflict in Darfur is not neatly divided into Arab (Muslim) north versus African (Christian) south, although there certainly are elements of this. Rather, a more accurate portrayal would be to see this as (Arab) livestock growers and (African) farmers fighting over destitute and desolate land. The UN Secretary-General, Ban Ki-Moon, has described Darfur as the world's first 'global warming' conflict, in the sense that the war is being fought over ever-diminishing resources caused by environmental devastation in this region. The conflict in Darfur highlights that the distinction between economic rights and political rights is not always a clear and distinct one. Moreover, this conflict shows that economic deprivation can and often will lead to violations of civil and political rights. At the time of writing, this war has resulted in more than 2,700 villages being destroyed, upwards of 400,000 people killed, and another 2.3 million having had to flee their homes and communities.

Is this genocide? In July 2004, the US Congress passed a resolution labelling Darfur as 'genocide', and in September 2004 Secretary of State Colin Powell also used this term. Moreover, in a speech to the United Nations, President George W. Bush also termed the situation in Darfur as constituting 'genocide'. This is the first time that senior US government officials have applied the term to a current crisis and invoked the Genocide Convention. Yet Bush's use of the term 'genocide' did not produce the anticipated results, a US or international intervention.

Not everyone agrees that there has been genocide in Darfur. This was the finding of an independent report commissioned by the UN (2005), which based its conclusion on the following two factors: (i) the various tribes that have been the object of attacks do not appear to make up ethnic groups distinct from those groups that are carrying out these attacks; and (ii) there is no indication of an intent to destroy an ethnic group as such, but rather individual villagers have been killed selectively, while other villagers have been allowed to remove themselves. The problem is that while international lawyers and government officials continue to debate whether there is genocide in Darfur, the widespread killing continues, albeit at a much lower rate than at the height of atrocities in 2003–4.

Box 6.5. **The ICC indictment of President Bashir**

One of the more noteworthy developments in the Sudan was the indictment handed down by the International Criminal Court against Sudanese President Bashir in spring 2009. This was the first time a sitting head of state has been subjected to this process. Bashir's response was to remove from the country most of the international relief agencies that had been providing assistance, thereby making a dire humanitarian situation even worse. At the time of writing, the international community had no meaningful reaction to this. Thus the indictment could well be seen as a symbolic act that carried with it severe negative human rights consequences.

Democratic Republic of the Congo, 1997–present

Although the conflict in the Darfur region of Sudan has received the lion's share of public attention, the single most violent country in the world over the course of the past decade has been the Democratic Republic of the Congo (DRC, known as Zaïre from 1971 until 1997, and (Belgian) Congo before then). The history of the DRC has been one marked by civil war and corruption. After its independence from Belgium in 1960, the country was immediately faced with an army mutiny and an attempted secession by the mineral-rich province of Katanga. A year later, its prime minister, Patrice Lumumba, was killed by troops loyal to army chief Joseph Mobutu, who were assisted by Belgian and US operatives.[1]

Mobutu seized power in 1965. For more than two decades, he served as a bulwark against communism and the United States rewarded him well – at the time of his death in September 1997 he was reputed to be one of the five richest people in the world. After the end of the Cold War, Mobutu was thought to be expendable, and in 1997 the neighbouring country Rwanda invaded Zaïre in an attempt to locate Hutu militias. This provided the opportunity for anti-Mobutu rebels to seize power and install Laurent Kabila as president of Zaire – a country he would then go on to re-name the Democratic Republic of the Congo. Within a short period of time, the DRC became the site for Africa's own version of a world war. With the support of Rwanda and Uganda, rebel groups attempted to overthrow the Kabila regime, which was supported by Angola, Namibia and Zimbabwe. This developed into a five-year war, resulting in the loss of an estimated three million lives, either as a direct result of fighting or because of disease and malnutrition. A peace agreement was reached in 2003, but with little effect. Since then, an additional two million people have died, and it is estimated at the time of writing that nearly 1,000 individuals die every day from war-related causes. Throughout this time and in the face of nearly 5 million deaths, no meaningful humanitarian intervention has taken place.

Sierra Leone, 1991–2002

The civil war in Sierra Leone began in 1991, when the Revolutionary United Front (RUF) first attacked in the eastern part of the country on the Liberian border. The war was fought in large part out of dissatisfaction with an ineffective and corrupt government and because of mismanagement of the country's diamond resources. The RUF's

---

1 The Belgian government has since acknowledged and apologized for its involvement in Lumumba's assassination (Kerstens 2007). However, the US government has yet to do so.

strategy was based on terrorizing the population, and they did so by killing large numbers of civilians and through physical mutilation, including the amputation of arms, legs, lips and ears. By 1995, the RUF was on the verge of taking control of Freetown, the nation's capital, but it was driven back, not by an international force but by mercenaries from Executive Outcomes, a private security firm founded in South Africa.

In April 1996, Ahmad Tejan Kabbah, a former UN diplomat, was elected president. He was subsequently overthrown in a military coup but then reinstated after a successful intervention by the Nigerian-led Economic Community of West African States Monitoring Group (ECOMOG). In January 1999, RUF launched yet another offensive, but were rebuffed by ECOMOG forces. In July 1999, the Kabbah government signed the Lomé Peace Accord, which granted the RUF representation in the government, and the UN Security Council established the United Nations Mission in Sierra Leone (UNAMSIL) with an initial peacekeeping force of 6,000. In May 2000 the human rights situation deteriorated yet again, and the British government responded by sending in a military force (Operation Palliser) that helped restore order (Collier 2007). Although there was a series of subsequent minor uprisings, in January 2002 President Kabbah declared the civil war officially over. At that point, between 30,000 and 75,000 people had died, while thousands suffered from gross human rights violations, including torture, starvation and mutilation.

Both of these operations in Sierra Leone, that led by ECOMOG, and then the British-led Operation Palliser, were successful humanitarian interventions, but a significant period of time went by before these interventions were undertaken.

Liberia, 1989–96 and 1999–2003

Liberia has gone through two major civil wars. The first lasted from 1989 until 1996. It initially involved the government led by President Samuel Doe, who assumed office through a military coup in 1980, fighting against two rebel groups, one led by Prince Johnson and the other by Charles Taylor (whose son, Chucky, was mentioned in Chapter 3). The second began in 1999 and lasted until 2003.

In September 1990, Doe was captured and killed. However, fighting continued between forces loyal to Johnson and those commanded by Taylor. In 1991, the United Liberation Movement of Liberia for Democracy (ULIMO) was formed, made up primarily of former Doe supporters, and they entered the fray as well. In 1993, ECOMOG was able to get the warring parties to agree to a peace agreement, and the UN Security Council established the UN Observer Mission in Liberia (UNOMIL) to support this effort. However, fierce fighting broke out again in May 1994 and continued until another peace agreement, largely brokered by Ghanaian President Jerry Rawlings, was reached in August 1995. But this was short-lived, and fighting erupted again in April 1996. Yet another peace agreement was eventually reached, resulting in national elections being held in July 1997. Aided by massive voter intimidation, Taylor was elected president, obtaining some 75 per cent of the national vote. However, his election served to quell much of the violence, at least for some short period of time. It is estimated that upwards of 200,000 Liberians were killed during the first civil war and many more than this sent into exile.

The country's second civil war began in 1999, and it proceeded much like the first war in that the government, now led by Taylor, was fighting against two rebel groups. In 2003 a single US Marine amphibious group of just over 2,000 troops, but deploying only 320 of them ashore, was able to play a vital role in facilitating the end of the civil war (Kuperman 2009). This example and Operation Palliser in Sierra Leone show that humanitarian interventions do not have to be large-scale undertakings. Also recall General Dellaire's assertion that with a well-trained force of 5,000 troops (not peacekeepers), genocide in Rwanda could have been avoided altogether.

Uganda, 1987–present

This decades-long war is primarily a conflict between forces of the Uganda government and the Lord's Resistance Army (LRA). In 2004, UN Under-Secretary-General Jan Egeland described this as one of the worst humanitarian disasters in the world. Children are routinely abducted and either conscripted or forced into sexual slavery. In 2005 the International Criminal Court issued its first arrest warrants against the LRA leadership, although there have been no further developments from this. Moreover, there has been no other meaningful international involvement, and the conflict and the abduction of children continues unabated.

Conclusion

Although humanitarian intervention is widely recognized in international law, there have been a number of problems in practice. As we have seen, there have been several instances when states have claimed that they are taking action against another country for humanitarian purposes but are primarily pursuing their own national security interests. Equally problematic has been the fact that there are several places in the world where it seems to be in no state's interest to intervene in an attempt to prevent gross and systematic human rights violations. The primary reason for this is that humanitarian intervention has always been viewed as being discretionary. A state might intervene, but it is generally assumed that international law does not require such intervention. However, we would suggest that this reflects an even deeper failure, namely the inability or unwillingness to recognize that states have human rights obligations outside their own national borders.

It is important to keep in mind that there also have been a number of successful humanitarian interventions. In these cases (i.e. Somalia, Kosovo, East Timor), a state (or a group of states) has placed its own military personnel in harm's way in an attempt to halt human suffering in another country. This is no small feat. What have been lacking are discernible criteria for when and how humanitarian interventions should take place. We now turn to a recent initiative that seeks to establish these legal principles.

The Responsibility to Protect (R2P)

In the light of the many problems associated with humanitarian intervention – the charge that it is an infringement of state sovereignty; the willingness to intervene in some countries but not in others; the manner in which intervention has at times been carried out; and the issue of whether intervention without UN Security Council authorization is legal – UN Secretary-General Kofi Annan plaintively asked this question at the 2000 Millennium Summit:

> If humanitarian intervention is, indeed, an unacceptable assault on sovereignty, how should we respond to a Rwanda, to a Srebrenica – to

gross and systematic violations of human rights that offend every precept of our common humanity?

Responding to the Secretary-General's challenge, in 2000 the Canadian government, along with several international foundations, created an International Commission on Intervention and State Sovereignty that was made up of distinguished academics and international policymakers who subjected the issue of military intervention to intense scrutiny. In December 2001 they published a report, *The Responsibility to Protect*. At the 2005 UN World Summit, world leaders unanimously declared that all states have a responsibility to protect their citizens from genocide, war crimes, crimes against humanity and ethnic cleansing, and that as members of the international community they stand 'prepared to take collective action' in cases where national authorities 'are manifestly failing to protect their populations' from these four ills (Bellamy 2009). In April 2006, the UN Security Council reaffirmed R2P and indicated its readiness to adopt appropriate measures where necessary.

The driving force behind the Commission's work is the deep commitment to spare the world of any more 'Rwandas'. In order to achieve this, the Commission set forth the following four objectives:

> To establish clearer rules, procedures and criteria for determining whether, when and how to intervene;
>
> To establish the legitimacy of military intervention when necessary and after all other approaches have failed;
>
> To ensure that military intervention, when it occurs, is carried out only for the purposes proposed, is effective, and is undertaken with proper concern to minimize the human costs and institutional damage that will result; and
>
> To help eliminate, where possible, the causes of conflict while enhancing the prospects for durable and sustainable peace. (International Commission on Intervention and State Sovereignty 2001: para. 2.3)

Certainly the most noticeable change is the different terminology used in the report. The Commission set forth several reasons why the traditional 'right to intervene' language has not been helpful:

First, it necessarily focuses attention on the claims, rights and prerogatives of the potentially intervening states much more so than on the urgent needs of the potential beneficiaries of the action. Secondly, by focusing narrowly on the act of intervention, the traditional language does not adequately take into account the need for either prior preventive effort or subsequent follow-up assistance, both of which have been too often neglected in practice. And thirdly, although this point should not be overstated, the familiar language does effectively operate to trump sovereignty with intervention at the outset of the debate: it loads the dice in favour of intervention before the argument has even begun, by tending to label and delegitimize dissent as anti-humanitarian. (International Commission on Intervention and State Sovereignty 2001: para. 2.28)

Beyond terminology, R2P presents a dramatically different notion of state sovereignty, shifting the understanding from sovereignty as control to sovereignty as responsibility. The report explains the significance of this change:

First, it implies that the state authorities are responsible for the functions of protecting the safety and lives of citizens and promotion of their welfare. Secondly, it suggests that the national political authorities are responsible to the citizens internally and to the international community through the UN. And thirdly, it means that the agents of state are responsible for their actions; that is to say, they are accountable for their acts of commission and omission. (International Commission on Intervention and State Sovereignty 2001: para. 2.15)

Where does the responsibility to protect lie? In the first instance, it is the territorial state. As the report explains,

The Commission believes that responsibility to protect resides first and foremost with the states whose people are directly affected. This fact reflects not only international law and the modern state system, but also the practical realities of who is best placed to make a positive difference. The domestic authority is best placed to take action to prevent problems from turning into potential conflicts. (International Commission on Intervention and State Sovereignty 2001: para. 2.30)

However, if domestic authorities fail to meet this responsibility, that is, if this state essentially forfeits its own sovereignty, then this task is placed in the hands of the international community.

> While the state whose people are directly affected has the default
> responsibility to protect, a residual responsibility also lies with the
> broader community of states. This fallback responsibility is activated
> when a particular state is clearly either unwilling or unable to fulfill its
> responsibility to protect or is itself the actual perpetrator of crimes or
> atrocities; or where people living outside a particular state are directly
> threatened by actions taking place there. This responsibility also
> requires that in some circumstances action must be taken by the broader
> community of states to support populations that are in jeopardy or under
> serious threat. (International Commission on Intervention and State
> Sovereignty 2001: para. 2.31)

Under traditional notions of state sovereignty, states enjoyed the prerogatives of sovereignty without question. R2P stands this premise on its head. Sovereignty is now something that states have to earn, and they do this by protecting their own people. If a state is not able or willing to do this, then this responsibility will be taken over by the international community.

What most significantly distinguishes R2P from humanitarian intervention is the nature and scope of state responsibility. Under the traditional approach, the sole focus was on the military intervention itself. Because of this, there was seldom, if ever, any discussion concerning an antecedent obligation to help avoid the humanitarian crisis altogether, or a subsequent obligation to help reconstruct a society after intervention had taken place. The Responsibility to Protect proposal offers a much broader approach, positing three separate but related obligations: the responsibility to prevent, the responsibility to react and the responsibility to rebuild.

Responsibility to prevent

The first duty of states is the responsibility to prevent humanitarian disasters from arising in the first place. The report sums this up nicely: 'Intervention should only be considered when prevention fails – and the best way of avoiding intervention is to ensure that it doesn't fail' (International Commission on Intervention and State Sovereignty 2001: para. 3.34). How is this to be done? To begin with, it is important to establish again that the primary responsibility for prevention rests with the territorial state. If states succeed in preventing humanitarian disaster within their borders, then there is no need to look any further to ensure prevention, and certainly not intervention. However, if the territorial state fails to meet its responsibility, then the states of the international community share an obligation to take whatever measures are necessary – 'more resources, more energy, more competence, more commitment' (para 3.40) – to prevent humanitarian disaster.

The R2P Report makes note of the increasing reluctance of some states to accept any internationally endorsed preventive measures for fear that 'internationalization' is a slippery slope that might lead to further involvement in the affairs of other countries. The report answers this by accepting the idea that many preventive measures are inherently intrusive and coercive. In the Commission's view it is important to acknowledge this, but it also highlights that it is equally important to make a clear distinction between carrots and sticks. This means that in the first instance at least, it is important to adopt measures that are non-intrusive and that are sensitive to national prerogatives. Beyond this, the report points out that if preventive measures are not taken, in many instances this will only lead to greater international involvement later on – in the form of military intervention. Thus, what R2P calls for is a change in mindset, from a 'culture of reaction' to a 'culture of prevention' that can only be accomplished by holding states accountable for their actions and by attending to preventive measures at the local, national, regional and global levels. As the report warns,

> Without a genuine commitment to conflict prevention at all levels –
> without new energy and momentum being devoted to the task – the
> world will continue to witness the needless slaughter of our fellow
> human beings, and the reckless waste of precious resources on conflict
> rather than social and economic development. The time has come for
> all of us to take practical responsibility to prevent the needless loss of
> human life, and to be ready to act in the cause of prevention and not just
> in the aftermath of disaster. (International Commission on Intervention
> and State Sovereignty 2001: para. 3.43)

Responsibility to react

R2P comes closest to looking like traditional humanitarian intervention in the second duty, the responsibility to react. To reiterate, R2P is based on the premise that military intervention should always be the very last option, and it is only when all other efforts have failed that this policy should even be considered. What should military intervention be based on and what should it look like? The report provides the following six criteria.

The first is 'just cause'. In the Commission's view, military intervention for human protection is only justified in the case of large-scale loss of life or the imminent threat of this taking place. In addition, the Commission lists various situations – widespread racial discrimination, systematic imprisonment or other repression of political opponents – where it feels that military intervention would *not* be warranted, although it notes that such human rights violations would be 'eminently appropriate' cases for the application of political, economic or military sanctions.

The second criterion for military intervention is 'right intention': the primary purpose of the intervention must be to halt or avert human suffering. The Commission expresses the strong view that overthrowing a regime is not a legitimate objective, although disabling that government's ability to harm its own people could well be an essential part of discharging its mandate of protection. In terms of occupation, the report is of the opinion that while this might be unavoidable for some short period of time, this should not be one of the objectives of a military intervention, and all occupied territory should be returned to its 'sovereign owner' at the end of hostilities (or soon thereafter), or if that is not possible, administered on an interim basis under UN auspices.

Earlier in this chapter we focused on whether certain interventions truly were humanitarian or not. In many instances the intervening state had long been at odds with the country in which it was intervening. This, then, raised the question whether the military action was undertaken to assist and protect the human rights of citizens of this enemy state, or whether the intervening state had some ulterior motives, namely, the pursuit of its own national security interests. As the Commission points out, one of the best ways to ensure that the intervention is for the right reasons is if a multilateral force is engaged.

The third criterion is 'last resort'. This means that before military intervention is allowed to take place, all other peaceful avenues – diplomatic protests, appeals to the UN Security Council and General Assembly, economic sanctions – must first be attempted.

The next criterion, 'proportionate means', relates to the manner in which the military intervention is carried out:

> The scale, duration and intensity of the planned military intervention should be the minimum necessary to secure the humanitarian objective in question. The means have to be commensurate with the ends and in line with the magnitude of the original provocation. The effect on the political system of the country targeted should be limited, again, to what is strictly necessary to accomplish the purpose of the intervention. (International Commission on Intervention and State Sovereignty 2001: para. 4.39)

Furthermore, as in the case of humanitarian intervention, all rules of international humanitarian law must be observed throughout the military engagement.

The fifth criterion is termed 'reasonable prospects'. It means that the only military intervention that can be justified is that which has a reasonable chance of success. Related to that, interventions that have a high probability of escalating violence and conflict, rather than quelling it, should be avoided. As a result of this, military intervention will simply not be an option in various countries. Thus, although the human rights situation in the Chechnya region of Russia has long been a nightmare, any military intervention against Russia would give rise to the possibility of a broader conflict, including the use of nuclear weapons. So since a military intervention in Chechnya would carry a high risk of further escalating an ongoing conflict, it would not be justifiable under the R2P criteria.

The last criterion deals with the question of legitimate authority: what entity is to provide the authorization to engage in military intervention? As noted at the outset of the chapter, the UN Charter makes provision for humanitarian intervention dependent on Security Council authorization. The R2P report reiterates the central role that the Security Council must play in determining if, when, where, how and by whom military intervention should happen.

However, one of the great concerns for the Commission (and for many others as well) has been the Security Council's repeated failure to act. As the report puts it: 'There were too many occasions during the last decade when the Security Council, faced with conscience-shocking situations, failed to respond as it should have with timely authorization and support' (International Commission on Intervention and State Sovereignty 2001: para. 8.6). In some instances, such as Kosovo, this role was simply taken over by others. However, in other cases, most notably Rwanda, the Security Council's inaction led directly to genocide.

The Commission states that these events provide two important messages to the United Nations. The first is that if the United Nations does not act, this vacuum will be filled by individual states. The second and broader message relates to the overall stature and credibility of the UN if it cannot perform the most important task entrusted to it: maintaining international peace and security.

Responsibility to rebuild

The third and final duty that is placed on all countries under the Responsibility to Protect initiative is the responsibility to rebuild after military intervention has been completed. In certain ways, the responsibility to rebuild can be taken literally, in the sense of engaging in public works projects to rebuild houses, roads, buildings and bridges that were destroyed during the course of the fighting. But in addition to providing material support in this manner, there are several other vital steps in which the international community must engage. One of the most important of these is the provision of security. In the words of the Commission, one of the 'most difficult and important issues to be regularly confronted in the post-intervention phase relates to disarmament, demobilization and reintegration of local security forces' (para. 5.9).

After the completion of a military intervention, the rule of law needs to be (re-)established. Unfortunately, one of the hallmarks of a 'failed state', or one in which gross human rights violations occur, is the absence of a functioning judicial system. However, as the Commission report points out, it would ultimately be self-defeating if the task of protecting human rights and providing justice was simply left to the intervening force itself. The country in which the atrocities took place, even if this is a 'failed state', has to play a crucial role in establishing a system of justice and in protecting human rights. In essence, the role of the international community is to help the state to re-create itself. The question of establishing justice after a society has suffered from gross human rights violations will be addressed in the next chapter.

Conclusion

We fully share the view expressed by international human rights lawyer, Chris Joyner, who writes, 'If the "responsibility to protect" does emerge full-fledged as an accepted norm of international law, it will generate a revolution in consciousness in international relations' (Joyner 2007: 720). R2P is based on a completely different vision of state sovereignty. Under R2P, sovereignty *is* protection. And if a state cannot provide protection itself, this responsibility will be taken up by the international community.

We are not suggesting that the traditional approach to humanitarian intervention never worked; at times it worked very well – although there are just as many (if not more) cases when it did not work well. However, there are far too many humanitarian disasters in the world to begin with. Thus the biggest shortcoming of the current system is that there is no responsibility to work towards averting disaster in the first place. When a humanitarian disaster does arise – as it most assuredly will, especially when there is no obligation to prevent it – there is no real sense of responsibility for dealing with this situation. As we have seen, intervention might occur, but it also might not. Finally, under the traditional approach to humanitarian intervention all attention is focused on the intervention itself. What is seldom, if ever, considered is the broader responsibility to work toward ensuring that this humanitarian disaster does not occur again. R2P is vastly more consonant with human rights principles than what exists at the present time.

Although R2P represents a quantum leap forward, we shall close with two concerns that we have with the initiative. The first is the manner in which the responsibility to prevent is interpreted. It is not clear whether the responsibility to prevent only applies to the likes of mass atrocities and genocide, or whether there is a broader responsibility to prevent human rights violations of all kinds. As we explain in Part I, we believe the latter ought to be the case. Finally, it remains unclear whether the various responsibilities (prevent, react, rebuild) are moral obligations or whether they are legal obligations as well.

FURTHER READING

Economic sanctions

- Tomasevski, Katarina. 1997. *Between Sanctions and Elections: Aid Donors and their Human Rights Performance.*
  Tomasevski's concern is that economic sanctions provide a form of double victimization. The first victimization is the original human rights violation, while the second one is when outside states apply sanctions that have a severe impact on those already victimized. Written with great power and passion, Tomasevski demands that we look to see the way in which these practices serve Western political practices more than the cause of protecting human rights.

Humanitarian intervention and peacekeeping

- Howard, Lise Morjé. 2008. *UN Peacekeeping in Civil Wars.*
  An exhaustive source of case studies involving UN peacekeeping missions. Howard's treatment is fair and judicious as she points out why some have worked and others have not.

- Weiss, Thomas. 2007. *Humanitarian Intervention: Ideas in Action.*
  Weiss is one of the strongest proponents of the principle of humanitarian intervention and he draws up decades of his own work to explore the theory and practice of such efforts.

Democratic Republic of the Congo

- Hochschild, Adam. 1998. *King Leopold's Ghost.*
  Hochschild's page-turner deals with Belgian colonial practices in what is now the Democratic Republic of the Congo. As Hochschild explains at the outset, what prompted him to write this book was an offhand reference that he stumbled on that King Leopold of Belgium was responsible for the deaths of somewhere between five and eight million people.

Rwanda

- Gourevitch, Philip. 1998 *We Wish to Inform You that Tomorrow We will be Killed with our Families.*
  Gourevitch's book still provides the rawest and most insightful account of the 1994 genocide. What does the title signify? Read the book and find out for yourself.

RELATED FILMS

Rwanda

- **Hotel Rwanda** (Terry George, 2004). This true-life story of Paul Rusesabagina, a hotel manager who saved the lives of over a thousand Tutsis, is the Hollywood version of the Rwandan genocide.

- **Sometimes in April** (Raoul Peck, 2005). This is the 'other' film about the Rwandan genocide, starring a cast of African actors and centred on the relationship of two brothers, one who is involved with the Hutu genocide and the other who is married to a Tutsi woman.

Sudan

- **The Devil Came on Horseback** (Annie Sundberg and Ricki Stern, 2006). This film is told through the eyes of Marine Captain Brian Steidle, a former US military officer who served on a peacekeeping mission in Sudan and whose photographs were in large part responsible for alerting the international community to the atrocities taking place in that country.

Uganda

- **Invisible Children**: rough cut (Jason Russell, Bobby Bailey and Laren Poole, 2003). This film starts off as if it will be a silly story of young American college students cavorting around Africa. Instead, the story becomes engrossing when it focuses on the horrendous plight of children in northern Uganda who struggle mightily to avoid being kidnapped and pressed into servitude on behalf of the Lord's Resistance Army.

West Africa

- **Refugee All Stars** (Zach Niles and Banker White, 2005). This film is testament to the strength and will of refugees in the form of the Sierra Leone Refugee All-Stars, a (now) world-famous musical act that was formed by refugees from that country. The music alone is reason to watch this movie.

- **Pray the Devil Back to Hell** (Gini Retlicker, 2008). A group of women decide to take matters in their own collective hands to bring peace to Liberia.

Burma

- **Burma VJ** (Anders Ostergaard, 2008). This documentary thriller provides some of the first film footage of the repression of military rule in this country. The images themselves are startling, but what is even more remarkable is the bravery of the guerrilla camera crew.

Democratic Republic of the Congo

- **The Greatest Silence: Rape in the Congo** (Lisa Jackson, 2007). In this stunning documentary, Lisa Jackson shows how rape has become a part of twenty-first-century warfare. However, what the director also does is to give voice to the brave women who have somehow lived through this experience.

- **Lumumba** (Raoul Peck, 2000). This film focuses on Patrice Lumumba, the first prime minister of the newly independent Republic of the Congo. Lumumba governed for only two months before he was seen as being too independent, and was assassinated with the involvement of Belgian and US operatives.

chapter **7**

Rebuilding society in the aftermath of repression

'We cannot have peace of mind if we do not know what happened to our husbands and brothers.'

statement by a wife of a 'disappeared' man to an unnamed Amnesty International official.

'But the truth will not necessarily be believed and it is putting too much faith in truth to believe that it can heal.'

Michael Ignatieff (quoted in Minow 1998: 52)

In the preceding chapter we mentioned Sudan as a 'forgotten country'. Although a fair amount of publicity has been given to the massive levels of human rights violations that have afflicted this country, no humanitarian intervention has taken place, and the UN peacekeeping force (UNAMID) was strongly rejected by Sudan as a foreign invasion. Still, some day the violence will stop and soon thereafter the world's attention will turn to another crisis. However, efforts to bring truth, justice and a stable government to Sudan in these difficult circumstances will most assuredly not be given anywhere near the same level of attention by the world's media as putting an end to the physical violence. Yet achieving these goals is vital to the long-term prospects for peace, and arguably this will be a much more difficult and a much more complicated undertaking than stopping physical violence.

In this chapter we focus on the way in which countries that have suffered gross human rights violations attempt to deal with their past. How can society be rebuilt and made functional in the wake of such abuses? How can democratic governments and societies respectful of human rights be created? Should such societies prioritize bringing perpetrators to justice or rather focus on reconciliation and forgiveness? In the following, we concentrate on transitional justice, what it means, how it might be achieved and what the main obstacles are to realizing it.

Transitional justice centres on two key elements: truth and justice. It includes a 'set of practices, mechanisms and concerns that arise following a period of conflict, civil strife or repression, and that are aimed directly at confronting and dealing with past violations of human rights and humanitarian law' (Roht-Arriaza 2006: 2). A broader understanding of transitional justice includes how aspects of the economic, social and cultural environment can be utilized to establish justice by addressing and correcting past repression and inequality. For our purposes we concentrate on a narrower understanding of transitional justice, which uses political tools, in particular truth commissions, to deal with past gross human rights violations.

Obstacles to transitional justice

Before we can understand the difficulties of choosing and developing transitional justice mechanisms, we need to consider the obstacles such damaged societies typically face. Countries that are searching for transitional justice are, by definition, troubled ones, having recently experienced torment in connection with violent struggles and, most frequently, repressive regimes. The problems that transitional justice institutions must deal with are varied. In this section we examine five conditions that are inherent in such societies: the continued influence and power of past perpetrators; a weak, biased or non-existent judicial system; a poor economy; the omnipresent risk of renewed violence; and finally, continuing deep divisions within these societies. We now discuss each of these obstacles in turn.

One common problem when dealing with a violent past is that the perpetrators of the crimes continue to hold positions of power after peace has returned. For example, the repressive regime of Augusto Pinochet, which had been responsible for over 3,100 deaths and disappearances between September 1973 and 1990,[1] was ousted in an unexpected election defeat in 1990. But prior to the election, General Pinochet had arranged to remain commander-in-chief of the armed forces until 1998 and thereafter senator for life (a position that he and his supporters presumed would help him to steer free of prosecution) through an earlier amendment to the Constitution enacted when he was fully in control. In this context, one can understand the obstacles that faced those who wished to bring Pinochet and others responsible for repression under his regime to justice. Given Chile's violent past, many Chilean citizens and even some international human rights experts thought that another coup and the resumption of violence would be likely if the new government was too aggressive in its pursuit of justice. Similarly, thirty years after the mass killings at the hands of Pol Pot and the Khmer Rouge in Cambodia, that country has resisted most efforts to bring those responsible to justice, because even today some perpetrators still occupy positions of power.

---

1 These figures are those reported in the Rettig Report and the National Corporation for Reconciliation and Reparation in 1996.

A second difficulty in bringing those responsible for human rights violations to justice is that those countries that have suffered from repression frequently do not have very well developed court systems, or else the judicial system in place is biased towards the old regime. The case of East Timor, renamed Timor-Leste after independence, gives an extreme example of an underdeveloped legal system. Because East Timor had been occupied by Indonesia for twenty-four years, and there had been violent struggles during that time, particularly during the transition period to independence, the country was missing the basic infrastructure for self-rule, including a judicial system. When in October 1999 the UN Transitional Administration (UNTAET) was established in East Timor, 'there was only a handful of poorly trained East Timorese lawyers with little or no experience, no laws, no courts, no police force, no national military, no government departments, a few East Timorese doctors, no system for garbage collection, taxation or telephones' (Burgess 2006: 181–2). The UN and the relatively few educated citizens who were left had to build a legal system from scratch, without having nearly the number of qualified persons needed to fill the vacant positions in a workable justice system.

East Timor is an extreme case. More frequently, the main problem these countries face is that the justice system, although perhaps underdeveloped and under-funded, has been controlled by a repressive regime through removal of 'unco-operative' judges and has suffered from intimidation tactics, or is otherwise rife with corruption. The effects of intimidation do not dissolve overnight, so the influence over the courts of a repressive regime, frequently supported by the military, usually outlasts the regime itself. In the case of Chile, for example, the president of the Supreme Court, Enrique Urrutia Manzano, on behalf of the other justices, expressed his satisfaction with the military coup of September 1973 which had brought Pinochet to power. After the re-establishment of the civilian regime in 1990, a government inquiry concluded that the Supreme Court had co-operated with the abusive regime and indeed provided institutional assistance by granting immunity to those responsible for carrying out violence. Therefore human rights activists and critics of the Chilean regimes were not very trusting of the Chilean judiciary after Pinochet stepped down. Deep-rooted distrust of the justice system in the post-repression regime is common in other cases where judiciaries had been complicit in repressive policies.

A third obstacle that transitional justice efforts frequently face is that societies that have experienced human rights disasters are typically poor and underdeveloped. As an example, consider again the case of East Timor. Nearly the entire economic infrastructure had been destroyed by supporters of Indonesia as the result of a countrywide scorched-earth campaign. In Chapter 5 we have shown that there is a clear relationship between wealth and repression, where those countries that are most affected by repression are also least wealthy ones. The relative lack of economic well-being of these societies limits their ability to recover from past violence. Governments have only very limited resources to rebuild the country in general and to improve the justice system in particular. Restoring the infrastructure of a country is often a major and costly undertaking faced by countries in the wake of repression. The devastation and destruction caused by years of repression coupled with depleted economic resources provide a very difficult situation for any country. Frequently, new governments are faced with the dilemma of choosing between different, usually all very urgent, demands: should they spend their limited resources on improving the justice system, addressing the costs of prosecution and trials of human rights criminals in order to satisfy those who yearn for justice? Or should they give priority to demands from the populace for improved economic conditions, such as providing access to adequate housing and education for their people? Rebuilding the social and economic structure with very limited human and monetary resources puts a major obstacle on the path to recovery from previous repression.

This brings us to another obstacle to achieving justice and reconciliation. Whatever paths and priorities a country chooses to rebuild, it will invariably generate disagreement and opposition. Because of the recent history of these societies, there is oftentimes reasonable fear of renewed violence. Most post-repression regimes are relatively new, which means that they cannot build on a long institutional history or tradition. Political regimes define how a government and its citizens interact with each other and how the government can use its power. Over time, rules and regulations become part of the common language of that country, and citizens know what types of behaviour they are likely to see from their government. As a result, trust and legitimacy does not occur immediately. Newly established post-repression regimes are therefore often viewed with suspicion and mistrust. Opposition forces within the country may be more likely to challenge these new regimes because of the perception that they are illegitimate. Thus this lack of legitimacy (or simply the perception of such) and the potential of renewed violence from opposition groups is another problem often faced by post-repression societies.

A final obstacle to achieving justice and bringing out the truth about the past in post-repression societies is that people will have a strong identification with an in-group and antipathies toward an out-group. Ethnicity poses a sensitive issue when people strongly identify with one group and perceive members of another group as enemies. Examples where human rights violations were carried out along ethnic lines include the mass killings in Bosnia and Rwanda and the apartheid regime in South Africa. If repression were concentrated on one particular ethnic or religious section of the population, the ties in that section are likely to have become stronger during the period of repression due to the suffering people shared as members of that group. A strong identification with a minority group that has previously suffered violence at the hands of the majority makes it even more difficult for survivors to leave the past behind and to live as one people with the majority group. Particularly problematic are situations where political power is concentrated in the hands of one ethnic group. Marginalized ethnic groups often find it difficult to put their trust in the political and judicial system if those institutions are filled with members of another group. There is often the fear of the minority that the majority will misuse political, or military, power and not adequately accommodate the needs of the minority. For example, one of the main strategies of the Rwandan government at the beginning of the twenty-first century in order to avoid a repetition of the 1994 genocide is to minimize the role of ethnic identity in favour of a stronger feeling of citizenship. However, it is not always the minority that suffers from violence at the hands of the majority, as the apartheid regime in South Africa makes painfully clear. With these obstacles in mind, we now turn to a discussion of two predominant approaches to transitional justice.

Objectives of transitional justice

The search for solutions to societal problems that arise in the wake of grave human rights abuses involves the choice of transitional justice institutions. As mentioned above, transitional justice is an effort to re-establish a system of fairness following human rights disasters in order to move society away from the violence and instability of the past towards a more stable and less violent future. The underlying assumption of transitional justice is that violence and instability result from past injustices and that those injustices must be addressed before progress can be made towards a more peaceful and stable society.

The definition of transitional justice we offered above is a rather general one, and we adopt it purposely so that it encompasses several different conceptions of what transitional justice involves. We have not yet addressed some rather pivotal issues: what does it mean to address the injustices of the past? What might be done to move towards justice? How and why would this be expected to translate into a more peaceful, stable society? Transitional justice experts disagree on these issues. In order to provide an overview of current thinking in this area, we examine various points of view on what objectives are believed to be important.

Mechanisms of transitional justice go back as far as 411 BC when Athenians carried out retribution against the preceding oligarchy and enacted new laws to prevent future violence.[2] In the following, we concentrate on efforts to develop transitional justice institutions during the late twentieth and early twenty-first century. The evidence presented in this chapter shows that although experiences with transitional justice have been mixed, we have learned a few lessons about how to better achieve transitional justice goals.

Transitional justice institutions are designed to achieve three goals. The first one is to achieve justice – indeed, this goal is so important that it appears as a part of the term 'transitional justice' itself. We do not offer a detailed discussion of the definitions of justice here, leaving such undertaking to political philosophers such as Plato and others.[3] Instead,

---

2 See Elster (2004) for a discussion of historical cases of transitional justice.
3 See, for example, Plato's *Republic* (360 BC).

in the next section we distinguish between two different meanings, or paths: the retributive and the restorative approaches. In order to achieve justice, the institutions aim to hold those who are guilty of past abuses accountable for their actions. Hence their goal is to achieve justice by punishing those responsible for the crime. But dealing with justice by identifying perpetrators and punishing them for their crimes does not necessarily help the victim, other than (perhaps) to bring the victim, or the victim's survivors, a sense of closure.

When one looks at justice from the victim's perspective, however, punishing the perpetrator does little to address the loss of the family. If a father has been killed, the family is still without at least one – and perhaps its only – breadwinner. A second aspect of justice that concerns transitional justice scholars addresses the issue of how the losses felt by the victim can be mitigated and the victim's conditions improved. Reparations programmes are one example of a government policy meant to achieve, or approximate, 'justice' from the perspective of the victim in the wake of human rights abuses.

The second goal of transitional justice institutions is to find and disseminate the truth of what happened during the period of human rights violations. Many experts believe that it is important that members of society – victims, abusers, accomplices and bystanders – learn what has happened. One of the main purposes of the truth commission, which has become one of the fixtures of modern efforts at transitional justice, is to find the truth about human rights atrocities and then to communicate that truth to the whole society. The South African Truth and Reconciliation Commission (TRC) shows just how much importance can be attached to bringing out the truth, where perpetrators could receive amnesty in exchange for fully disclosing their past crimes. Obviously bringing out the truth is more complicated than it sounds. What is 'the truth' about a pattern of events when tens of thousands, or even hundreds of thousands, of people were killed and their families left suffering? Can the truth be told in a single document? Some have argued that this is too much to expect from transitional justice institutions. Others have argued that the most one can hope for is that a new 'national myth' is created that will allow society to move on. Depending on the nature of the past violations, different aspects of 'the truth' can become more important. The emphasis can be more on bringing out knowledge of what happened or on the perpetrators' acknowledgement of their past wrongdoings. For example, the human rights violations that occurred under military rule in Latin America during the 1970s and 1980s were characterized by the disappearances of regime opponents. In such cases being able to find out what actually happened to loved ones is crucial for the victims' families. In other regimes, such as in eastern Europe during the Cold War, the extent and nature of human rights violations were well known, but what was lacking was acknowledgement by the perpetrators.

A final goal of transitional justice is reconciliation. The theory behind this is that, at some level, people need to reconcile with one another for society to move on. In many cases the victims and the perpetrators of the abuses (and the supporters of each of these groups) must live together in one society. Members of groups that formerly were opposed to one another will have to deal peacefully with one another on a daily basis for a stable society to develop. Some argue that, for this to happen, they must be able to look at the past empathetically, by putting themselves 'in the other's shoes'. Perhaps this is asking for too much, especially when one considers the magnitude of the victims' losses. Would you be able to see the killing of your loved one from the perspective of the perpetrator who often, in the case of human rights abuses, might have been convinced that what (s)he was doing was in the best interest of society? And then, even more difficult, would you be able to reconcile with that person? Clearly, some can. As an example, consider the story of the parents of Amy Beale, a young American scholar who had travelled to South Africa. She was stoned to death by a mob of black men in August 1993. The leaders of the mob were arrested and sentenced and then applied for amnesty as part of the South African Truth and Reconciliation Commission. Amy's parents, Linda and Peter Beale, flew to South Africa to attend the amnesty hearings. They witnessed the killers' testimony – and supported their release.

It is probably too much to ask for this degree of reconciliation from all victims or their families. Not all parents would express the same degree of empathy as did Linda and Peter Beale, nor would many parents be able to forgive as easily as they, who were motivated in part by the belief that their daughter, a very loving and forgiving person, would have wanted them to act in the same way.

Even if that is too much to ask, there is still a place for reconciliation. At the very least, members of the recovering society need to be reconciled to the extent that they are willing to respect each other's rights.

The retributive approach

As noted before, there are some differences among experts on transitional justice regarding which of the above goals – justice, truth and reconciliation – are most important, whether they are all realistically achievable or whether they are mutually exclusive to a certain degree. To simplify these disagreements we can distinguish between two different approaches to transitional justice, one emphasizing a retributive approach, and the other a restorative one.[4] Those who are concerned with achieving retributive justice focus on holding those responsible for crimes accountable, which involves imposing punishments commensurate with the crime. This approach concentrates more on the perpetrator than on the victim. The idea behind retributive justice is that the rule of law must be established and justice levied for past wrongs.

International justice institutions

Retributive justice may be pursued through various legal institutions, including the country's own domestic court system, the court system of another sovereign state or through newly developed international legal institutions. The first institutions of transitional justice in modern history are the Nuremberg Trials that began in Germany and the International Military Tribunals (IMT) proceedings in Tokyo that were set up by the Allied Forces immediately after the end of the Second World War. The decision to bring Nazi and Japanese war criminals to trial was an important human rights milestone that preceded the creation of the UN and the promulgation of the UDHR. At the Nuremberg trials in Germany, twenty-four

---

4 We do not mean to imply that there are two discernable camps that disagree strongly with the goals of the other. Indeed, most frequently scholars and activists who would fit into one camp would acknowledge the importance of the efforts of the other, and view efforts towards retributive and restorative justice as complementary. See, for example, Minow (1998), Hayner (2002) and Ratner and Abrams (1997).

high-ranking government and corporate leaders were prosecuted, and nineteen were convicted. At the IMT proceedings in Tokyo, twenty-five defendants were prosecuted and all were convicted. There were also 'subsequent proceedings' against lower-ranking officials in both of these countries. This was the first time in history that the leading political, military and economic leaders of a country were held accountable to the world community for their actions.

Despite the historical significance of these proceedings, these trials did little to engage ordinary German and Japanese citizens and make them confront their own role in supporting the war machines in their respective countries. Instead, these prosecutions seemed to have the opposite effect of providing the false notion that all the 'guilty parties' had now been held to account. Ian Buruma, one of the most astute observers of post-war Germany and Japan, has argued that the Auschwitz (1965) and Majdanek (1975–1981) trials had a much greater impact on the German people than the post-war trials did (Buruma 1994). One reason for this is timing. Immediately following the war the German people were poor and exhausted. Their most pressing concern at that time was survival, not justice. However, after a number of years of prosperity, the German people (or at least the vast majority of them) were more receptive to examining the nature of Nazi rule and were horrified by these 'revelations'.

More recent examples of international institutions of transitional justice, which have been inspired by the Nuremberg and IMT model, include the establishment of the International Criminal Tribunal for the former Yugoslavia (ICTY) to investigate and prosecute war crimes during the Bosnian conflict, and the International Criminal Tribunal for Rwanda (ICTR), which is engaged in trying some of those responsible for the 1994 genocide in that country. Both tribunals have successfully prosecuted high-ranking war criminals from those countries. But they also have their problems. For example, the proceedings are held without any Serbian or Rwandan judges serving on these panels. Furthermore, these tribunals are not in the countries where the atrocities took place; the ICTY is based in The Hague and the ICTR in Arusha, Tanzania. Because the proceedings are far removed from the citizens of these countries, they are unable to engage fully in the process.

To address some of these shortcomings, Rwanda created a local judicial response, gacaca courts, as briefly discussed in Box 7.1. Gacaca is based on traditional mechanisms for dispute resolution and it emphasizes popular participation in the trials. Roht-Arriaza explains the advantages of such a local-level approach to providing justice:

> Local-level justice processes can create a much tighter sense of community ownership than those that take place in far-off capital cities or, worse still, foreign lands. They can provide a more understandable process, one untainted by the perceived unfairness or remoteness of formal legal structures often inherited from a colonial power. They can also play a role … in allowing neighbors who have been on different sides of a conflict to re-engage and to coexist. (Roht-Arriaza 2006: 11–12)

Box 7.1. **Gacaca courts**

The creation of the gacaca courts in Rwanda addressed various problems that are inherent in post-conflict societies; the courts combine elements of both redistributive and restorative justice. After the genocide, Rwanda's legal system had been devastated, the vast majority of its personnel dead or in exile. At the same time, over 120,000 people, nearly 2 per cent of the population, had been imprisoned on charges related to the genocide. Dealing with all the accused would have been impractical and would have completely overwhelmed the ICTR. The ICTR was also criticized for a lack of involvement of the victims and for not facilitating the reconciliation of society, an aspect of key importance to the restorative approach discussed later in the chapter.

Gacaca courts were set up throughout the country. A panel of popularly elected lay judges held public trials of those who were accused of lower-level crimes. Timothy Longman describes the process:

> The vast majority of those alleged to have participated in the genocide will be judged before their neighbors and families and sentenced by a group of their peers serving as judges … [T]he gacaca process will require each community to develop a record of how the genocide occurred in their community and to determine those responsible for carrying it out and those who were victims, and it will establish mechanisms for providing reparations to survivors. (Longman 2006: 207)

Perhaps the most important international justice institution of all is the International Criminal Court (ICC), a permanent tribunal based in The Hague that can try individuals for one of four international crimes: genocide, crimes against humanity, war crimes and the yet to be defined crime of 'aggression'. The ICC came into being on 1 July 2002, when its founding treaty, the Rome Statute of the International Criminal Court, came into force. The ICC can only exercise jurisdiction in cases where the defendant is a national of a state party, or the crime has been committed on the territory of a state party, or if the matter has been referred to the Court by the UN Security Council. The ICC is designed to serve as a complement to domestic courts, and it is prevented from acting unless national courts are either unable or unwilling to investigate or prosecute such crimes. The ICC does not have any law enforcement officials at its disposal and it is dependent on the co-operation of the broader international community. To date, the ICC has got off to a careful start, opening up investigations into four situations: Northern Uganda, the Democratic Republic of the Congo, the Central African Republic and the Darfur region in Sudan. The ICC's first trial began in January 2009 against the Congolese militia leader Thomas Lubanga.

Domestic courts and regional tribunals

The forum of first resort to lawyers and victims is the court system of the country in which the abuses took place. We highlight two examples where those responsible for human rights violations have been held to account by their own states: the prosecution of the Greek military junta (Box 7.2) and the proceedings in the aftermath of Argentina's Dirty War' (Box 7.3).

Box 7.2. The prosecution of the Greek military junta

The civilian government in Greece that came to power in 1974 after seven years of military dictatorship immediately began to prosecute those responsible for the 1967 military coup and those responsible for committing torture. Harry Psomiades describes the larger social and political meaning of these trials:

> [T]he trials, which received widespread radio, television, and press coverage, served to demystify the dictatorship. The trials made possible

the exposure of seven years of maladministration, repression, scandal, corruption, and conspiracies and depicted a regime much worse than even the military had imagined. The details of torture, particularly of distinguished senior military officers by subordinates, were most offensive to the professional officer class. The statements and the demeanor of the accused revealed to many their pettiness and their incompetence and destroyed within seconds the military image of the strong man. The trials exposed the 'supermen' without their clothes, and what the public and the officer corps saw, they did not like. (Psomiades 1982: 264)

Box 7.3. **Prosecutions for Argentina's Dirty War**

Argentina's Dirty War lasted from 1976 until 1983, following the country's military defeat in the Falkland Islands war in 1982. During this time, nearly 9,000 persons 'disappeared' and tens of thousands were detained without being charged with specific crimes. In 1983, the democratically elected president Raul Alfonsín ordered the arrest and prosecution of the nine military officers who had comprised the three military juntas from 1976 to 1983. In 1986, amidst rumblings in the Argentine military, the Congress passed the 'Full Stop' law that established a 60-day deadline for the filing of any complaints or charges against alleged torturers, and it followed this with the passage of the 'Due Obedience' law, which established an irrebuttable presumption that military personnel accused of committing human rights abuses were acting under orders and were not able to question the legitimacy of such orders. In 2005 the Supreme Court annulled both laws.

But, as discussed earlier, the domestic approach is not always possible because most of these countries are either poorly developed or possess hopelessly corrupt justice systems. Another possible instrument for pursuing retributive justice in a particular country is the legal system of another sovereign nation-state. Based on the principle of universal jurisdiction, those suspected of particularly heinous human rights violations can be tried in the courts of any country, regardless of the relationship with the country in which the abuses took place. In recent years, Spain has been particularly aggressive in invoking universal jurisdiction in an attempt to hold accountable those thought to be responsible for human rights abuses in Chile and Argentina. This includes the extradition request by the Spanish magistrate Baltasar Garzón to have the former Chilean dictator, Augusto Pinochet, extradited from Britain, which we have discussed in Chapter 3.

An equally noteworthy effort was Belgium's universal jurisdiction law. This statute was the broadest in the world in terms of the crimes that it covered, but also because it did not require a specific link between Belgium and either the suspect, the victims or events (Ratner 2003: 889). In 2001 the government tried and convicted two Rwandan nuns and two Rwandan men for their role in the genocide in that country. Soon thereafter a criminal complaint was filed against the Israeli Prime Minister Ariel Sharon for his role in the 1982 massacre in Palestinian refugee camps in Lebanon. In March 2003, seven Iraqi families requested an investigation of former US President George H. W. Bush and several high-ranking US officials for their role in the 1991 Persian Gulf War. In June 2003, US Secretary of Defense Donald Rumsfeld threatened that Belgium risked losing its status as the home of NATO headquarters unless it moderated its laws.[5] The Belgian government responded by severely curtailing its universal jurisdiction law.

Table 7.1 summarizes advantages and disadvantages of different institutions that are aimed at bringing about retributive justice. In general, national or even local institutions, such as gacaca courts in Rwanda, benefit from being geographically and culturally closer to the past events. International justice institutions, on the other hand, often have more resources at their disposal, including highly qualified lawyers. Looking at the advantages and disadvantages of various institutions, it is not surprising that over time various hybrid institutions have developed, trying to combine the best of these different approaches, such as in Timor Leste, Cambodia and Kosovo.

The most impressive hybrid tribunal has been the Special Court for Sierra Leone, which was the result of a treaty between the UN and the government of Sierra Leone, in order to hold accountable 'persons who

---

[5] Henry Kissinger is a critic of universal jurisdiction (see, e.g., Kissinger 2001). His criticism no doubt stems from his fear that he might be subject to prosecution in countries with universal jurisdiction statutes because of his activities as an advisor to President Nixon, and later as secretary of state during the Vietnam War.

Table 7.1 **Advantages and disadvantages of retributive justice institutions**		
	Advantages	**Disadvantages**
Justice system of affected country	• Often perceived to be more sensitive towards the issue • Use of local knowledge • Process highly visible, as such contributes to closure and truth finding	• Potential corruption and bias in favour of the old repressive regime • Sometimes limited resources • Often lack of experience
Justice system of another country	• Potentially more objective handling of cases • Limited pressure of supporters of perpetrators	• Limits sense of closure for victims • Potentially limited acceptance of affected country
International justice institution	• Highly qualified lawyers • Substantial international visibility • Setting standards for related cases	• Limits sense of closure for victims • Potentially limited acceptance in affected country

bear the greatest responsibility for serious violations of international humanitarian law and Sierra Leonean law'. The Special Court has concurrent, but primary, jurisdiction with Sierra Leone's national courts and it is composed of eight trial and appeals judges, three appointed by Sierra Leone and five appointed by the UN Secretary-General.

The Court sits in Sierra Leone and it made its impact felt immediately. In June 2003, the Special Court indicted the Liberian president, Charles Taylor, for war crimes related to his role in Sierra Leone's war, constituting the first time that a sitting head of state has been indicted for war crimes. And earlier that same year, the Special Court arrested Sam Hinga Norman, a former Minister of State Security for Sierra Leone, on charges of crimes against humanity. What was most significant about Norman's arrest is that it offered evidence that a victorious party could be held to the same standards as those who had been defeated (Tarin 2005: 520). Sierra Leone also established a Truth and Reconciliation Commission (TRC) to investigate lesser crimes. We come back to the case of Sierra Leone at the end of this chapter.

Substantial effort has been made to expand legal remedies, and possibilities for retributive justice have therefore increased in recent decades. We are clearly not at the point where dictators are deterred from committing abuses because they are afraid of being thrown into jail after their terms in office. But the trend, when viewed from the perspective of human rights advocates, is clearly in the right direction. Criminal prosecutions are not, however, simply about putting the 'bad guys' of the old regime behind bars, as happened after the fall of communism in eastern Europe (Gibney 1997). Rather, such proceedings should help advance societal understanding and the process of democratization. While the retributive approach concentrates on the perpetrators and aims at holding the guilty accountable for their past wrongs, the restorative approach puts the reconciliation of society at the centre of the transitional justice process.

The restorative approach

The most dominant approach to healing hurt societies seeks not just retribution, but concentrates on the restoration of society. While the retributive approach focuses primarily on the perpetrator, the restorative approach turns more attention to the victim. Proponents of restorative justice aim to move beyond holding the guilty accountable by trying to achieve broader goals through a variety of means outside the normal legal institutions. As Burgess puts it, 'Accountability may be the most essential ingredient to healing the past, but it is the total answer to neither justice nor reconciliation. Punishment will not by itself heal the past wounds, which are so commonly the cause of renewed hostilities and the occurrence of new violations' (Burgess 2006: 176).

The primary aim of restorative justice is to facilitate the 'healing of the wounds' left by past atrocities. To achieve this aim, two elements are stressed in the restorative approach: truth and reconciliation. Truth finding and the promulgation of truth are important values; establishing knowledge and acknowledgement of past human rights violations is seen as a key component in moving forward and rebuilding a society. Before any healing can take place, an account of what happened is necessary. This often goes beyond establishing who carried out particular violent acts, which is also part of the retributive approach of establishing justice and accountability. Victims and their relatives often want to understand the wider picture – for example, who acted as informant and what the command structure and incentives were that led to these crimes. Jon Elster identifies several agents that are involved in the process of transitional justice.

> First, there are the *wrongdoers*, the perpetrators of the wrongs on behalf of the autocratic regime. Second, there are the *victims* who suffered from the wrongdoings. Third, there are the *beneficiaries* of wrongdoing. To these we may add the category of *helpers*, who tried to alleviate or prevent the wrongdoings while they were taking place, and that of *resisters*, who fought or opposed the wrongdoers while these were still in power. A further category is that of the *neutrals*, who were neither wrongdoers, victims, helpers, nor resisters. (Elster 2004: 99, emphasis in orginal)

This categorization hints at the complex picture of past human rights violations and shows how difficult it can be to establish the 'truth' of what happened. From the viewpoint of restorative justice, bringing out the truth is essential, as it is the first step towards the perpetrators accepting responsibility for their actions, which in turn forms the basis for reconciliation.

The second focal point of restorative justice is reconciliation, reconciliation of individuals, such as reconciling the wrongdoer with the victim, but also reconciliation of different groups within society. Often these individuals come from ethnically different groups that reflect wider inequalities and historical animosities between these groups. Therefore the goal of restorative justice is to contribute to the reconciliation of these groups in order to reduce the risk that renewed violence and human rights violations will break out again. A key element for achieving reconciliation is that victims, offenders and their communities are actively involved in the process of transitional justice (Batley 2005). Often this includes the use of traditional systems of justice, such as was done in Rwanda and East Timor. Howard Zehr summarises the restorative approach with the following key questions:

- Does it address harms and causes?
- Is it victim oriented?
- Are offenders encouraged to take responsibility?

- Are all three stakeholder groups involved?
- Is there an opportunity for dialogue and participatory decision-making?
- Is it respectful to all parties? (Zehr, quoted in Batley 2005)

Patrick Burgess describes how the implementation of the restorative approach was envisaged by the Community Reconciliation Processes (CRP) that formed the key element of the East Timorese Commission for Reception, Truth and Reconciliation (CAVR):

> A perpetrator who burned houses returns from West Timor, feeling vulnerable and afraid. He approaches the CAVR's local representatives and provides them with a statement including admissions of his actions. This statement is forwarded to the Office of the General Prosecutor (OGP), which decides whether it is appropriate to be dealt with by CRP instead of prosecution. If approved, the CAVR establishes a five-person panel in the community affected by the crimes. The panel conducts a public hearing at which the perpetrator admits his wrongs and apologizes. Community elders and spiritual leaders attend and incorporate traditional practices into the hearing. Victims are able to address and question the perpetrator directly, community members also contribute and a decision is made as to what the perpetrator needs to do to be accepted back by the community. If he accepts the offer, and completes any required acts he will receive full immunity from future prosecution. (Burgess 2006: 184)

The implementation of the CRP programme was judged to be very successful. More than 1,500 such processes took place between April 2002 and March 2005, 500 more than had been hoped for originally. Eighty-five of these cases did not receive the approval of the OGP and were then dealt with by criminal prosecution. The main shortcoming of this process was that as participation in these programmes was voluntary, not all perpetrators chose to be part of this process. Another major weakness was that key perpetrators and officers in charge of planning the violence remained outside the CRP programme, as these were Indonesian military commanders and militia leaders living outside the territorial boundaries with which the CRP was concerned. But, despite these problems, this reconciliation process seems to have contributed substantially to facilitating the healing process in society, which is reflected so well in the following statement of a community elder at the closing of a CRP hearing:

> In 1999 we saw the Indonesian soldiers and militia leave. On May 20, 2002 we celebrated our independence as a nation. But it is only today that we as a community can be released from our suffering from this terrible past. Let us roll up the mat, and this will symbolize the end of all of these issues for us. From today we will look only forward. Let us now eat and dance together, and celebrate the future. (quoted in Burgess 2006: 193)

Truth commissions as a means towards restorative justice

Truth commissions, or what are sometimes referred to as truth and reconciliation commissions, are the most commonly used tool under the restorative approach. In her influential book *Unspeakable Truths*, Priscilla Hayner defines a truth commission as 'an *official* investigation into a *past pattern of abuses*' (Hayner 2002: 23, emphasis in original). They 'focus on the past, ... investigate a pattern of abuses over a period of time, ... are a temporary body ... [and] are officially sanctioned, authorized, or empowered by the state' (Hayner 2002: 14).

According to Hayner, truth commissions have five basic aims. The first and perhaps the most important one is to find out the truth about the past atrocities. Truth commissions attempt to get at the truth by taking testimony from those involved in the abuses that occurred. A commission can establish some areas of agreement and define issues of debate. A truthful report can help, or in some instances force, persons to accept the past by confronting them with a balanced treatment of the situation. This aspect is particularly important in cases where the country's violent recent history is already widely known but continues to be denied. Under such circumstances, truth commissions aim to establish not only knowledge but also acknowledgement of the past violations.

The second goal of truth commissions is to focus on the victims, in contrast to trials, which tend to focus on the accused. Truth commissions can recommend reparations programmes designed to correct inequities, or at the very least to serve as a small, symbolic payment designed to acknowledge the wrongs that were committed.

The third goal of truth commissions is to establish a sense of justice and accountability. This aim is closely linked to the retributive approach, as truth commissions can help to hold perpetrators accountable for their acts. For example, reports produced by truth commissions can provide evidence that is later used in trials of the accused.

The fourth goal is to make recommendations for the future. In particular, truth commissions evaluate the role played by various institutions, such as the police, the military and the judiciary, in the abuses and recommend reforms that are designed to prevent history from repeating itself.

Finally, truth commissions aim to promote reconciliation in society (Hayner 2002: 30). The idea behind this is that one has to know the truth about the wrongs that were committed, and by whom, before one can reconcile with the perpetrators or members of the perpetrating group. Yet the goal of reconciliation is controversial at best, as Hayner herself acknowledges. Although truth commissions may contribute to this goal for some individuals, they might well serve to stir up past enmities, resulting in further violence. Perhaps the best we can hope for is that truth commissions contribute to the ability of groups to respect each other's rights, to learn from the negative effects caused by past violence and to agree not to use violence to achieve political goals in the future.

Are truth commissions successful in achieving the goals and in improving a post-atrocity situation? Although the utility of truth commissions has not yet been supported by systematic social science studies (mainly because the phenomenon is rather new), many politicians, human rights and transitional justice activists and scholars believe them to be helpful. However, what is certain is that truth commissions are increasingly being employed as a means of addressing post-conflict situations.

Case study: the South African Truth and Reconciliation Commission

The South African Truth and Reconciliation Commission (TRC) was created by the South African parliament to investigate the human rights violations that occurred under the apartheid regime during 1960–94. The apartheid regime was characterized by the systematic violation of political and civil rights, as well as the economic, social and cultural rights, of non-whites by the government, which was in the hands of the white minority, and by the violent struggle of the armed wing of the African National Congress (ANC) against this repressive regime. Outlined in the Promotion of National Unity and Reconciliation Act, the aim of the TRC was

> to provide for the investigation and the establishment of as complete a picture as possible of the nature, causes and extent of gross violations of human rights ... emanating from the conflicts of the past, and the fate or whereabouts of the victims of such violations; the granting of amnesty to persons who make full disclosure of all the relevant facts relating to acts associated with a political objective committed in the course of the conflicts of the past during the said period; affording victims an opportunity to relate the violations they suffered; the taking of measures aimed at the granting of reparation to, and the rehabilitation and the restoration of the human and civil dignity of, victims of violations of human rights; reporting to the Nation about such violations and victims; the making of recommendations aimed at the prevention of the commission of gross violations of human rights. (Promotion of National Unity and Reconciliation Act, No. 34 of 1995, 26 July 1995)[6]

The chair of the TRC, Archbishop Desmond Tutu, believed that although a purely retributive justice might be attractive in some instances, it was not advisable in the case of South Africa. Unlike the cases that were brought by the Allies in Nuremberg against Nazi leaders, as well as similar trials and tribunals that followed Nuremberg, participants in the South African process would have to live and interact with one another on a daily basis. Thus the primary focus has to be on the relationship of South Africans and their ethnic communities.

The TRC was made up of three committees: the Human Right Violations Committee recorded statements of victims and witnesses, the Amnesty Committee processed applications for amnesty, and the Reparations and Rehabilitation Committee prepared recommendations to a reparations programme. To what extent did the South

---

6 The full text of this act can be accessed at www.doj.gov.za/trc/legal/act9534.htm.

African TRC achieve the core aims of truth commissions as discussed above? It becomes clear from the quote above that a key focus of the Commission was to 'clarify and acknowledge the truth'. Over 21,000 victims and witnesses gave testimony, and this process was covered extensively by newspapers, radio and television. To further facilitate the process of truth finding, the Commission had the power to grant individualized amnesty 'to those who fully confessed to their involvement in past crimes and showed them to be politically motivated' (Hayner 2002: 43). Unlike for some other truth commissions, such as in Sierra Leone, the perpetrator did not have to show remorse or apologize for the wrongdoings to qualify for amnesty. Over seven thousand individuals applied for amnesty under this 'truth-for-amnesty' programme.

The TRC also focused on the 'needs and interests of the victims'. This was, among others, addressed with the procedure to claim for amnesty. To be considered for amnesty in the case of gross human rights violations, the perpetrators had to be available to be questioned by the victims, among other criteria. As above, this element focused on allowing the victims and their families to find out what really happened. Additionally, the Commission made detailed recommendations for a reparations programme, although in the end there were long delays to reparation payments, which also were far lower than the amount recommended.

Although at its core the TRC was decidedly focused on restorative and not retributive justice, it also impacted on criminal prosecutions and therefore contributed, to a certain degree, to justice and accountability. Almost 5,400 amnesty applications out of just over seven thousand in total were refused, although few trials were actually held. For example, the killers of the anti-apartheid activist Steve Biko were denied amnesty because they claimed the death to have been accidental, and since only politically motivated crimes could be considered for amnesty, it was denied in this case. Yet one could argue that granting amnesty defies justice and accountability – which is what some victims' families claimed. They took the TRC to court, arguing that its amnesty-granting power was unconstitutional. However, the South African Constitutional Court ruled in favour of the Commission (Hayner 2002: 44). Some also questioned whether the amnesty process was at odds with international law (Dugard 1997).

Restorative and retributive justice: complement or contradiction?

· ·

In this chapter we have discussed two approaches to transitional justice, the restorative and the retributive approach. Both approaches aim to establish justice, truth and reconciliation in the wake of repression, yet with different emphases. While the retributive approach focuses primarily on the perpetrator and on bringing those responsible for the past wrongs to justice, the restorative approach emphasizes the role of the victims, the establishment of a common history and the larger reconciliation of a society. Yet just as hybrid criminal justice institutions have developed that bring together and utilize both national and international actors, so also have hybrid approaches developed that combine the retributive approach, represented by criminal prosecution, with the restorative approach, generally represented by truth and reconciliation commissions. For example, the Sierra Leone Truth and Reconciliation Commission (TRC) coexisted with criminal prosecutions held by the Special Court for Sierra Leone. This dual approach was a result of circumstances and not explicitly planned at the outset (Horovitz 2006; Schabas 2006). The UN High Commissioner for Human Rights described the relationship between the TRC and the Special Court as follows:

> The TRC and the Special Court were established at different times, under different legal bases and with different mandates. Yet they perform complementary roles in ensuring accountability, deterrence, a story-telling mechanism for both victims and perpetrators, national reconciliation, reparation and restorative justice for the people of Sierra Leone. (UN Doc. E/CN.4/2002/3, para. 70, quoted in Schabas 2006: 35)

As this quotation highlights, using both tools in transitional societies enables countries to make use of the advantages of both approaches. But this combination also brings difficulties. In the case of Sierra Leone, for example, there was never a formal agreement about co-operation or information sharing between the two bodies (Schabas 2006). The Special Court was unwilling to share information with the TRC, while the work of the TRC in establishing the 'truth' and a record of what happened would have been severely hampered had they shared their information with the Special Court.

In East Timor it was intended from the outset to adopt 'a twin track to the question of accountability and reconciliation with the country's difficult past, combining retributive and restorative justice through criminal trials as well as a Commission for Reception, Truth and Reconciliation (CAVR)' (Reiger 2006: 143). The courts were intended to prosecute 'serious crimes', while the CAVR concentrated more on lesser crimes and focused on establishing the truth and bringing about reconciliation. Similarly, the gacaca trials in Rwanda, which we have briefly discussed in Box 7.1, were an attempt to combine the goals of restorative and retributive justice by prosecuting the guilty (using a traditional, non-Western approach) while at the same time involving victims in the process and working towards reconciliation.

Since Nuremberg, different institutions and formats have been tested, all aimed at helping societies that come out of a period of violence and repression to deal with their past and to move toward a more promising future. Given the difficult circumstances under which these societies try to establish transitional justice, it is quite remarkable that some progress has been made in so many countries towards this goal.

FURTHER READING

Transitional justice

- Buruma, Ian. 1994. *The Wages of Guilt: Memories of War in Germany and Japan.*
  Buruma analyzes the manner in which these two states have coped with their
  role in bringing about the Second World War.

- Hayner, Priscilla B. 2002. *Unspeakable Truths: Facing the Challenge of Truth
  Commissions.*
  Hayner is generally recognized as the world's leading authority on truth
  commissions and the thorough and insightful nature of her book demonstrates
  why this is.

- Roht-Arriaza, Naomi and Javier Mariezcurrena (eds.). 2006. *Transitional Justice
  in the Twenty-First Century.*
  This volume provides the most extensive analysis of the attempts by various
  institutions at the international, regional, national and sub-national levels to
  bring perpetrators of human rights violations to justice.

- Schabas, William. 2007. *An Introduction to the International Criminal Court*,
  3rd edn.
  Schabas is one of the important figures in the realm of international criminal
  law and this book has already become one of the leading texts on the newly
  created International Criminal Court.

RELATED FILMS

International justice mechanisms

- **The Reckoning** (Pamela Yates, Paco de Onis and Peter Kinoy, 2009). This
  documentary provides a behind-the-scenes view of the work of the International
  Criminal Court (ICC). Featured prominently in this film is the Chief Prosecutor,
  Luis Moreno-Ocampo, as well as members of his staff, as the viewer gets a good
  feel for the legal and political intricacies of the ICC's work.

- **Carla's List** (Marcel Schupbach, 2006). Like *The Reckoning, Carla's List* intends
  to provide a fly-on-the-wall account of the life and work of Carla Del Ponte
  during the time when she was the Chief Prosecutor at the International Criminal
  Tribunal for the former Yugoslavia.

- **Milosevic on Trial** (Michael Christoffersen, 2007). A documentary on the trial
  before the ICTY of Slobodan Milošević.

- **Judgment at Nuremberg** (Stanley Kramer, 1961). This is a classic movie with some
  of the biggest Hollywood stars, including Spencer Tracy and Burt Lancaster. The
  film focuses on the prosecution of four Nazi judges for war crimes. *Judgment at
  Nuremberg* very effectively raises the issue of the relationship between the law
  and larger notions of 'justice'.

Truth and reconciliation

- **Long Night's Journey Into Day** (Frances Reid and Deborah Hoffman, 2000). This
  moving film offers an insightful look into the workings of the South African
  Truth and Reconciliation Commission. The viewer is exposed to a wide range

of individuals – some of them human rights victims and some human rights violators. The story begins with Amy Beale's parents, mentioned earlier in this chapter, and it shows that there are different kinds of truth and different levels of reconciliation.

- **My Neighbor, My Killer** (Anne Aghlon, 2009). Focusing on one small hamlet in Rwanda, Aghlon's camera tells the story of the victims and perpetrators of the 1994 genocide and the role of the gacaca courts in bringing justice and closure.

chapter **8**

Towards the future

This brief concluding chapter focuses on three related issues. The first involves how human rights have come to be conceptualized. As we have noted before, there has been a strong tendency to equate human rights with atrocities carried out in distant lands with no seeming or apparent connection with our own lives. In that way, human rights have been limited to 'other' people – other than ourselves, that is.

Under this approach, starvation in Ethiopia is seen only as Ethiopia's human rights problem; torture in Egypt is seen only as Egypt's human rights problem; the AIDS epidemic in South Africa is seen only as South Africa's human rights problem, and so on. As the reader will know by now, we reject this thinking. Just as human rights are themselves universal, so is the responsibility to protect human rights universal as well. At the very least, many of the things that affect the lives of everyone, such as health care, education, environmental quality, food safety, working conditions and so on, involve human rights.

The second point we want to highlight is that it would be wrong to be fatalistic about the prospects of human rights for the future. We take the opposite view because the empirical evidence, from around the globe, is on our side. For example, during the Second World War, the Nazi regime in Germany committed probably the worst genocide in the history of humankind. Yet with the victory of the Allied forces this extensive repression was not only terminated, but within a relatively short period of time Germany established a stable regime that respects most human rights most of the time. More recently, the Rwandan genocide in 1994 seemingly destroyed a whole country, which is now working hard towards re-establishing itself as one nation, implementing traditional means to establish reconciliation and justice as briefly discussed in Chapter 7. On yet another continent, Argentina suffered widespread repression during the Dirty War under military rule during the late 1970s and early 1980s. Today, despite having experienced economic collapse at the beginning of the twenty-first century, the country has a good record of generally protecting human rights. Turning our eyes to Asia, Timor-Leste has emerged from an extremely violent recent past. On the road to the country's independence in 2002, at least 100,000 people of this tiny country died under Indonesian occupation. Only a few years after the end of the devastating occupation, the new country underwent a process of restoration and reconciliation, which has provided some healing and a new basis for the future of the country. There are many more examples of states that once suffered unimaginable atrocities in terms of violations of physical integrity rights and that have changed their fortunes dramatically, including Nicaragua, Sierra Leone, El Salvador, Algeria, Brazil, Liberia, Chile, Uruguay, to name just a few. Of course, one also needs to remember that it is only about forty years ago when racial discrimination was commonplace in the United States – and today the country is headed by its first black president.

Within academia, there is a growing community that tries to answer the question of why human rights violations occur, using empirical analysis, just as we have done in Chapter 5. This will allow us to accumulate more detailed but also wider knowledge that is based on real-world observations of why so many people have their human rights violated and are therefore unable to lead lives in human dignity. There is a small, but growing, body of work that attempts to assess the risk of future human rights violations to provide policymakers with the information that enables them to prevent human rights disasters from happening in the first place. More research is also being done on the practical question of how societies can best deal with past atrocities, as we have highlighted in Chapter 7 on judicial proceedings and truth commissions on transitional justice. And there are many more topics and questions on human rights that attract more attention from scholars but that we have not discussed, for example, how foreign aid or trade impact on human rights, or how the popularization of the media, such as the use of the internet, can be used to improve human rights across the globe.

We hope, and expect, that this increased academic attention to the topic of human rights will further improve our understanding of the politics of human rights, of why and under what conditions they are most likely to be violated, and when they are most likely to be respected. The next and crucial step is to translate this improved understanding into actions that enable more and more people to lead their lives in dignity.

The larger point is that what seems impossible is anything but. It also needs to be said that most human rights violations occur because we allow them to happen. To be sure, thousands of people die of starvation and malnutrition each day, and the number of chronically hungry people has, for the first time, crossed the one billion mark. But this is not a situation that cannot be changed. From 1969 to 2004, the proportion of the world's population who suffered from hunger dropped from 30 to 17 per cent.[1] At the G8 Summit early July 2009, the eight countries pledged to contribute $20 billion over three years towards ensuring food security in poorer countries. Of course, promises are one thing and commitment can be quite another. Nevertheless, this reflects the G8's responsibility to work towards providing economic rights for people in less fortunate countries.

Many young people are attracted to electoral politics, and rightly so. This, after all, is where real change can take place. Yet human rights are often either completely ignored or relegated to a specific event or country (e.g., China). During the 2008 presidential campaign in the United States, for example, nearly the entire discussion on human rights concentrated on whether the US military base at Guantánamo Bay, Cuba, that housed 'enemy combatants' should be closed or not.

We do not mean to suggest that this particular issue was not vitally important. But our point is that there are many more important human rights issues, at home and abroad, that require our attention. Human rights should be the defining political issue – whether it is in local politics, regional politics, national politics or international politics.

Finally, to work towards the realization of human rights requires a lifelong interest in and commitment to human rights. In essence, human rights are about the way in which each one of us treats the rest of humanity. When human rights are viewed this way, it becomes clear why this is such an extremely important subject, academic and otherwise.

---

1 This figure is based on a report, 'G8 to commit $20bn for food security', *Financial Times*, 10 July 2009.

Bibliography

PUBLICATIONS

Abouharb, M. Rodwan and David Cingranelli. 2007. *Human Rights and Structural Adjustment*. New York: Cambridge University Press.

Akpan, Uwem. 2008. *Say You're One of Them*. New York: Little, Brown.

Alston, Philip. 2005. 'Ships passing in the night: The current state of the human rights and development debate seen through the lens of the Millennium Development Goals', *Human Rights Quarterly* 27: 755–829.

—2006. 'Reconceiving the UN human rights regime: challenges confronting the new UN Human Rights Council', *Melbourne Journal of International Law* 7: 185–224.

Amnesty International. Annual reports, available at http://thereport.amnesty.org/.

Association of the Bar of the City of New York and Center for Human Rights and Global Justice. 2004. *Torture by Proxy: International and Domestic Law Applicable to 'Extraordinary Renditions'*. New York: ABCNY and NYU School of Law.

Batley, Mike. 2005. 'Restorative justice in the South African context.' In T. Maepa (ed.), *Beyond Retribution: Prospects for Restorative Justice in South Africa*, Monograph no. 111. Pretoria: Institute for Security Studies, with the Restorative Justice Centre, available at www.iss.co.za/pubs/Monographs/No111/Chap2.htm.

Bellamy, Alex. 2009. *A Responsibility to Protect: The Global Effort to End Mass Atrocities*. Cambridge: Polity.

Brody, Reed. 2006. 'The prosecution of Hissène Habrè: international accountability, national impunity'. In Naomi Roht-Arriaza and Javier Mariezcurrena (eds.), *Transitional Justice in the Twenty-First Century, Beyond Truth versus Justice*. New York: Cambridge University Press, pp. 278–300.

Burgess, Patrick. 2006. 'A new approach to restorative justice – East Timor's community reconciliation processes'. In Naomi Roht-Arriaza and Javier Mariezcurrena (eds.), *Transitional Justice in the Twenty-First Century, Beyond Truth versus Justice*. New York: Cambridge University Press, pp. 176–205.

Buruma, Ian. 1994. *The Wages of Guilt: Memories of War in Germany and Japan*. New York: Farrar, Straus & Giroux.

Carey, Sabine C. 2009. *Protest, Repression and Political Regimes: An Empirical Analysis of Latin America and Sub-Saharan Africa*. London: Routledge.

Carey, Sabine C. and Steven C. Poe (eds.). 2004. *Understanding Human Rights Violations*. Aldershot: Ashgate.

Cingranelli, David L. and David L. Richards. 1999. 'Respect for human rights after the end of the Cold War'. *Journal of Peace Research* 36: 511–34.

Collier, Paul. 2007. *The Bottom Billion: Why the Poorest Countries Are Failing and What Can Be Done about It*. Oxford University Press.

Coomans, Fons and Menno Kamminga (eds.). 2004. *Extraterritorial Application of Human Rights Treaties*. Antwerp: Intersentia.

Crawford, James. 2002. *The International Law Commission's Articles on State Responsibility: Introduction, Text and Commentaries*. Cambridge University Press.

Davenport, Christian, 1995. 'Multi-dimensional threat perception and state repression: an inquiry into why states apply negative sanctions', *American Journal of Political Science* 39: 683–713.

Davenport, Christian. 2007. *State Repression and the Domestic Democratic Peace*. New York: Cambridge University Press.

Davenport, Christian and David A. Armstrong. 2004. 'Democracy and the violation of human rights: a statistical analysis from 1976 to 1996', *American Journal of Political Science* 48: 538–54.

De Schutter, Olivier. 2008. 'The right to food', the interim report of the Special Rapporteur on the right to food, submitted to the UN General Assembly, 21 October.

Donnelly, Jack. 2003. *Universal Human Rights in Theory and Practice*. Ithaca: Cornell University Press.

—2007. *International Human Rights*, 3rd edition. Boulder: Westview Press.

Dugard, John. 1997. 'Is the truth and reconciliation process compatible with international law? An unanswered question: Azapo v. President of the Republic of South Africa', *South African Journal on Human Rights* 13: 258–68.

Elster, Jon. 2004. *Closing the Books*. Cambridge University Press.

Farmer, Paul. 2007. 'From "marvelous momentum" to health care for all', *Foreign Affairs*, January/February.

Fein, Helen. 1995. 'More murder in the middle: life-integrity violations and democracy in the world', *Human Rights Quarterly* 17 (1): 170–91.

Gammeltoft-Hansen, Thomas. 2010. 'Extraterritorial obligations and international refugee law', in Mark Gibney and Sigrun Skogly (eds.), *Human Rights and Extraterritorial Obligations*. Philadelphia: University of Pennsylvania Press.

Garrett, Laurie. 2007. 'The challenge of global health', *Foreign Affairs*, January/February.

Gibney, Mark. 1997. 'Prosecuting human rights violations from a previous regime: the East European experience', *East European Quarterly* 31: 93–110.

—2002 'On the Need for an International Civil Court', *Fletcher Forum of World Affairs* 26: 47–58.

—2008. *International Human Rights Law: Returning to Universal Principles*. Lanham, MD: Rowman & Littlefield.

Gleditsch, Nils Petter, Peter Wallensteen, Mikael Eriksson, Margareta Sollenberg and Håvard Strand. 2002. 'Armed conflict 1946–2001: a new dataset', *Journal of Peace Research* 39: 615–37.

Gourevitch, Philip. 1998. *We Wish to Inform You that Tomorrow We Will Be Killed with Our Families*. New York: Picador.

Gurr, Ted Robert. 1986. 'The political origins of state violence and terror: a theoretical analysis'. In *Government Violence and Repression. An Agenda for Research*. Michael Stohl and George A. Lopez, (eds.), Westport, CT: Greenwood.

Hafner-Burton, Emilie M. 2005. 'Trading human rights: how preferential trade agreements influence government repression', *International Organization* 59: 593–629.

Hall, Christopher Keith. 2007. 'The duty of states parties to the Convention against Torture to provide procedures permitting victims to recover reparations for torture committed abroad', *European Journal of International Law* 18: 921–37.

Hathaway, Oona. 2002. 'Do human rights treaties make a difference?', *Yale Law Journal* 111: 1935–2041.

Hayner, Priscilla B. 2002. *Unspeakable truths: Facing the Challenge of Truth Commissions*. New York: Routledge.

Henderson, Conway. 1991. 'Conditions affecting the use of political repression', *Journal of Conflict Resolution* 35(1): 120–42.

Hertel, Shareen and Lanse Minkler (eds.). 2007. *Economic Rights: Conceptual, Measurement, and Policy Issues*. New York: Cambridge University Press.

Hochschild, Adam. 1998. *King Leopold's Ghost*. Boston: Houghton Mifflin.

Hoodbhoy, Mehlika, Martin S. Flaherty and Tracey E. Higgins. 2005. 'Exporting despair: the human rights implications of US restrictions on foreign health care funding in Kenya', *Fordham International Law Journal* 29: 1–118.

Horovitz, Sigall. 2006. 'Transitional criminal justice in Sierra Leone'. In Naomi Roht-Arriaza and Mariezcurrena, (eds.), *Transitional Justice in the Twenty-First Century, Beyond Truth versus Justice*. New York: Cambridge University Press, pp. 43–69.

Howard, Lise Morjé. 2008. *UN Peacekeeping in Civil Wars*. Cambridge University Press.

Howe, R. Brian and Katherine Covell. 2005. *Empowering Children: Children's Rights Education as a Pathway to Citizenship*. University of Toronto Press.

Hunt, Paul. 2007. Report of the Special Rapporteur on the right of everyone to the enjoyment of the highest attainable standard of physical and mental health, United Nations Human Rights Council.

—2008. 'Promotion and protection of all human rights, civil, political, economic, social and cultural rights, including the right to development', Report of the Special Rapporteur on the right to everyone to the enjoyment of the highest attainable standard of physical and mental health (Addendum), Human Rights Council, 5 March.

Ignatieff, Michael. 2001. *Human Rights As Politics and Idolatry*. Princeton University Press.

—2004. *The Lesser Evil: Political Ethics in an Age of Terror.* Princeton University Press.

Ikelegbe, Augustine. 2001. 'Civil society, oil and conflict in the Niger Delta region of Nigeria: ramifications of civil society for a regional resource struggle', *Journal of Modern African Studies* 39: 437–69.

International Commission on Intervention and State Sovereignty. 2001. *The Responsibility to Protect.* Ottawa: International Development Research Centre.

Joyner, Christopher. 2007. '"The responsibility to protect": humanitarian concern and the lawfulness of armed intervention', *Virginia Journal of International Law* 47: 693–723.

Kerstens, Paul. 2007. '"Deliver us from original sin": Belgian apologies to Rwanda and the Congo', in M.Gibney et al. (eds.), *The Age of Apology: Facing up to the Past.* Philadelphia: University of Pennsylvania Press.

Kinney, Eleanor and Brian Clark. 2004. 'Provisions for health and health care in the constitutions of the countries of the world', *Cornell International Law Journal* 37: 285–355.

Kissinger, Henry A. 2001. 'The pitfalls of universal jurisdiction', *Foreign Affairs*, July/August.

Kozol, Jonathan. 1991. *Savage Inequalities: Children in America's Schools.* New York: HarperCollins.

Kuper, Andrew (ed.). 2005. *Global Responsibilities: Who Must Deliver on Human Rights.* New York: Routledge.

Kuperman, Alan J. 2009. 'A small intervention with a big payoff: Liberia 2003', paper presented at the annual meeting of the International Studies Association, New York.

Landman, Todd. 2005. *Protecting Human Rights: A Comparative Study.* Washington, DC: Georgetown University Press.

—2006. *Studying Human Rights.* London: Routledge.

Lauren, Paul Gordon. 1998: *The Evolution of Human Rights: Visions Seen.* University of Pennsylvania Press.

Lawson, Stephanie. 1993. 'Conceptual issues in the comparative study of regime change and democratization', *Comparative Politics* 25: 183–205.

Lee, Chris, Ronny Lindström, Will H. Moore and Kürşad Turan. 2004. 'Ethnicity and repression: the ethnic composition of countries and human rights violations'. In Sabine C. Carey and Steven C. Poe (eds.), *Understanding Human Rights Violations.* Aldershot: Ashgate.

Longman, Timothy. 2006. 'Justice at the grassroots? Gacaca trials in Rwanda'. In Naomi Roht-Arriaza and Javier Mariezcurrena, (eds.), *Transitional Justice in the Twenty-First Century, Beyond Truth versus Justice.* Cambridge, NY: Cambridge University Press, pp. 206–28.

Mason, David. T. 2004. *Caught in the Crossfire: Revolutions, Repression, and the Rational Peasant.* Lanham, MD: Rowman & Littlefield.

Mayer, Jane. 2008. *The Dark Side: The Inside Story of How the War on Terror Turned into a War on American Ideals.* New York: Doubleday.

Minow, Martha. 1998. *Between Vengeance and Forgiveness: Facing History after Genocide and Mass Violence*. Boston: Beacon Press.

Mitchell, Neil J. 2004. *Agents of Atrocity: Leaders, Followers, and the Violation of Human Rights in Civil War*. New York: Palgrave Macmillan.

Mitchell, Neil J. and James M. McCormick. 1988. 'Economic and political explanations of human rights violations', *World Politics* 40: 476–98.

Morsink, Johannes. 1999. *The Universal Declaration of Human Rights: Origins, Drafting and Intent*. Philadelphia: University of Pennsylvania Press.

Most, Benjamin A. and Harvey Starr. 1989. *Inquiry, Logic and International Politics*. Columbia, SC: University of South Carolina Press.

Muller, Edward N. 1985. 'Income inequality, regime repressiveness and political violence', *American Sociological Review* 50: 47–61.

Mutua, Makau. 2001. 'Savages, victims, and saviors: the metaphor of human rights', *Harvard International Law Journal* 42: 201–45.

—2002. *Human Rights: A Political and Cultural Discourse*. Philadelphia: University of Pennsylvania Press.

Narula, Smita. 2006. 'The right to food: Holding global actors accountable under international law', *Columbia Journal of Transnational Law* 44: 691–800.

Natsios, Andrew. 2008. 'Beyond Darfur', *Foreign Affairs*, May/June.

Nowak, Manfred. 2007. 'The Need for a World Court of Human Rights', *Human Rights Law Review* 7: 251–9.

Orakhelashvili, Alexander. 2007. 'State immunity and hierarchy of norms: why the House of Lords got it wrong', *European Journal of International Law* 18: 955–70.

Perry, Michael. 1998. *The Idea of Human Rights*. New York: Oxford University Press.

Poe, Steven C., 2004. 'The decision to repress: an integrative theoretical approach to the research on human rights and repression'. In Sabine C. Carey and Steven C. Poe (eds.), *Understanding Human Rights Violations: New Systematic Studies*. Aldershot: Ashgate.

Poe, Steven C. and C. Neil Tate . 1994. 'Repression of human rights and personal integrity in the 1980s: a global analysis', *American Political Science Review* 88: 853–72.

Poe, Steven C., Sabine C. Carey and Tanya C. Vazquez. 2001. 'How are these pictures different? A quantitative comparison of the US State Department and Amnesty International human rights reports, 1976–1995', *Human Rights Quarterly* 23: 650–77.

Pogge, Thomas. 2002. *World Poverty and Human Rights: Cosmopolitan Responsibilities and Reforms*. Cambridge: Polity Press.

Powell, Emilia Justyna and Jeffrey K. Staton. 2009. 'Domestic judicial institutions and human rights treaty violation', *International Studies Quarterly* 53: 149–74.

Power, Samantha. 2002. *'A Problem from Hell': America and the Age of Genocide*. New York: Basic Books.

Psomiades, Harry. 1982 'Greece: From the Colonel's Rule to Democracy', in John Herz (ed.), *From Dictatorship to Democracy: Coping with the Legacies of Authoritarianism and Totalitarianism*. Westport, CT: Greenwood Press.

Rapport de la Commission Nationale Indépendante Chargée de Rassembler les Preuves Montrant l' Implication de l' Etat Français dans le Génocide Perpetré au Rwanda en 1994, 15 November 2007, available at www.scribd.com/doc/4531960/Report-on-Frances-complicity-in-Rwandan-Genocide-in-French.

Ratner, Steven R. 2003. 'Belgium's War Crimes Statute: a postmortem', *American Journal of International Law* 97: 888–97.

Ratner, Steven R. and Jason S. Abrams. 1997. *Accountability for Human Rights Atrocities in International Law: Beyond the Nuremberg Legacy.* Oxford: Clarendon Press.

Reiger, Caitlin. 2006. 'Hybrid attempts at accountability for serious crimes in Timor Leste'. In Naomi Roht-Arriaza and Javier Mariezcurrena (eds.), *Transitional Justice in the Twenty-First Century, Beyond Truth versus Justice.* Cambridge, New York: Cambridge University Press, pp. 143–70.

Report of the International Commission of Inquiry on Darfur to the United Nations Secretary General. 2005, available at www.un.org/News/dh/sudan/com_inq_darfur.pdf.

Richards, David L., Ronald D. Gelleny and David H. Sacko. 2001. 'Money with a mean streak? Foreign economic penetration and government respect of human rights in developing countries', *International Studies Quarterly* 45: 219–39.

Roberts, Adam. 2002. 'The so-called "right" of humanitarian intervention'. In *Yearbook of International Humanitarian Law,* vol. 3: 2000. The Hague: T.M.C. Asser, pp. 3–5.

Roht-Arriaza, Naomi. 2006. 'The new landscape of transitional justice'. In Naomi Roht-Arriaza and Javier Mariezcurrena (eds.), *Transitional Justice in the Twenty-First Century, Beyond Truth versus Justice.* Cambridge, New York: Cambridge University Press, pp. 1–16.

Roht-Arriaza, Naomi and Javier Mariezcurrena (eds.). 2006. *Transitional Justice in the Twenty-First Century.* Cambridge University Press.

Rummel, Rudolph. 1997. *Power Kills: Democracy as a Method of Nonviolence.* New Brunswick, NJ: Transaction Publishers.

Sachs, Jeffrey. 2005. *The End of Poverty: Economic Possibilities for Our Time.* New York: The Penguin Press.

SCFAIT Report (Canada). 2005. House of Commons, Standing Committee on Foreign Affairs and International Trade, 1st Sess., 38th Parl., Fourteenth Report: Mining in Developing Countries and Corporate Social Responsibility.

Schabas, William. 2000. *Genocide in International Law: The Crime of Crimes.* Cambridge University Press.

Schabas, William A. 2006. 'The Sierra Leone Truth and Reconciliation Commission'. In Naomi Roht-Arriaza and Javier Mariezcurrena (eds.), *Transitional Justice in the Twenty-First Century, Beyond Truth versus Justice.* Cambridge, New York: Cambridge University Press, pp. 21–42.

Schabas, William. 2007. *An introduction to the International Criminal Court,* 3rd edn. Cambridge University Press.

Schmitt, Paul. 2009. 'The future of genocide suits at the International Court of Justice: France's role in Rwanda and implications of the Bosnia v. Serbia decision', *Georgetown Journal of International Law* 40: 585–623.

Seck Sara. 2008. 'Home state responsibility and local communities: the case of global mining', *Yale Human Rights and Development Law Journal* 11: 177–206.

Sen, Amartya. 1981. *Poverty and Famines.* Oxford University Press.

Shacknove, Andrew. 1985. 'Who is a refugee?', *Ethics* 95: 274–84.

Shue, Henry. 1980. *Basic Rights: Subsistence, Affluence, and US Foreign Policy.* Princeton University Press.

—1988, 'Mediating duties', *Ethics* 98: 687–704.

Skogly, Sigrun. 2006. *Beyond National Borders: States' Human Rights Obligations in International Cooperation.* Antwerp: Intersentia.

Sunstein, Cass. 2004. *The Second Bill of Rights: Why We Need It More than Ever.* New York: Basic Books.

Tarin, Danielle. 2005. 'Prosecuting Saddam and bungling transitional justice in Iraq', *Virginia Journal of International Law* 45: 467–545.

Tomasevski, Katarina. 1997. *Between Sanctions and Elections: Aid Donors and their Human Rights Performance.* London: Pinter.

United Nations, Committee on Economic, Social and Cultural Rights. 1990. General Comment 3: The Nature of States Parties' Obligations Fifth session.

—1999. General Comment 12: Right to Adequate Food, Twentieth session, UN doc. E/C.12/1999/5.

—2000. General Comment 14: The Right to the Highest Attainable Standard of Health. Twenty-Second Session.

—2002. General Comment 15: The Right to Water, Arts. 11 and 12 of the International Covenant on Economic, Social and Cultural Rights, Twenty-Ninth session.

United Nations, Concluding Observations of the Committee on Economic, Social and Cultural Rights: Ireland, 05/06/2002, UN Doc. E/C.12/1/Add.77 (Concluding Observations/Comments).

—Committee Against Torture. 2005. Conclusions and Recommendations of the Committee against Torture: Canada.

—Human Rights Committee. 2006. Concluding Observations of the Human Rights Committee: Canada.

United Nations Development Programme. 2008. *Human Development World Maps (2008 update)*, available at http://hdr.undp.org/en/statistics/data/.

US Department of State. Country report available www.state.gov/g/drl/rls/hrrpt/.

Vandenhole, Wouter. 2007. 'Third state obligations under the ICESCR: a case study of EU sugar policy', *Nordic Journal of International Law* 76: 71–98.

Walker, Scott and Steven C. Poe. 2002. 'Does cultural diversity affect countries' respect for human rights?', *Human Rights Quarterly* 24: 237–63.

Weiss, Thomas G. 2007. *Humanitarian Intervention: Ideas in Action.* Cambridge: Polity Press.

Weschler, Lawrence. 1990. *A Miracle, A Universe: Settling Accounts with Torturers.* New York: Pantheon.

Whelan, Daniel. 2010. *Indivisible Human Rights: A History*. Philadelphia: University of Pennsylvania Press.

Yanik, Lerna. 2006. 'Guns and human rights: major powers, global arms transfers, and human rights violations', *Human Rights Quarterly* 28: 357–88.

Zehr, Howard. 2002. *The Little Book of Restorative Justice*. Intercourse, PA: Good Books.

Ziegler, Jean. 2005. 'The right to food', Report of the Special Rapporteur on the right to food, Economic and Social Council, Commission on Human Rights, 61st sess.

Zolberg, Aristide, Astri Suhrke and Sergio Aguayo. 1999. *Escape from Violence: Conflict and the Refugee Crisis in the Developing World*. New York: Oxford University Press.

CASES

International courts

European Court of Human Rights
Ireland v. United Kingdom, Series A, No. 25, ECHR 1 (1978).

Soering v. United Kingdom, App. No. 4038/88 [1989] ECHR 14 (7 July 1989).

Banković et al. v. Belgium et al., App. No. 52207/99 ECHR (2001), 41 ILM 517.

Human Rights Committee
Sergia Euben Lopez Burgos v. Uruguay, Communication No. 12/52 (5 June 1979), UN Doc. Supp. No. 40 (A/36/40) at 176 (1981).

International Court of Justice
Arrest Warrant of 11 April 2000 Democratic Republic of the Congo v. Belgium, [2002] ICJ Rep. 3.

Case Concerning the Application of the Convention on the Prevention and Punishment of the Crime of Genocide (Bosnia and Herzegovina v. Serbia and Montenegro), Judgment of 27 February 2007, available at www.icj-cij.org.

Domestic courts

Canada
Bouzari v. Iran, Ontario Superior Court of Justice (2002).

Suresh v. Canada (Minister of Citizenship and Immigration) [2002] 1 SCR 3, 2002 SCC 1.

Israel
Public Committee Against Torture in H.C. 5100/94, Israel v. Israel [1999].

United Kingdom
Regina v. Bow Street Metropolitan Stipendiary Magistrate and Others. Ex parte Pinochet Ugarte (no. 3), Judgment of March 24, 1999, (2000) 147.

United States

Filartiga v. Pena-Irala, 630 F. 2d 876 (2d Cir. 1980)

Matter of Kasinga, Board of Immigration Appeals (en banc), 1966.

Sale v. Haitian Ctrs. Council, 509 US 155 (1993).

Index